CIVILIZATION AND HEALTH

CIVILIZATION AND HEALTH

BY

WOODS HUTCHINSON, A.M., M.D.

Author of " Studies in Human and Comparative Pathology,"
" Instinct and Health," " Preventable Diseases,"
" We and Our Children," " Com-
mon Diseases," etc.

BOSTON AND NEW YORK
HOUGHTON MIFFLIN COMPANY
The Riverside Press Cambridge
1914

Published November 1914

CONTENTS

CIVILIZATION AND HEALTH

CIVILIZATION AND HEALTH

CHAPTER I

THE DISEASES OF CIVILIZATION

NOTHING is more dangerous than strict logic — which is not quite sure of its premises. Some of the most damnable errors of history have been perfectly sound, logical conclusions from data which everybody knew to be sound and no one even doubted, — but which afterwards turned out to be false. Nothing outside of a book ever goes on to its full logical conclusion. Especially is this true in the realm of disease. To paraphrase Hamlet's famous lines, —

> For by strict justice
> None of us should see salvation.

From the number and deadliness of the maladies that lie in wait for us we have no logical right to expect to survive; and yet we are here in defiance of logic. Of course, this world is a dangerous place and few of us ever get out of it alive; yet the race goes right on living, somehow, undaunted in spite of the new and terrible diseases that medical science keeps discovering.

It is easy enough to construct a prognostic for any disease which will be perfectly logical and absolutely appalling. All you have to do is to show by vital statistics that it is increasing at a certain rate per annum; that this rate is so many times greater than the rate of increase of the race; *therefore*, within so many years or decades the disease is certain to exterminate us. The latest disease to be submitted to this simple formula for calculating the date of the end of the world — for it does not make the faintest difference to us how long and stupidly the world goes on spinning after we have stopped, the real end of the world is when *we* end — is that clogging of the body-filters known as Bright's Disease.

The method is simplicity itself, and as convincing as it is simple. There appears to be no escape from its awful conclusion. From unimpeachable vital statistics taken from the records of certain cities and areas in these United States, it is shown that the deaths from Bright's Disease have increased in the past ten years one hundred and thirty-five per cent. As the rate of increase of the community from natural causes during the same time has been only fifteen per cent, it is perfectly obvious that it can only be a matter of five or six decades before we shall all be dead of Bright's Disease.

The only trouble with the method is that it proves too much. In fact the same modern Jeremiah who has constructed such a terrible horoscope for us under the sign of Bright's Disease has illustrated this defect by incautiously taking up another modern disease which he regards as a menace to the future of the race, namely, insanity. Applying the same formula here, he actually has the hardihood and heartless cruelty to announce that, at present rates of increase, every American-born citizen will have become insane by 1966, forgetting, apparently, that at least half of us are to be dead of Bright's Disease before that time.

And when you come to consider the claims as race exterminators of nearly a dozen equally-to-be-dreaded pathologic perils, such as appendicitis, cancer, heart disease, tuberculosis, alcoholism, meat-eating, cigarettes, race suicide, sugar, and syphilis, it is obvious that within half a century there will not be enough human beings left to go round among the diseases and furnish one meal a day to each. So that the process finally lands us in the consoling conclusion that just as surely as the human race becomes extinct so will the diseases, for lack of anything to feed upon; and perhaps the second conclusion may get ahead of the first. Certainly we are at liberty to take our choice between them and believe — as we generally do in matters of logic and conviction — whichever of the two we personally prefer.

We may even find ourselves in the frame of mind of the little boy in John B. Gough's story, who, one Sunday afternoon, was shown a picture of Christian martyrs being thrown to the lions in a Roman arena. After he had gazed at it like one fascinated for some ten or fifteen minutes, his mother asked him if it did not make him feel sorry for the poor Christians.

"Yes," he said, "I'm sorry for the poor Christians, but I'm a great deal sorrier for that poor little lion over there in the corner that hasn't got any Christian."

Our sympathy may waver between our luckless

posterity and the poor diseases that have no further material to feed on.

Every disease, like every dog, has its day; and this appears to be the day of Bright's Disease. The professional prognosticators and other prophets of evil have had their eye upon it for some time, ever since we began to get away from the "Dispensation-of-Providence" view of disease and that picturesque fatalism, so well illustrated by the Turkish pasha, who, when asked by an English consul for a list of the deaths in his province for the last ten years and the causes thereof, replied that there was no such list, for the labor of making it would be great and the foolishness thereof still greater, since these things happened according to the will of Allah which none could attempt to change without impiety.

When we began insisting upon knowing just what we died of and what could be done about it, we began to discover both some very encouraging and some rather alarming facts. The encouraging side of the shield was that nearly all the acute diseases and infections, like typhoid, tuberculosis, pneumonia, smallpox, cholera, et cetera, were considerably, and in most instances rapidly, decreasing. But, on the other hand, came the obverse side, that another, less fatal but still formidable group of diseases seemed to be steadily increasing. Chief among these last are ranked Bright's Disease, insanity and other diseases of the nervous system, heart disease, and cancer.

As this is — we are pleased to believe — a civilized age, and these diseases are increasing in this age, the conclusion was promptly jumped to that these were diseases of civilization and in some peculiar way dependent upon its new conditions. The next natural and indeed inevitable step in this hand-me-down logic was to sally forth among modern conditions and with as little delay as possible pick out and apprehend those which were responsible for these modern diseases.

The manner of fixing responsibility was, unfortunately, in some instances almost as summary as the judicial procedures of frontier times in California, where whenever a crime was committed the authorities exclaimed, "*Fiat justitia, ruat cœlum!*" and went forth and hanged a Chinaman. Whatever conditions were newest or most unpopular or most prominent at the time were immediately accused of being the causes of the new diseases. This was the method, in fact, of the Jeremiah of 1966, who asserts, with all the confidence in the world, that meat-eating, alcohol, and theater-going are the causes of these maladies.

On the same principle, he might just as well have incriminated postage stamps, paper collars, and suffragettes. For the sole connection between the effect and its alleged cause was that they were both modern!

The reasoning is of the childish naïveté of the logic of the savage, to whose mind it is a striking point of resemblance between a cow and a comet that they both have tails. In fact, the whole argument about the so-called "diseases of modern civilization" is riddled with uncertainties, not to say absurdities.

In the first place, we have no valid proof that these diseases are any more common now than they were fifty, a hundred and fifty, or five hundred years ago. Diseases are "new" only in the sense of having been recently discovered, and they are discovered as Columbus discovered America or Watt the power of steam — they had always been there, but we had not had intelligence enough to recognize them!

Strange as it may seem, we have no positive proof of the origin of a single new serious disease since the dawn of recorded history. At least seventy per cent of all our serious diseases were well known to the Greeks and probably to the Egyptians. And the probability is that nearly half the remainder were also in existence then, though Bright's Disease, for instance, was only clearly recognized and traced to its anatomical cause, the kidney, some eighty years ago by Dr. Richard Bright, of Guy's Hospital, London, whose name it now bears. It had certainly existed for centuries, and probably for thousands of years before that. Obviously, any statement as to its being more or less common in the nineteenth century than, say, the fourteenth, can be nothing better than the merest guess.

The second fault in the argument about modern diseases and their menace is, that our systems and methods of vital statistics are so exceedingly new and young. There are no complete public or official records, of more than the mere bald fact of births and deaths, which date back more than fifty years, except for certain very limited areas and groups. The majority of our vital statistics are barely thirty years old, and even less than that in America.

Last and greatest of all comes the uncertainty as to

how much of an apparent increase simply means better and prompter recognition of the disease.

Obviously, after a disease has been discovered it is some time before it becomes sufficiently well known to be readily recognized by the rank and file of the medical profession, and still longer before the laity come to believe in it and have any clear idea of its nature. Almost every new disease when it is first discovered is believed to be as rare as it is new; but often, when its picture has been distributed to the rogues' galleries of our hospital wards and consultation rooms all over the medical world, it comes to be recognized as quite a common criminal.

Such was the case with appendicitis, and in lesser degree with those two diseases which are exciting so much alarm at present — infantile paralysis and cerebro-spinal meningitis.

The former, for instance, is now pretty generally recognized as the real "Ethiopian in the woodpile" of those numerous stories of children who were let fall from their mother's or nurse's arms in infancy, and later developed a life-long lameness or paralysis, while cerebro-spinal meningitis has been helping to stock our blind asylums and our schools for deaf-mutes for centuries. As both popular and professional intelligence in regard to a disease increase, and more and more of the cases that occur are recognized and reported, it will appear to be increasing, and often at an alarmingly rapid rate.

Bright's Disease furnishes a very pretty illustration of the way in which diseases "increase" in modern times, and are manufactured by the very means devised for their recognition. The rapid, recent increase in frequency of Bright's Disease has run parallel with, and probably been chiefly due to, a most harmless and wholesome phenomenon, namely, the spread of the habit of life insurance and the consequent frequent examinations for albumen in the urine.

It is safe to say that we should not have upon our mortality records more than half as many cases of Bright's Disease as we now have had it not been for this widespread habit among business men of insuring their lives and having routine examinations of the urine made. Almost the first question that a doctor asks nowadays of a patient in whom he discovers Bright's Disease is, "When were you last examined for life insurance?" as such an examination is usually the first thing which attracts the patient's attention to the condition of his kidneys.

The same is true, though in lesser degree, of heart disease and of tuberculosis. There can be little question that the regular habit of careful physical examination set on foot by the life insurance companies has been of great hygienic value to the community, prolonging thousands of valuable lives and saving other thousands by warning them of their danger in time to take effective steps for its cure. Quite unintentionally the insurance companies are saving lives as well as insuring them; and now that they are becoming intelligent enough to do this intentionally and devote part of their huge surpluses to the active prevention of disease, they will add still more to the benefits which they confer upon and reap from the community.

There is a surprising amount of truth in the shrewd old Spanish proverb, "Threatened men live long." One of the many cheering features of modern medicine is that there is almost no known disease whose diagnosis is now equivalent to a death sentence, and scarcely a single disease in which a sufficiently early recognition is not merely half but nine tenths of a cure. Almost everybody knows that Bright's Disease is a disease of the kidney, and that it is connected with, and proclaimed by, the appearance of albumen in the urine. Every one is equally sure that its discovery is an intimation to make one's will and set one's house in order.

This last has proved, fortunately, to be one of the familiar overleaps of popular opinion. It was natural enough because, twenty or thirty years ago, a case of Bright's Disease was usually not recognized, nor even brought under the eye of a physician, until it had been in existence for years and had seriously damaged both kidneys and produced changes in the liver, heart, and nervous system which were beyond repair. Nowadays, although the presence of albumen in the urine is always a serious and disquieting symptom, yet it does not inspire the terror-stricken panic which it used to cause. We know that a great number of different influences may cause albumen to appear temporarily in the urine, so that a large number of cases of albuminuria are curable, or will get well of themselves.

Even if albumen persists in the urine it may be only due to an inflammation or damage of a small part of one kidney, and the kidney has wonderful powers of compensation, especially when assisted by the skin and the liver. So that by the skillful utilization of all the reserve powers of nature, by dieting, bathing, sweating, and the sparing use of certain helpful drugs, especially purges, we can hold the situation in balance, and keep the blood sufficiently purified for years and even decades; in fact, until the patient dies of something else.

The more carefully and broadly we consider the problem of the so-called diseases of civilization, the chronic decays of later life, the more we are impressed with the importance of attacking and preventing the spread of the ordinary acute infections. These were long regarded as dangerous chiefly on account of their immediate mortality, which is bad enough; but we are now finding that the damage they do by the marks and scars which they leave upon the hearts, kidneys, and nervous systems of those who survive them, though slower in showing itself, is almost as serious a matter in the long run as the immediate deaths they cause.

Sanitarians have been accused of saving children from the diseases of infancy, scarlet fever, and diphtheria, and young adults from pneumonia, tuberculosis, and typhoid, only to have them die in middle life from Bright's Disease and diseases of the heart and nervous system. Indeed, such real increase in these diseases as may have occurred is probably due to this fact. But now we know that the large majority of these so-called "diseases of later life" are the results of the innocent-looking little diseases of childhood. The so-called "new" diseases of civilization are chiefly due to our old enemies, the infectious diseases of barbarism.

We have no reason to dread the future, for almost everything that is new in our civilized conditions is an improvement, from a health point of view, upon the situation of our fathers and of our grandfathers, legends of the Good Old Days notwithstanding.

Even the overcrowding in our slums of which we hear so much is not half so bad or so unsanitary as the walled cities of the Middle Ages, or the dark, damp, undrained peasant's hut or laborer's cottage of fifty years ago.

The strains upon our nervous system, instead of being greater, are probably less than in any previous age of battle, murder, and sudden death; and the wear and tear upon our disgestions is certainly less, for food is far better, more abundant, and better cooked than ever before.

Stamping out completely, as will be done for most of them within fifty years, our infectious fevers and diseases will not cause us to live forever, but we shall certainly have to invent some other diseases to die of in later life than Bright's Disease, heart disease, and paralysis.

The new diseases of civilization are chiefly the results of the old diseases and conditions of barbarism. The remedy for the evils of civilization is more civilization!

CHAPTER II

THE DAWN OF THE NEW DOCTOR

IT was the boast of the cynics of the Renaissance that they believed nothing — save that ginger was hot in the mouth. And we know nothing certain about medicine a hundred years hence, save that it will taste bitter — and that none of us will be here to take it.

Moreover, it is probable that the bitterness of the medicine of the future will be tasted rather by classes than by individuals, by corporations than by children. And its after-effects will be even more salutary than they are now. The doctor of the future will prescribe for the community, rather than for the individual; then he will get lasting results instead of temporary ones. And the community will both take and administer his doses.

Of course it goes without saying, that huge progress will have been made upon the purely curative or reparative sides of the science and art of medicine — new drugs, wonderful antitoxins, marvelous surgery. But all this will simply have become only the Repairs and Alterations Department of a great Race-Building and Nation-Construction business, such as the world has never yet seen.

It is as certain as anything can well be, on this mundane sphere, that we shall have discovered an antitoxin for almost every known infection plague, but it is almost equally certain, and much more to be hoped, that we shall, long before the year 2014, have wiped out of existence all of these enemies of humanity, by preventing their spread and insisting upon wholesome and human conditions of life and work for all classes, and have as little use for our antitoxins as we now have for antidotes against snakebite.

And a good riddance the infections will be, for, although it may be faintly urged in their defense that they weed out a few of the weaklings and the unfit, they perform this slight racial service in about the clumsiest, most painful, and most expensive manner conceivable. And even those who survive them are not only not a whit the better for the experience, but often permanently the worse. Too often they carry the scars of them to their graves, and land in these the sooner on account of them.

Moreover, in the fight against them many a hoary error, many an ancient injustice, will fall. Indeed, the fight against contagious diseases is one of the most hopeful in its certainty of victory, one of the best worth while in the value of its conquests, and one of the prettiest quarrels that ever appealed to those who really love a fight, which includes eight tenths of male humanity when it is healthy — to say nothing of the New Woman.

The next two decades will see thousands of eager-eyed youngsters enlisting for the war. There are few ventures in which they can embark with better chances of winning their spurs, as the real knights of the twenty-first century, than in the new practice of medicine.

It is practically certain that the laboratory of our synthetic chemists will have provided us with an array of new wonder-working drugs; that we shall have remedies specially created for particular disease conditions, from the knowledge of the effects of their chemical composition upon those chemical changes in our tissues which, when harmonious, we call life, when inharmonious, disease; that the physiological chemist, by his tireless analyses of the juices and secretions of all our glands, our organs, and our tissues, will be able to determine just what substances are the secret of their activity and what other acid, or salt, or globulin controls that activity and keeps it within the bounds of health. When these have been determined and supplied to us in pure form, we may possess a whole new Materia Medica of Nature's own remedies, with which we can stimulate whatever activity of whatever organ in the body we may find to be deficient, or check whatever may be in excess. It might even give us the power of temporarily filling the place and doing the work of any organ in the body which might have become disabled, and thus tide the organism over a period of otherwise fatal defect and enable it to regain its physiological balance.

But it is equally certain that we shall increasingly regard even such wondrous remedies as these as we already do our drugs — as mere makeshifts, patches and plasters, apologies for previous neglect, whether ignorant or culpable. As one of our leaders of medicine has already prophetically declared: "He is the best physician who best knows the worthlessness of most drugs."

Drugs are of priceless value when needed, but they are at best emergency measures of most temporary utility, — emetics for arsenic, bandages upon spurting arteries. The more effective they are in the right place, the more harmful in the wrong one. The medicine of the future will know but few drugs, and know those so exceedingly well that it will thoroughly understand just when not to use them.

It will devote at least three times as much time to keeping its patients well as it will to curing them after they are sick. It will save a man's life with drugs in order that it may cure him afterward with Nature's real remedies — food and fresh air.

There can be no question that surgery will have continued on that marvelous upward bound which began with the discovery of antisepsis, barely half a century ago. It has already reached the point of being able to remove with neatness, dispatch, and safety anything that appears to be superfluous in the body, whether a tumor, or an organ which is out of date, like the appendix, the ovary or, according to Metchnikoff, the large intestine.

It has made an encouraging start in the direction of substituting or engrafting healthy organs, or portions of them, in the place of diseased ones removed.

And while it hardly seems probable that it will be able to go so far as to invade the realm of religion, and give one convicted of physiological sin, such as rheumatism, a new heart, or "administer to a mind diseased" by supplying a new and healthy brain, yet it is within the limits of possibilities that by the year 2014 it will be able to graft in a piece of supplementary liver or kidney, or suprarenal or thyroid gland, which will be of the greatest temporary utility as a life preserver.

At the same time the more successful and effective the medicine of the future becomes, the less the surgeon will have to do. There will always remain a wide and incalculably useful field for his splendid skill in the repair of congenital effects and of unavoidable accidents, in the removal of tumors and of portions of the body which have become fatally diseased and threaten to involve the entire body in their destruction.

But if there were no tuberculosis, for instance, there would be comparatively little surgery of the spine or of the hip. The abolition of blood-poisoning and of venereal disease would do away with two thirds of all abdominal and pelvic operations, while enforcement of humane and proper laws against avoidable accidents in industry and travel would cut down bone-settings and amputations to the same degree.

By the year 2014 we may, perhaps, have a National Department of Public Health, with a doctor in the Cabinet, to balance the five lawyers! And we may even have come up to the level of Japan and given our army medical department full authority to prevent disease among our soldiers in the field.

But this is a dream rather than a prophecy. Certainly the new doctor will work with the architect in designing new buildings, especially schoolhouses, apartments, and theaters; with the engineer in city planning and laying out new additions; with the amusement promoter in devising new plays and sports for the people, and lose his present too exclusive association in the popular mind with the druggist and the undertaker.

The medicine of a century hence will concern itself largely with three great tasks: The intelligent control and supervision of the production and distribution of food; the study and improvement of education, and the rational adjustment of hours and conditions of work.

It will concern itself with the production and preparation of food, rather than the production and preparation of drugs, because it knows that its only permanent results in the direction of improving health will be won by the former instead of by the latter. The kitchen is the best laboratory, and the doctor of the future may even take rank with the cook as a public benefactor.

The medical colleges of 2014 will teach the botany, geographical source, and methods of production and preparation of foods as carefully as they now do those of drugs. And their graduates will be able to play their part in a great National Commission, or Board of Food Supply and Distribution, which will spend as much time on this really vital problem as our governments now do on the tariff, the income tax, and how to sink as many of your neighbor's ships and kill as many of his citizens as possible in a given time.

The next sanitary problem would be to see that each individual got his proper share of that supply. For if there be anything that the medicine of the future is sure of, it is that no community can afford to allow any child born into it to grow up without a full and abundant supply of food, as well as air and liberty.

To permit anything short of this is simply to breed criminals and paupers, and the ancestors of more criminals, defectives, and paupers. No matter what its first cost, it will save the State five times that amount in the long run.

There will be difficulties in the way, but these could be overcome by patient and intelligent study, especially as our sister profession of the law would probably by that time have also moved forward and become a positive help to progress instead of a hindrance.

The doctor of the year 2014 will work shoulder to shoulder with the teacher. He will see to it that education shall train and develop the whole child, instead of just the expanded bulb at the top of him, leaving the rest of him to shift for itself in the intervals that remain. The new medicine will make schooling a thing of the open air instead of stuffy rooms, of fields and gardens instead of printed pages, of deeds instead of words.

It will fit children for life by living, instead of by reading in books how it should be done. It will not allow the schoolroom to interfere with the playground. It will fit instruction to the growing brain just as food to the stomach and exercise to the muscles.

Every child will be under its watchful eye from the day of its birth, to see that it is not robbed of any of its birthrights; that its eyes are keen and clear, not bleared by disease or dirt; its hearing sharp, not blunted by adenoids; its teeth sound and white, not ragged and poisonous, and its back straight and sturdy, not bowed by premature toil, or burdens no child should carry.

Any guaranty of life, liberty, and the pursuit of happiness without these things is little better than a mockery. And the medicine of 2014 with the community behind it, will see that whosoever shall cause one of these little ones to offend, shall find that it were literally better for him that a millstone were hanged about his neck.

It is idle to lavish instruction upon starving children, or to strew mathematical pearls before brains fogged and dulled with sleeping in a beehive or a rabbit warren.

Perhaps by 2014 teachers may recognize that it is as important for a child to correctly bound and describe his liver as the countries of Europe, or the States of the Union, and to know at least as much of his own interior as he does of that of Hindustan. Education for life will include a sound, working knowledge of the body machine that he has to live and work with; of what food fuels will best and most economically supply it with energy; how its bearings are to be watched and its gears regulated; and how to make roadside repairs.

When every child is taught with his A B C's something of the dangers of impure water; of the different dirts that may get into it — from typhoid bacilli to the toxin of the yeast germ — and how to fight them; that dirty milk has slaughtered more innocents than a thousand Herods; that the fly is both a pest and a pestilence breeder, a product of filth and a cause of disease; that consumption is bred solely by the spit of consumptives, in the underfed and overworked; that malaria and yellow fever can be spread only by mosquitoes, and the black death solely by fleas and rats,— then the community will rise up and demand of its officers that they protect its life and its health, as well as — nay, rather than — its property.

They may even live up to Lord Palmerston's pregnant saying, that for every death from typhoid somebody ought to be hanged. The child of the future will be taught that it is treason to the State and a crime against biologic morals to give aid, shelter, or comfort to any of these — its enemies.

The medicine of the future will be deeply concerned with the distribution and conditions of work in the community. The three great foundation stones of national health and efficiency are food, housing, and work, but the greatest of these is work, for food and housing depend upon wages, and wages upon work.

Vigorous, blood-stirring work that calls for the best a man has in him, within the reasonable limits of his powers, is wholesome, invigorating, and upbuilding — the very mainspring of progress and the foundation of morality. Beyond these limits, it shortens life, dulls intelligence, and degrades morality.

No intelligent community can afford to allow any of its members to habitually go beyond this limit, or to shirk their proper share.

The medicine of the future will carefully and lovingly study and consider every child brought into the school and shop, for by that time no one will be able to tell where one ends and the other begins — both will alike be educational. The best and most priceless product of any factory or shop is the type of man that it turns out.

No industry is profitable to the State which shortens the lives or the stature of its workers. What will it profit a nation to gain the commercial supremacy of the world and lose its own physique and stamina?

Every human institution originated as a makeshift. Danger is the mother of wit, and even most of our sciences were born in emergencies. The first astronomer was a rain-doctor, a caster of horoscopes, an averter of evil stars. The first chemist dealt in charms and amulets, in mad-stones and love-philters, and later spent his life in the search for the Elixir of Youth and the Philosopher's Stone. Naturally, the practice of medicine began with the hurried administration of herbs and roots as antidotes, the driving away of disease demons with tom-toms and incantations, and for generations after it had emerged into the light of reason it chiefly occupied itself with reducing fevers, emptying poisoned stomachs, tying spurting arteries, purging, blistering, bleeding. In short, the doctor always has been, and is yet, what our Indian wards would term "The Man-Called-in-a-Hurry" to do something right away quick. Hence the extraordinary but now departed vogue of emetics, purgatives, and the lancet — relics of barbarism all.

In the language of Scripture his function has been chiefly to pull his neighbor's ox — or the other quadruped — out of a pit. He has been a General Emergency Man, and the profession a sort of social "Wrecking Crew" or "Breakdown Gang," for so many centuries that it is difficult to consider him seriously in any other capacity. Yet this is precisely what the New Doctor is demanding — to be regarded in a different light, as a preventer instead of a curer, an active promoter of health instead of a mere arrester or mitigator of disease. We doctors want to be associated in the minds of our patients with the grocer, the teacher, and the builder instead of the minister and the morgue.

One of the greatest obstacles to this forward step is the ancient and time-honored financial relation between doctor and patient, the principle on which the doctor is paid. What can the physician do in the effective prevention of disease if he is never called until after the patient is "sick enough to need a doctor"? Is it reasonable to expect the medical profession to devote its best energies to the prevention of disease when it is paid only in proportion to the amount of sickness that actually occurs? It is one of the finest and most convincing proofs that human nature has something more in it than pure selfishness — that gold is not the thing which man prizes most highly — that the medical profession, even under this absurd and irrational system of remuneration, has been and is, in season and out of season, the most persistent foe of disease, the most unselfish advocate of, and insister upon, sanitary reforms. No claim for anything heroic or angelic in doctors on this score. Simply that they are men like other men, and the two things that a real man most loves to do are: first, to fight; and second, to be of service to his country. We doctors have grown to hate disease instinctively, as a terrier hates a polecat, — to attack it on all occasions, whether it touches us or not, and to hound it eagerly to its lair for the sheer joy of battle and the chase.

We are tired of being so exclusively called to "lock the stable door after the horse is stolen." We are not so much losing faith in drugs as gaining confidence in Nature and her remedies: fresh air, pure water, sound food, exercise, and sleep. These are the only remedies we really believe in as means of permanent cure or genuine improvement of the race. Drugs are mere stop-gaps; tourniquets on a spurting artery, of priceless value in emergencies, but only of most temporary utility. We would a hundred times rather prevent a germ or a poison from getting into the body than inject an antidote or an antitoxin after it has pierced the citadel. Drugs or mental influence may help, but Nature alone cures.

Coöperation, solidarity, mutual helpfulness is the keynote of the century. Originally the doctor had to fight disease single-handed with such weapons as he carried at his saddle-bow. Then it was found necessary to unite with his fellow-physicians for coöperative study and investigation, first of the cure and then of the causes of disease. Thanks to the new science of bacteriology, born of this medical coöperation, the causes of most of our deadliest diseases have been clearly and unmistakably discovered. Now a further step in coöperation is necessary, and that is the assistance of the community to stamp out these diseases bodily by removing both their causes and the conditions which favor them. The ideal of the New Doctor is Service — service to the people, with the people, for the people. We have pushed the battle against disease almost as far as we can, unaided; now we are calling for help from the community.

This new fighting shoulder-to-shoulder of physician and patient is coming about in two ways. First, and at present most striking, is the assumption of hygienic and sanitary functions by the State. This is rapidly becoming a prominent — and bids fair soon to be the leading — political question of the day, involving, as it does, problems not merely of health and happiness, but also of efficiency, of crime and dependency, of economics and morality. No further reference need be made to this feature of the union between the doctor and the community except that within fifty years at least from one fourth to one third of our present number of physicians to the thousand of population will be in the employ of the State and devoted to what may be broadly termed the social treatment of disease, as health officers, school physicians, mine and factory inspectors, directors of food production, and superintendents of prisons and asylums. Crime is, broadly considered, largely a medical problem. Probably half our criminals are born so, and could be recognized and isolated before they could do any harm as easily as so many epileptics or imbeciles, while most of the other half are made by bad hygienic or social surroundings in childhood. Put our criminal and defective classes in the care of intelligent physicians and biologists instead of stupid policemen and ignorant, precedent-worshiping lawyers, and the crime problem would be half-solved within three decades.

There is no longer any question that the health officer, the public physician, should devote himself chiefly to prevention. The problem now is how the private physician, or family doctor, may be enabled to do the same. The spirit of our present scheme of relations between patient and physician might be summed up as "Millions for cure, but not more than ten cents for prevention." It is so arranged as to insure the maximum of dosing and drugging with the minimum of prevention. It is, of course, both our privilege and out duty to point out to our patient, at the same time that we give him the prescription which is to relieve his immediate discomfort, the bad physical habits which have led to or caused his disease and to urge him to reform them in future. Much influence for permanent cure can be and is exerted in this way. But by many of our patients this excellent and wholesome advice is looked upon as a dose of scolding to be swallowed with the medicine and then forgotten.

One of the chief reasons for the futility of this advice is that it costs nothing. What the patient pays for is the prescription — the advice is thrown in gratis. And, as that grotesque but shrewd philosopher and student of human nature, Josh Billings, long ago remarked: "Whut people gits fer nothin' they ginerally valleys at about whut they giv fer it!" Make a patient pay for advice, whether he gets a prescription or not, and he is at least five times as likely to follow it.

To meet these new conditions — the increasing desire of the better class of physicians to do more radical and effective health work, and the increasing demand of the more intelligent class of patients for sound, hygienic advice and instruction how to live, instead of drugs — a readjustment of our relations would be highly advisable. The plan suggested for consideration is, briefly: That physicians should be engaged by the year instead of by the visit or case. That each individual or family should engage a medical attendant for a term of twelve months, agreeing to pay him a specified salary in advance, either in full or in quarterly or semiannual payments, as preferred. For this sum, which would vary according to the size and financial and social position of the household, the physician would agree to examine thoroughly every member of it at least twice a year and to render all medical services required except operations or treatments demanding the skill and training of a specialist. The physician would further agree, in consideration of the sum specified, to make an annual or semiannual inspection of the sanitary condition of the house and premises of his client, and to offer such suggestions as he saw fit in regard to the diet or habits of life of the

family; in short, to act as general adviser on all matters
of hygiene or therapeutics. The system might briefly,
and perhaps not inaptly, be described as a scheme of
"health insurance."

The advantages of such a plan are obvious. Certain
objections to it, perhaps, equally so. To take the former first, the new relation would make us not merely
physicians, but also sanitary inspectors and health
advisers to all our families. We could condemn the
well which was too near the cesspool or privy-vault
without having to wait for typhoid to break out in
the family. We could screen the water-butt or kerosene the duck pond or water garden, instead of adding the insult of quinine to the injury of malaria.
We could, personally, see that windows would open
and bedrooms would ventilate, instead of waiting
until the flower of the flock was smitten with the
White Plague of the North. We could order removed
the garbage-heaps and manure-piles which breed that
not least of the plagues of Egypt, the fly. We could
weigh one child and measure another and take the
blood count of a third, and detect malnutrition,
arrested development, and anæmia at their very be-
ginnings; then regulate food, exercise, and school
hours accordingly. We could discover tuberculosis
in the stage when nine tenths of it can be cured. We
could follow the children of our families to their schoolrooms, the adults to their offices and workshops, and
thus make the pressure upon insanitary schoolhouses,
unventilated workshops, and stuffy offices too powerful to be resisted.

Should any of our family clientele fall ill, they would not have the slightest inducement to delay consulting us. Indeed, moved by a not unnatural desire to get their money's worth out of us, they would probably hasten to do so at once. This would put us in control of the case in those hours or days which are worth at least five times as much for curative purposes as any which succeed them. Nine times out of ten a case seen early is a case half-cured. We would be perfectly at liberty to make as many visits as we thought best, without being accused of "running up a bill," and to keep the patient under observation and care until we were satisfied that every possible danger of relapse or complication was over and he was really cured.

As it is now, half our patients disappear from our view just as soon as they begin to feel markedly better, believing that the medicine will complete the cure and unwilling to incur the expense of further visits. Fully half, if not two thirds, of our most serious chronic troubles of the heart, the kidneys, the brain, and the nervous system are the results of half-cured attacks of acute infectious diseases, from "colds" and tonsillitis to typhoid.

Now as to the objections. They are real, and some of them weighty, but most of them could be obviated by a little intelligent planning and mutual consideration. First of all would be the difficulty of fixing an appropriate fee for services of such variable character and incalculable amount. But, of course, the law of averages runs in sickness just as it does in births, deaths, incomes, and life expectancies, and as there are scores of companies now that insure against sickness, and hundreds that insure against death, for a fixed annual sum, there would be little serious difficulty in working out, from the data afforded by our census reports and vital statistics, an average "morbidity" per capita for each age, sex, and social condition in the community. From this could be constructed a scale of annual payment which would be reasonably safe to cover the average expenses for medical attendance of each individual and family, and by a mutual agreement between the medical societies and the community these could be adopted as fees, just like the present fees charged for visits, for office treatments, for operations, for confinements, etc. However, if this objection be too strenuously insisted upon, it would be perfectly feasible to divide the scheme in two, as it were, and let each individual or family engage a physician to inspect his house and place of business and examine each member thoroughly at least twice a year for a fixed sum, and then to render the medical services required, either at a fixed rate per visit or treatment or according to the usual fee bill of the locality.

Unfortunately, any arrangement for medical services by the year would be looked upon with suspicion by a considerable percentage of the medical profession, on account of the bad odor into which this plan of attendance has been brought by the friendly societies, sick-benefit clubs, and fraternal organizations on this side of the Atlantic, in England and France, and the *Kranken-Kassen* in Germany and

Austria. This is not due to any inherent vice of the plan, but simply to the fact that these clubs have, for the most part, been formed chiefly for the purpose of getting medical attendance of some sort for their members at the lowest possible rate. They go about the matter in the most mercenary fashion imaginable, advertising the number of their members and the great social and practical advantages to be derived from the honor of becoming their physician, and then invite bids for the job-lot of work from all the impecunious physicians of the neighborhood. The result, naturally, has been that contracts have been taken at ridiculously and outrageously low rates, such as twenty-five and even fifteen cents a visit, medicine included, with the inevitable concomitant that the work has been badly and hastily done and the services often of the poorest quality.

Finally, as to the expense and practical bearings of such a readjustment. At first sight these would appear to be the greatest stumbling-block; but as a matter of fact, they would form one of its greatest advantages. We should be enabled to take advantage of the two great principles, coöperation and the law of averages; and instead of either underpaying the doctor or overloading the patient we should be enabled to save money for both. This is the kernel of good in the sick-club and benefit societies' plan, and while it has been used almost exclusively for the benefit of the patient there is no reason why it might not, like every good bargain, be made profitable to both parties. "But," some one will at once ask, "how can any adjustment possibly be made by which the community shall pay little or nothing more and yet get better and more useful service, and at the same time the doctor receive no less?"

The problem is a wide and interesting one. But the answer may be briefly phrased in the statement that the community could abundantly well afford to pay twice what it now does for being cured and patched up as best may be, for being kept well and avoiding the frightful waste of time, life, money, and nerve-strain due to preventable disease. The doctor, on the other hand, could well afford to render medical services for an average of less than half his present fees, if he could get these fees from all his patients and be reasonably sure of collecting them.

As the situation stands now, nearly one fourth of the community is treated at hospitals, dispensaries, and other charitable institutions. Another fourth the doctor treats for nothing, through the involuntary mechanism of inability to collect his bill or of reductions on account of poverty. And scarcely one half of the community pays him according to the rates laid down in the fee bills, which, naturally, have to be made large enough to cover.

This is bad economics in every way. The free hospitals and dispensaries encourage pauperism, not to say sponging, and are attended by hundreds of thousands of individuals in comfortable and even comparatively well-to-do circumstances. While, on the other hand, hundreds of thousands of the self-respecting poor, who would gladly pay a moderate fee every month or every year out of their wages to "a doctor of their own," as they express it, feel unable to meet the regular "doctor's charges," and hence either go to the hospitals, join a sick-benefit club, or worst of all, go without medical services altogether except in extreme emergencies.

If workable, the new scheme would do more than any other step that could be taken to put something like thirty per cent of our entire population upon a self-respecting basis in regard to their needs in sickness and in health, to improve their general welfare, happiness, and efficiency, and to solve the great free hospital and dispensary problem. Think of having every worker in our industrial army under the care of an intelligent, public-spirited physician, who had pledged his honor to keep him and his family in as perfect health as possible! The sanitary laws of factory, mine, and workshop would almost enforce themselves under the incessant fire of such a battery of criticism as that!

The actual expense of such an arrangement and the fees to be charged would, of course, have to be determined and adjusted by a high-minded and intelligent commission of sanitarians, business men, workingmen, and physicians, but it will be safe to say that it would, even in actual fees and money expended for drugs and nursing, be little or no greater than that of our present slipshod, hand-to-mouth plan. This can be roughly estimated by two different methods. One, the actual amounts now received by physicians as incomes from their practice. The other, the proportion of physicians to the population and the amount they would have to receive from each individual to give them an adequate income. From the first point of view it can be promptly stated that the average income of even thoroughly trained and competent physicians is much lower than is usually supposed.

A series of inquiries was set on foot some years ago by one of our medical journals, and, to the surprise of all parties concerned, it was found that the average net income of the practicing physician in these United States was in the neighborhood of twelve hundred dollars a year; and this, of course, refers only to fully qualified, registered, graduate physicians. On this basis it is easy to calculate that if each physician had a clientele of four hundred individuals paying him five dollars apiece per annum he would receive as good an income as he does at present, allowing him eight hundred dollars for office expenses, carriage, telephones, etc.

Further, the average sum actually received from each of his families by a physician in good class of practice is much smaller than is usually supposed. I had occasion to look into this question some years ago and was kindly given access to the books of four of my professional brethren whom I had selected as types suitable for the purpose. One had his practice in a little country town, chiefly among farmers — a typical country doctor. The second was in a small town of about five thousand population, and the third and fourth had rather high-class practices in a Middle Western city of some fifty thousand inhabitants. I went over their books and picked out a list of from fifty to one hundred families who had been regular patients for three years or more, then ascertained the number of persons in each family and calculated the income derived from each. To my surprise the average amount received *per capita* ranged from a dollar and a half per annum in the country district to four dollars per annum in the city. So that an average of five dollars per annum would have given these physicians a better income than they were actually receiving.

Finally, from the broad point of view, the number of physicians in these United States who are registered as in active practice, is, according to the last reports, something like one hundred and forty-five thousand — doctors of all sorts: regular and irregular, allopath, homœopath, hydropath, osteopath, psychopath, good, bad, and indifferent. This, divided into our ninety-five million population, gives about six hundred and fifty inhabitants for each physician.

It may be remarked in passing that this is the highest proportion of physicians in any country in the civilized world, the percentages ranging from one in fifteen hundred in Great Britain, one in two thousand in Germany, one in thirty-five hundred in Italy, and so on down to one in six thousand in Russia, and one in twelve thousand in Turkey. It may be a mere coincidence, but the United States, with the most doctors, has the lowest death-rate, and Turkey, with the fewest, has the highest.

Upon the law of averages, if each doctor in these United States had his average six hundred and fifty souls as patients and received from them an average of five dollars a year each, he would be sure of a reasonable living and a better average income than he receives at present. The rates quoted are, of course, purely suggestive; the actual "premiums" would probably have to be considerably higher at first, to cover contingencies, epidemics, bad bills, etc., and the fact that only a small percentage of the community would at first enter into the scheme. They would, of course, be minimum, and any one who wished more elaborate, or specially skillful, services could pay higher. The more competent a physician the more families he would get, as at present, and if he wished to limit the amount of his practice he could raise his fees. A special rate should be fixed for the laboring-classes and those receiving less than, say, sixty dollars a month. This need not at most exceed the rate already paid by many miners, mill-workers, and others to the "company doctor," of seventy-five cents a month for a single man and twenty-five cents a month additional for each member of a married man's family.

Let the community pay for being kept well instead of being cured and patched up, and the doctor be enabled to devote his energies to building up the health of the entire community instead of dancing attendance upon the whims of the successful one third or one fourth, and the physical welfare and happiness of the race would be immensely improved.

CHAPTER III

THE drug habit is a survival of savagery — an amusing after-echo of the old primitive belief that disease was a mysterious, semi-personal sort of creature, which clutched you or "possessed" you, and had to be shaken off or driven out. A patient in convulsions, for instance, would be naïvely but not unnaturally supposed to be struggling in the grasp of some demon; or perhaps an evil spirit was inside him trying to get out. Naturally, we eagerly sought for some other half-personal, equally mysterious agency like an incantation, the juice of an herb plucked in a certain stage of the moon, or finally, a drug, to banish or neutralize this malign possession. Nor can we afford to laugh at our childish and grotesque ancestors. There are scores of drugs, favorite popular remedies, in widespread use to-day, whose claims rest on no more substantial basis than such a one as the stage of the moon in which they were gathered, and whose healing powers are, naturally — pure moonshine.

Yet this is no disproof of the fact that there are plenty of drugs which are most effective and helpful *when properly used*. The change in our attitude toward drugs is almost as complete as that which we have already considered toward disease. Drugs are no longer regarded as specifics, cures, antidotes, which in some mysterious way will neutralize the equally mysterious influence of disease; but simply as edged tools, as knives, whose effects will depend entirely upon the skill with which they are used.

It is not too much to say that the medical profession to-day no longer believes that any drug (with a few exceptions, like quinine in malaria, mercury and the antitoxins) will cure a disease as such. All that it will do is so to modify conditions as to help the body in its fight against disease. We are no longer content, in the biting phrase of Voltaire, to "pour drugs of which we know little into bodies of which we know less." What will help one patient may harm another, and what may be beneficial in the early stage of a disease will be useless or even injurious in a later stage. In the language of Captain Cuttle, the effect of a drug, like "the bearin' of an obserwation," "depends on the application on it." It is neither rational, nor safe, blindly to swallow down a drug which is highly recommended in a certain disease and expect it to "do the rest." There is no such thing as a universal cure for a disease, nor even a remedy which can be relied upon as "a good thing to take" at any and all stages of it.

It must, therefore, be frankly recognized at the outset in considering the advantages and disadvantages of patent medicines that, broadly and philosophically speaking, two risks have to be taken with all of them: the risk that the medicine, though a useful remedy in this disease, may not fit your particular case or stage of it; and the further risk that you may not have the disease you think you have, in which case, of course, the poor medicine will be a hopeless misfit. Bearing these facts in mind, it is obviously only the course of prudence and good sense to avoid all powerful or drastic remedies of this class, such as, if they do not do good, have the power to do harm. Remedies, therefore, which are advertised to cure immediately, "like magic," "overnight," that are guaranteed to cure every case or money refunded, that "have never been known to fail," etc., are good things to let alone, even if you give credence to their claims. Usually, as a matter of fact, the claims of these "sure cure" remedies are based upon one of two things: prevarication, or some narcotic, most commonly opium, or alcohol.

There is also another universal source of risk which it is only fair to mention and then leave the reader to attach to it as much or as little weight as he chooses, and this is the impossibility of knowing what you are taking. It may surprise many to learn that, strictly speaking, a paper on patent medicines ought to be almost as short as the famous chapter on snakes in Iceland, which consisted of the words, "There are no snakes in Iceland." The vast majority of so-called patent medicines have nothing that is patented about them, except the name or trade-mark. To really patent a remedy it would be necessary to disclose its ingredients and to prove that they had never before been used for the cure of this disease; and this, for obvious reasons, is the last thing that the proprietors of these remedies would think of doing. The composition of the remedy is their most valued secret, which naturally they guard with jealous care, and it is inevitable in the nature of the case itself that any one who takes a dose of it is taking it in the dark. If he chooses to run that risk, it is one of his inalienable rights and privileges; but let him remember that — to paraphrase Voltaire — he is taking a drug of which he knows nothing for a disease of which he knows less, for his guess at its nature may be entirely wrong.

Not even an analysis of the remedy by a government chemist will help him, because the rigid secrecy as to its composition, which is maintained for commercial reasons, enables the manufacturers to change the formula at any time, according to variations in the prices of the different drugs, or the denunciation of one or other of them as injurious. Some well-known patent medicines in the United States have changed their formulas three or four times within the last five or six years.

However, the bulk of patent medicines to-day do not contain anything that is very dangerous, partly on account of the activity of state and federal chemists under the new Pure Food Laws, the agitation which led up to them, and the requirement that the names and amounts of all dangerous drugs shall be printed upon the label; and partly from the fact that most dangerous drugs cost too much to allow them to make their modest thousand per cent of profit. So that if the careful housemother who is stocking up her family medicine-chest wishes to fill her shelves with "Golden Discoveries," and "Arapahoe's Tonics" and "Old Dr. So-and-So's Favorite Prescription," she can do so with less risk of poisoning any of her family than ever before.

The liniments, sprain-cures, and plasters are an old and very favorite class of remedies. For the most part they do little harm and are often quite helpful. Most of them contain substances more or less irritating or stimulating to the skin, such as ammonia, camphor, Spanish fly, etc., and redden the surface by drawing an increased amount of blood to it, which latter by its nutritive and antitoxic effect may help to relieve local infections and disturbances. Their effects, however, are almost purely local, and the belief that anything is absorbed or rubbed in from them into the joints, or into the system generally, is almost entirely without foundation. The more vigorously the liniments are rubbed in, the greater the benefits from their use, for this amateur massage is the principal curative thing about them. The only oil or grease that can be made to "limber up" a stiff joint is "elbow grease."

Another great group of advertised remedies, which are in themselves comparatively harmless in moderate doses, are the laxatives and "antibilious" preparations and pills. The habit of indiscriminately taking cathartics is not a good one, but it is one of the distinguishing habits of the human species, and if you must indulge in it, the various "teas" and "tongue-cleaners" and pleasant pellets can be taken with comparatively little risk beyond some extra and unnecessary griping. Similarly, such aids to digestion, dyspepsia cures, etc., as contain pepsin, pancreatin, or other digestive ferments, are comparatively harmless and, like the milder carminatives and aromatics under the name of "gingers," "pepper teas," "hot drops," etc., will often give considerable temporary relief. The class of remedies for the relief of acidity and fermentation in the stomach, especially those chiefly composed of charcoal, magnesia, soda, ginger, etc., also do little harm, and in many cases will give a good deal of relief. It must, however, be remembered that this relief for the most part is only temporary, and that all those remedies containing soda in considerable amounts, while they check the acidity for the time, increase it later if used too frequently or habitually.

Kidney remedies, cures for Bright's disease, kidney bitters, etc., should be regarded with suspicion, for the reason, first, that the famous group of symptoms beginning with pain in the back, etc., are not the symptoms of Bright's disease at all. In the second place, there is no remedy known to medical science which is in any direct and specific way a cure, or even generally helpful, in Bright's disease.

The group of blood-purifiers, skin-cleansers and internal complexion-improvers should also be treated with considerable reserve. Many of them are more or less harmless, mere decoctions of innocuous roots, herbs, etc., whose principal healing virtues reside in their taste and color. But not a few of them, especially those that claim the most brilliant and constant results contain iodide of potassium, mercury, or small amounts of arsenic, all of which, though useful medicines in their proper place, are edge-tools that it is anything but safe to play with in the dark. The backbone, so to speak, of the group is iodid of potassium, even in those most strenuously claiming to contain only harmless vegetable compounds; and this drug, while helpful in certain special conditions, is exceedingly depressing, both to the appetite and to the general health, in continued doses.

An interesting group of patent medicines is that roughly outlined as the bitters, the tonics, and the "bracers." These all owe their vogue to the widespread and not unnatural belief that a medicine which will make a sick man well will make a well man better. This is, or course, a pure delusion, which will not bear a moment's careful thinking, inasmuch as the only reason why a medicine, for instance quinine in malaria, makes a sick man feel better is that it relieves him of some of his pain or discomfort. A dose of quinine, which would be like the gate of heaven to a malarious patient, if taken by a healthy man, would simply make his stomach burn and his head ring — make him feel less comfortable instead of more so. A dose of medicine will make a sick man feel better, it is true, but never quite as well as he feels in health. Even powerful tonics like quinine, strychnine, digitalis, etc., will not add a particle to the sense of well-being in a healthy individual, nor can they be depended upon to brace up a sick one, except just in those particular conditions in which the organ or tissue upon which they act is diseased.

There is only one class of drugs that can be uniformly relied upon to make an individual who is out of sorts or below par for any reason feel better for a time, and that is the class of narcotics — opium, alcohol, cocaine, chloroform, etc. We are now coming sadly to the conclusion that nearly all so-called "stimulants" are really mild narcotics in disguise, and owe their bracing, "feel-better" effects chiefly to the temporary relief of discomfort. The relief, of course, is only temporary; instead of neutralizing the poisons of fatigue or disease which are already present in the system, another one has been added to them. The depression that follows the exhilaration is greater than that which preceded it; another and larger dose is required, and so the pitifully familiar tragedy proceeds.

There is no known drug that will add in the slightest degree to the strength or vigor of the human body, and no "tissue-builder" on earth except food. The only universally reliable "bracer" is exercise in the open air and sleeping with your windows open, and the only permanent tonics to the body are fresh fruit, red meat, and green vegetables.

A dollar's worth of cream contains ten times the "strength" of any dollar-bottle of tonic ever invented. Eat plenty of real foods, the best you can raise or buy, and you'll have little need of either patent foods or patent medicines. Any remedy which universally, or even in the majority of all cases, produces a sense of exhilaration and improvement is pretty sure to contain a "cheater" of some sort, usually either alcohol or opium.

It is, perhaps, hardly necessary to say that these conclusions upon *a priori* grounds are absolutely supported at every point by the results of the analyses of all this class of remedies. The majority of them contain as much alcohol as whiskey, and some of them more.

The pain-relievers, agony-killers, colic cures, etc., which claim to relieve promptly and surely, should be regarded with suspicion for the same reason — that they are likely to contain either opium or chloroform. While these are perfectly legitimate in skilled hands in some conditions, it is obvious that they are exceedingly unsafe for indiscriminate family use. Moreover, as we have already seen, their use in digestive and bowel troubles is now regarded as bad practice until a thorough and intelligent effort has been made to get rid of the cause. Some, however, of these pain-relievers contain merely strong aromatics and "hot stuffs," with intestinal antiseptics, and now that the Pure Food Law compels the printing upon the label of the amounts of opium, cocaine, chloroform, or alcohol present, it is possible to discriminate between the dangerous and the comparatively harmless.

The indiscriminate use of cough-mixtures should be avoided for reasons already discussed, namely, that most of them are likely merely to smother the symptom without doing much to relieve the cause.

The only known drug to be relied upon to stop a cough within a few hours is opium, and the temptation to use it in popular remedies for scoring speedy cures is, or course, very great.

Of soothing-syrups, "babies' friends," and teething-mixtures of all sorts it is fortunately necessary to speak only in the past tense. They were a scandal and a disgrace, both to the intelligence and the maternal affection of civilization, and have slaughtered more innocents than a hundred Herods. Opium is harmful enough to an adult, but nearly twice as dangerous to a child.

There is progress in patent medicines, as elsewhere, and of late years a huge and very popular group of remedies has sprung up which makes no claim to be descended from the formula of an Indian chief, or the seventh son of a seventh son, or a revelation in a dream in the last century, but is frankly and confessedly modern, namely, the "Headache Cures." These, as the analyses compelled by the Pure Food Law disclose, contain usually one of the by-products of the distillation of coal-tar, namely, acetanilid, phenacetin, antipyrin, etc., known as the "coal-tar remedies." They have the merit of producing the effects claimed for them, in that they frequently relieve the headache, and, if people must take a narcotic, are much preferable to opium, being milder in their action and less actively poisonous.

But they are narcotics, nevertheless, in their action, and while opium strikes at the great vital centers in the medulla, controlling the breathing and the circulation, they strike at the heart; and where this organ is already weakened, or too large doses are taken, serious depression and collapse will follow, with often fatal result. They will also produce a condition of chronic poisoning if taken too frequently. If we could be sure that the dose were small enough and that our hearts were perfectly sound, these remedies might be used in moderation; but unfortunately the commercial safeguard which prevents the putting of too large amounts of real drugs into a patent medicine, namely, their expense, is entirely removed here, as the commonest, and unluckily most effective and most poisonous, of the coal-tar remedies, acetanilid, can be produced at an expense of only a few cents a pound. Hence the desire to produce quick and brilliant results is likely to lead to the inclusion of this drug in these capsules and cachets in dangerously large amounts.

Of course, the use of these remedies for the relief of headache is subject to the same underlying objection as that to the use of all mere pain-relievers — that they cure symptoms without relieving the cause. And this is peculiarly objectionable in the case of headache, in that it at the same time deprives us of one of our most valuable danger-signals of something going wrong, and often of impending breakdown or disease.

There is no royal road to health any more than to learning. The only sure way to keep well is to *be* well, to live well. And fortunately this is not half so hard as it sounds. Our attitude toward sickness, even in this twentieth century, is still far from rational. There is too much of the panicky and spasmodic about it. In spite of the cold, statistical fact that our chances of dying in the next twelve months are only about one in seventy, we persist in regarding death as an ever-present terror and in keeping ourselves unconsciously in the attitude that it is dangerous to be alive.

Though we have a whole procession of indisputable figures, showing that even of those attacked by serious disease only about two in a hundred die, we cower in the shadow of approaching death as soon as we become ill, and would give all our earthly possessions for something that we could swallow in the assurance that it was an infallible remedy, a "sure cure."

Consequently, our constant search and most eager longing in the realm of health and disease still is, not for some rational, natural methods which would increase the already heavy balance in our favor, but for some single procedure, some mysterious substance which will, as we say, "act like a charm" and relieve us "as if by magic" when we become ill or imagine ourselves to be so.

Prevention is as much safer and sounder than cure as legitimate business operations are than gambling or wildcat speculation. Yet we still like to do things "by magic" and are keenly on the lookout for cure-alls.

Nowhere is this tendency more strikingly and amusingly illustrated than in the various recipes one hears so confidently offered for "keeping well." The name of these is legion, but they nearly all have two or three characteristics in common. First, they are not really preventives, but cures, attempts to patch up matters after trouble has already occurred. Second, they are pathetically and often ludicrously ineffective, many of them absolutely worthless. Third, such of them as have some positive effect are apt to be too radical, and may even aggravate the trouble they are supposed to cure.

The vast majority of them, however, are practically harmless and owe such success as they have to the wonderful remedial power of Nature, which she has been perfecting these ten million years past. Their main fault is that they encourage ignorance or neglect of the laws of health and the principles of prevention, and train us to rely upon patching and covering up after the defect has shown itself, instead of upon sound building and good materials beforehand. They are survivals of our strong desire for a short cut which will get us swiftly and with little effort out of the trouble into which carelessness or ignorance has brought us.

Take, for instance, such a simple, everyday matter as the care of the teeth. Every one knows, or should know, that tartar upon the teeth is simply the result of failure to brush and clean them properly. But such commonplace advice as this has little that is attractive about it, and means such a lot of trouble, not merely every day, but three or four times a day. Here is a published cure for tartar, which apparently only needs to be used twice a week: "Buy five cents' worth of pumice-stone, and clean your teeth twice a week with it, and notice how the tartar disappears."

This is one of the cures that "works." The tartar will disappear and something else with it — that is, the polish of the enamel, the natural glass which coats the teeth and is their principal protection against decay. Tartar is bad enough, but too much pumice-stone may be worse. By cutting and scratching the natural surface of the teeth it will merely lay the foundation for the accumulation of more tartar and make openings for the acids of the food and the juices of the mouth to attack and eat away the teeth. Brush the teeth and gums thoroughly after every meal and at bedtime with a moderately stiff brush, with plenty of cool water to which a little mild alkali, like bicarbonate of soda, or some local antiseptic may be added once or twice a day, and let the brushing include not merely the teeth, but the gums and the inside of the lips and cheeks as well, and you will have no need of pumice-stone.

Another popular remedy which enjoys a surprising reputation and is frequently confidently brought forward as a sure cure is the familiar exposure of wounds, particularly of the foot, to the smoke of burning woolen cloth. This is most confidently recommended not only certainly to "take all the soreness out" of an inflamed wound, but absolutely to prevent lockjaw or tetanus.

The only proper way of curing an inflamed wound is to keep the dirt out of it. It makes little difference where this dirt comes from. It is pretty sure to contain germs of some sort. And while fortunately most of these are not actually poisonous, they are none of them of any assistance in the process of healing, and it is always best to be on the safe side and keep them out. This can be done, in eight slight wounds out of ten, by thorough washing with boiled water and then bandaging with a dressing containing a layer of absorbent cotton, which is impervious to germs. If made by a knife which has been used for cutting meat, cheese, fish, etc., or by a dirty nail or tool, some non-poisonous antiseptic, like formalin, may be added to the water, a teaspoonful to a pint, or one of the numerous peroxides or dioxides of hydrogen applied full strength. If, however, the wound be of any severity or depth, or much dirt of any kind has got in, it is better to have it seen by a physician, as one or two thorough antiseptic dressings at the beginning may save weeks of suffering and disability.

As for curing tetanus, this is due to a perfectly definite bacillus, and can be cured by nothing except the antitoxic serum prepared for the purpose. And even this must be used very shortly after the wound is made, in order to give a reasonable prospect of a cure. This bacillus has the curious habit of living in the alimentary canal of our friend the horse, and hence is found in garden soils which have been enriched with stable manure, and in the dust and dirt of our city streets. This explains why wounds of the feet and hands, and particularly the former, are more likely to be followed by lockjaw than those of any other part of the body, because they are more exposed to contamination with garden soil or city dust. Fortunately, while a very serious, it is not a very common, infection. Probably not more than one wound in five hundred, even of the feet, is likely to be followed by it.

Thorough and scrupulous cleansing and keeping the wound protected from the entrance of further dirt will probably prevent eight tenths of it. For some reasons, which we do not yet understand, wounds made by toy pistols, fire-crackers, and other explosives of this sort, seem peculiarly liable to be followed by it.

In such wounds as this, and others into which considerable amounts of garden soil or city dust have been rubbed, it is advisable and a reasonable protection to have the antitoxin applied to the wound at the first dressing. This is within reach of any physician, and is now provided at stations all over the city on the Fourth of July by modern city boards of health. But smoking the wound after the infection has got two or three days' start in the system is about as rational as inhaling the medicine-pipe of the Voodoo doctor, of which it is, indeed, a belated survival. There is no known remedy under heaven which can be relied upon to "take the soreness out" of a wound after it has become inflamed. The only way is to keep the soreness out of it in the first place, in the shape of dirt.

Somewhat akin to this "smoke cure" for a partially inflamed wound is the great group of lotions, liniments, and oils which are so widely relied upon to take the soreness out of bruises and sprains and inflamed joints. These usually possess a small amount of rational basis for the confidence reposed in them. Many of the lotions contain alcohol, — the immortal "arniky" and "camfire," for instance, — which partly by counter-irritant effect, but still more by the rapidity with which it evaporates, producing a sense of cooling, relieves the pain and promotes the natural processes of healing.

Others, like the liniments, contain very strong irritants, such as turpentine, ammonia, Spanish fly, etc., which by their power of reddening the surface — that is to say, of distending the blood-vessels of the part and engorging it with blood — bring the natural antitoxins of the body to the spot in larger amounts. No small part, however, of the virtue of these depends upon their pungent and powerful odor, which makes the patient gasp for breath and water at the eyes, but fills him with a corresponding confidence in their "strength" and healing power.

Lastly, there are the oils of various sorts, from the simple and inoffensive goose-grease to such eccentricities as rattlesnake-oil, skunk fat, or oil of angleworms. These are positively useful to the extent that they are soothing and protective. Furthermore, they are usually recommended to be "well rubbed in," which, if the inflammation be not too acute, gives valuable massage treatment. But the thing which is most highly valued in them is their odor, like the liniments, or their color — this preferably red, like the life-blood, or yellow, like the sunlight. A good, deep, saturated brown, especially if it stains the skin and smells to high heaven, is highly prized. The methods of adding this color to the oil are numerous, and some of them unique. One recently recommended is to use the red seeds of the St. John's-wort (hypericum). These are gathered in the autumn, placed in a bottle, covered with oil, and hung in a sunny place until the oil develops a deep red color. So long as it retains its color it is said to be a sure cure; but when it fades —

no color, no cure. This red oil should be doubly effective, for it has two claims to popular confidence — its color and the fact that hypericum is a very old herb of power, regarded as possessed of all sorts of magic virtues, especially in the direction of healing, since the earliest times. Cold-blooded, modern medicine, however, can find little or no basis for these claims and has practically discarded it, so that it is barely mentioned now in the list of remedies, and then chiefly as a historic memory.

The most fruitful field for these short cuts back to health lies in the realm of cough remedies and cold cures. Their name is literally legion, for hardly a drug can be mentioned, hardly a substance discovered, which is capable of being either swallowed or inhaled, that has not been recommended as a cough remedy. It is an axiom in modern medicine that the existence of a long list of remedies for a particular disease means one of two things — either that none of them has much effect, or that the disease tends to get well quickly of itself. In this instance both happen to be true. Eight tenths of all colds are mild infections, which run their course until the body has time to produce an antitoxin or antibody to stop their further progress. As this process in reasonably healthy individuals is usually carried out in from four to six days, anything which happens to be given in that time stands a fair chance of getting a reputation as a cure.

The only sure cure for colds and coughs is to avoid the infections and the foul air of ill-ventilated rooms

and buildings in which they breed; to keep the body
toned up to fighting pitch, by cold baths and an abundance of fresh air, especially in the bedroom; and if
the infection does get a foothold, to assist Nature in
her fight against it by rest in the open air, and promoting elimination through the skin, bowels, and kidneys.

As for cough remedies, few of them, however renowned, have any particular effect in stopping a cough,
and what is more to the point, they would n't be of
much value even if they did. A cough never killed any
one. It is merely the surface symptoms of what may
possibly be a serious condition, but in ninety cases
out of a hundred is a trifling temporary disturbance of
the upper air-passages.

Contrary to popular impression, it is most commonly due not to any deep-seated changes in the lungs,
but to conditions of the nose, palate, or upper throat,
especially of the larynx, or voice organ. In the small
percentage of instances in which these throat irritations depend upon deeper conditions, merely to relieve the cough has little or no effect upon these natural underlying conditions. Many and many a poor
consumptive has been deluded into his grave by a
false sense of security produced by cough mixtures,
which stopped his cough, but did nothing whatever
to cure his tuberculosis. The great majority of cough
cures are little more than deadeners of the sensitiveness of the upper air-passages, and far too many of
them contain narcotics, such as chloroform and the
various derivatives of opium.

The domestic cough cures have the virtue usually of

being free from injurious elements, but whether they be the immortal and indispensable onion, honey and tar, an eggshell dissolved in vinegar, or the smoke of the fragrant cubebs, they all depend for their virtue chiefly upon some temporary effect upon the sensitiveness of the throat and upper air-passages. Whether the cougher will get well, however, depends not in the slightest degree upon them, but only upon the resisting power of his system, whether in the case of a cold or in a deeper and more serious malady.

They are for the most part quite harmless, except that they are usually either so sweet or so pungent and vile-tasting that they interfere with the appetite and upset the digestion. Their local soothing effect is good in so far as it relieves discomfort and prevents the patient from being kept awake. But they are an admirable illustration of a far too common method of medication — simply relieving surface symptoms, like trying to cut down a tree by lopping off its topmost boughs. Cough cures as a class are among the most useless, the most irrational, and from the strong temptation of their makers to put in them chloroform or some form of opiate in order to produce a positive effect, the most dangerous of remedies. As illustrating the attitude now taken toward them, it might be remarked that in our open-air sanatoria for consumptives practically no remedies are given to stop the cough. That disappears as if by magic as soon as the disease is started on its way to recovery, by the open-air life and overfeeding, often within four or five days or a week.

A cough that hangs on is a danger-signal that should be heeded, and not smothered by " dopes."

Another belief which is widely prevalent is that it is very good for weak eyes to bathe them frequently in salt water. This is certainly harmlessness and simplicity in itself, and excellent so far as it goes; but it does n't go very far. It is useful both for the sense of coolness and relief which it often affords and because you cannot use your eyes while you're bathing them.

The only real cure for eight tenths of all weak eyes is a properly fitted pair of spectacles. Bathing in the saltiest of water will have no more effect in curing them than sluicing down an overdriven engine with a hose. There is always a definite cause for weak eyes — look for it. The medical profession is finding that properly fitted glasses, properly arranged light, and avoidance of overwork will cure ten times as many sore eyes as eye-lotions, eye-drops, or salve of any description.

There may be, of course, some acute inflammation or definite local disease, and these should be treated at once by a competent specialist. But even the vast majority of chronic inflammations of the eye, such as redness, watering, crops of styes, have been found to be due to some error of refraction and relieved by proper-fitting glasses. When these have been secured, the sufferer from weak eyes will not merely be relieved from his local discomfort, but will be given nearly double his former working power, and will often find that many other disturbances, such as neuralgia, sick headaches, and nervous dyspepsia will disappear.

In fine, don't tinker with symptoms; look for the cause, and remove it. Don't try to lock the stable door after the horse is stolen, but train your horse to bite strangers. Attack is the best defense. Keep your body at good fighting weight, and you can defy disease. Sunlight, food, fresh air, and exercise are the only cure-alls known. Don't worry about disease and what to take when you're sick, but work for health.

CHAPTER IV

ANY time is better than the present, to our minds. Actually, it's the only time we have. Yet most of us prefer mentally either to live in the future or to dwell in the past; probably because the present is too real, too insistent. It can neither be glorified by the golden light of memory, nor warmed with the roseate hues of anticipation and hope. Indeed, few days — or men — can be idealized until they are dead! The Golden Age has alway been in the past, and heaven on the top of some Olympus or in some realm above the clouds untouched by time.

This was the spirit of the past, of the Dark Ages, which still survives amongst us. The spirit of to-day just reverses this. Forward the good that is, instead of passively bowing at the shrine of the good and the gods that were — or more frequently, never were! Work, which is Worship of the God of Things as They Are, is the religion of the twentieth century. And Service, not Holiness, is the Master Word!

Few better illustrations of this worship of the past and belittling of the present can be found than our opinion of our own physique "in these degenerate days"! However modestly and inconclusively we may be content to express ourselves upon the nebular hypothesis, or the negro question, or the future navigation of the air, we are quite sure, beyond the shadow of a doubt, that our ancestors in the Good Old Days — particularly in the "Old Country" — were taller, stronger, healthier, and longer-lived, to say nothing of their being more honest and patriotic than we are. This conviction rises to the dignity and universality of an article of faith. But what is it based on? Why should we be so ready to write ourselves down "degenerate sons of sterner sires"? The moment we apply the acid test of actual investigation of records, statistics, measurements, etc., to this pious belief, it shrivels and goes up in smoke, like most of the legends of the "happy days of yore." We may be degenerate, but there is no valid evidence of the fact. In fact, all such data and records as we have point in exactly the opposite direction. The human race is still moving steadily upward, as it has always done from the days of the jelly-fish and the sea-squirt.

We have been particularly sure of our American degeneracy because we were the newest among the nations, the latest experiment, as it were. We do things so differently from the way they were done before, and are making such a strange success at it along special lines, such wonderful progress in mere commerical and financial issues, — in dollar-hunting, in a word, — that we must be paying the penalty for this one-sided success in some form of shipwreckedness, either physical or moral.

Merely a decent sense of respect to their own ideals was sufficient to lead the older nations to this conclusion. So when they crossed the Atlantic to study our provincialism and to discover the penalties which we had paid for our unwholesome and rather shocking success, they naturally found them, and went home and wrote a book about it. Now we Americans have not the reputation of suffering from undue or excessive modesty. We generally take all that is due us and claim a little bit more, but in some instances our bashfulness and self-depreciation are really extraordinary, and this is one of them. We were even willing to accept ourselves at the valuation placed upon us by our critics, and much as we might resent their comments upon our manners, when it came to our health and our minor morals we were willing humbly to plead guilty. An amazing feature about the situation was that after crying " *Peccavi*," if we had plucked up courage to retort, "You 're another!" we should have checkmated our critics at once.

For by this universal kink in the psychology of mankind, our haughtiest visitors and critics were equally firmly convinced that their particular nation was also degenerate, as compared with the age of heroes two or more generations ago. All of which shows how easy and common it is to be mistaken when you shut your eyes and dream about things as they were, or will be, instead of looking them straight in the face as they are.

Not every visitor to our shores has come over for the purpose of writing a book, but many of them have, and they all feel able to write it at about the end of three weeks. The longer they are here, the less they feel able to, but they usually take time by the forelock and write, and the first thing they say is that the American race is going to the canines; that we are becoming emaciated, with high cheek-bones, lank jaws, and straight hair, like the native aborigines; that we bolt all our meals in about fourteen minutes each; that we waste the saliva which we need in our digestion on our sidewalks and our carpets; that we are dyspeptic, neurasthenic, and insomniac; that we worship the nimble dollar and chase it day and night; and that we live with a time-table in one hand and a newspaper constantly before our eyes. What else could we expect but that the race would degenerate?

As a rule, we have meekly accepted these statements. While we are the home of the free and the land of the brave and the chosen of destiny, when it comes to nerves and dyspepsia and fried foods and too much pie and strong coffee, we are ready humbly to admit that we are undermining our constitutions and ruining the good physique which we had inherited. We were almost willing to admit the allegation of *Martin Chuzzlewit*, that "Everything degenerates in America. The lion becomes a puma, the eagle a fish-hawk, and man a Yankee."

We were also sure that our teeth were the worst in the world, because we had the best dentists, and after they had developed here, they went abroad and swept the field.

That sort of thing went on for so many years that we were beginning to get used to it and meekly make the most of our ill-health and decrepitude.

Now for the actual facts in the case! It is of course

difficult to make precise comparisons upon some points, on account of the small number and imperfectness of the records one hundred years ago, and, in many districts, even to-day. Accurate and precise vital statistics of even such important definite and simple matters as birth, death, disease, length of life, height, weight, etc., are scarcely more than thirty-five or forty years old, even in the civilized countries of the world.

But such data as we can secure are practically all on one side, and that, most unexpectedly, shows a steady and well-marked improvement in every respect — physical, mental, and moral, for the past century. The only apparent exceptions are a declining birth-rate, an increasing divorce-rate, and an apparent increase in certain classes of crime, all of which, however, we share with all civilized countries.

To take first one of the simplest and crudest comparisons, that of mere bodily dimensions and size, even our most unsparing critics — and they, exercising the charming privilege of plain speaking within the family, have usually been our blood relatives — have admitted that as a race we were tall, though they generally added " and lanky" or "lathy," or angular, or other adjective to that effect.

The first opportunity to make this comparison upon a large scale came during the Civil War. Careful and accurate measurements were then taken by our army surgeons at the recruiting depots of some 200,000 recruits for the Union Army. These men were not only from all the States of the Union, but from every important nation of Europe and several of Asia; and the larger and more important of these were represented, not merely by hundreds, but by thousands in the lists.

Some years after the close of the war, two army surgeons, Gould and Baxter, collected and carefully studied all these recorded measurements with reference to nationality, age, climate, etc., with the distinctly unexpected result of finding that the height of the American-born soldier exceeded by nearly two inches that of the average of the foreign-born soldiers of the nations from which they were descended. Not only so, but further analysis showed that the greatest heights, chest expansions, and weights in the entire series were found in the recruits from those States which were of most purely American blood, in the sense of having been free from foreign admixture by immigration for at least one hundred years, so the majority of them were probably American from the third to the fifth generation.

The mountaineers of Kentucky, West Virginia, and their descendants in Ohio, Missouri, and Kansas showed the best record. The same class, it may be incidentally remarked, also furnished the tallest regiments to our army in the late Spanish War. So that, as far as heights are concerned, American degeneracy is of that curious negative type which expresses itself by growing taller than the races from which we were descended.

This, of course, might only have been due to the process of "spindling," — but when they came to study chest measurements, it was found that the girth of chest of our native-born recruits was nearly an inch greater than the average of the European-born. Again the mountaineers of Kentucky and their descendants had a further superiority over the European average. This might possibly have been attributed to our well-known oratorical propensities, gained by long practice in making the eagle soar. But when later, through the medium of our life insurance companies, we were able to contrast the weights of large bodies of men on both sides of the Atlantic, it was found that American policy-holders showed practically the same lead over Europe in weight that they did in height, in chest measurement, and longevity; i.e., up to about the fortieth year. After that the average weight was more nearly equal, indeed, somewhat greater, on the other side of the Atlantic, on account of their much more marked tendency to lay on flesh after that age. But, roughly speaking, weight above the average under forty is an indication of vigor and an advantage, — after forty, not necessarily so; indeed, often the reverse.

It is, of course, a matter of common, everyday observation that the average American traveling abroad very seldom feels himself at all undersized or below the average height in a crowd; in fact, he is very often conspicuous by his stature.

Corroboration of an unmistakable sort of our steady increase in height and size comes from a somewhat unexpected and almost whimsical source; namely, from the makers of ready-made clothing, gloves, shoes, etc.

The cutters of these firms are unanimous in their testimony that there has been a steady increase within recent years of the size of customers of all sorts, so that models for a given age, numbered a given size thirty years ago, will not fit their customers of that age to-day with any degree of comfort. In gloves and shoes, for instance, the sizes most in demand are actually from one to three trade sizes larger than they were thirty years ago.

This was brought out recently in the courts through a suit growing out of the refusal of a Western jobbing-house to accept a consignment of gloves because the latter were "Philadelphia sevens," instead of "Chicago sevens"!—this rate of increase and process of Americanization having been greater in the West than in the East.

Of course this has long been known in regard to the pedal extremities of the daughters of a great inland city, but this is treading on dangerous ground! This is, of course, only what might have been expected on *a priori* grounds from our superb and abundant supply of food, especially of meats, fats, and sugars, our freedom from starvation, and even from its second cousin, economy; our high wages, our broad acres of rich, verdant soil; our abundance of elbow-room and escape from stifling traditions and beliefs of all sorts.

But our believers in decadence promptly retort: "Just look at our awful habits of bolting our food, of hustling, of turning night into day, or working till we drop!" Those of us who survived might possibly have grown taller and chestier, but what of those who fell by the wayside?

Surely we are shortening our lives and raising our death-rates by this senseless, steam-driven rush of ourselves. About thirty years ago, we began to get mortality records which really covered all the population and were reasonably accurate and reliable. Upon contrasting these with the French, English, German, and Norwegian records, we were surprised to discover that instead of a higher death-rate than any of these, we had one of the lowest.

Certain of our large Western cities, indeed, have the lowest official death-rates of any towns of their size in the civilized world, some of them falling as low as nine per thousand living per annum, contrasted with fourteen, eighteen, and twenty. Part of this favorable showing is, of course, due to a higher percentage of adults in the population, due to immigration, and part to imperfect reporting of all deaths. But even when both these sources have been allowed for, our best American death-rates compare most favorably with even the best policed and sanitated European districts.

Our great cities long lagged behind on account of the notorious inadequacy of their governments, and for years ranged up alongside of Constantinople and St. Petersburg in their mortality records, but this reproach has now been wiped out, and New York and Chicago can both show rates that are only about one point per thousand living behind London and Berlin; in fact, New York has several times

within the last five years fallen below London's best
record.

All this time, however, our pessimists have been
holding back their strongest and best supported
charges, and they now bring them forward with a
triumphant air and defy us to disprove them. These
are: (1) that we don't live as long as they used to in
the good old days; (2) that the American child has
been literally spoiled within an inch of his life, until
he is a mere bundle of nerves and bad teeth. Both of
these statements are so universally accepted that it
seems at first sight hopeless to challenge them, and
that our wisest course would be to plead guilty and
pass on to the next count.

But we are not going to surrender without a fight,
and propose to take the attitude of the Irishman who,
when he was brought before the court and asked by
the judge to plead guilty, or not guilty, promptly replied: "Shure, how can I till, till I hear the ividence!"

The first thing that began to give us some glimpse
of hope as to the shortness of the average modern life
was that afforded by the attitude of those great philanthropic institutions, our insurance companies. No
one had better reason than they to know that American lives were becoming shorter, or that the expectation of life on this side of the Atlantic was less than
in Europe, but there they stood, immovable as the
rock of Gibraltar, doing business amid the wreck of
this decaying race and civilization at the same old
rates as were calculated forty, fifty, and seventy years
ago. They had not raised the premiums on account

of the lack of centenarians and they did not seem to be losing money at it either. And the result magnificently justified their patriotic attitude and rewarded their virtue. Nearly a decade ago, it was discovered that the actual average longevity here in America had increased thirty-five per cent since those rates were calculated, and the average expectancy of life at all years under fifty was greater by from five to eight years, and still the companies kept on doing business at the old rates — and are still keeping on! The average length of life of American whites is now about twelve years greater than it was thirty years ago.

Having heard the evidence, we decline pleading guilty on this count, and proceed to the next: That the health and morals of the rising generation are being ruined by the indulgent methods of their bringing-up. Here the case seems almost hopelessly against us. Everybody knows that the American child is spoiled; that he eats too much candy, goes to bed when he likes, has no reverence for his elders, and naturally grows up neurotic and excitable; begins to need false teeth at twelve, and glasses at fourteen; while reformers appear to find it difficult to express in percentages, without going above one hundred, the extent to which the American boy is addicted to cigarettes. Altogether the outlook of the future of the race is about as bad as it can be.

About fifteen years ago, some heartless scientists, regardless of the mental suffering which their researches must cause, began to apply the yardstick and the scales to the degeneracy of the rising generation. The most reckless offenders in this respect were Professor Peckham, of Milwaukee, Dr. Porter, of St. Louis, and Dr. Bowditch, of Boston. Here are their results, in which even he who runs may learn the fate of our civilization. The results were most damnably identical in all three of these cities, so that there is no escaping from their conclusions.

Upon the basis of over ten thousand measurements, the awful fact was shown that the average American-born boy at seventeen years of age is only five feet ten inches in height and weighs barely one hundred and thirty pounds, while the average German boy in similar schools is five feet four and one half, the average Irish boy is five feet six, and the average English boy the same. In short, the poor American children, that is those whose parents and grandparents were born in the United States, are from two to three inches taller and from three to six pounds heavier at seventeen years of age than those of any European nationality, with the exception of the Germans, who although much shorter, equal or exceed in point of weight.

When the comparison is carried a trifle further, we find that children born in these United States of foreign parents are taller and heavier than children of corresponding age in their fatherland; that children whose parents were born in the United States are again superior to those born of immigrants; and that the children whose grandparents were born in the United States give the highest measurements.

Another unexpected result of these measurements, which has done much to start the movement to put our education upon a rational basis, was that the taller and heavier the children were at every age, the farther advanced they were in the school standard, even under our present antediluvian system of grading. Children's minds tend to grow just as naturally and as irrepressibly as their bodies. Take care of their bodies, and their minds will take care of themselves!

American-born children in all these three cities were from one to two grades ahead of the foreign-born of their years, the only ones who could even tie them being those who equaled them in weight; namely, the Germans. Really, spoiling seems to agree with the average American child! Of course it may be urged that mere size and bulk do not constitute vigor and endurance, and that our lack of measurable degeneracy in these respects may be due simply to our more abundant food and protection from overcrowding and more favorable average conditions of life generally. As to whether we really are stronger and tougher and longer-winded than our ancestors or their representatives of to-day on the other side of the Atlantic, is a little more difficult question to answer; but there are two straws which may be at least taken as indicating probabilities. One is such records as we possess of running, high jumping, putting the shot, and other athletic feats of the present century. These all point in the same direction as the other data, there being not a single record of the eighteenth century which has not been lowered anywhere from five to thirty per cent, and which is not still being further lowered year after year.

The other is the comparison with the descendants of our ancestor races on the other side of the Atlantic, who, having continued to live in their original environment, presumably more closely resemble our country ancestors than we do. This is furnished by those famous revivals of classic contests — the Olympic Games. In these our American athletes have carried off more prizes than any other nationality represented, with the exception of England, and more prizes in proportion to the number of competitors entered than any nation. Even though some of our English cousins may be inclined to think that a little too much of our lung power was expended in the ungracious exercise known as "roaring," and that some of the vigor of our Quadriceps Extensor was expended in kicking which would have been better utilized in the high jump, no one who scans the records could for a moment claim that the American race, as represented by its athletes, is physically degenerate, unless the whole world be so.

But what as to our record on the mental and moral side? Surely, the much-lamented strain of civilization is telling heavily upon us on this score. Success to-day is emphatically won by brain work, and more strain being placed upon that important organ, it must necessarily be breaking down earlier and more frequently; and here the records upon their face appear to be against us. The tabulated number of insane is steadily and constantly increasing, both absolutely and in proportion to the population. But when we glance at the records abroad, we find that a similar increase is taking place all over Europe, so that this progress of insanity is not a purely American symptom. Our records of insanity in the past were so gravely defective — only the most violent and most unmanageable cases being, as a rule, placed in public institutions and formally registered — that it is impossible to draw any positive conclusions one way or another. It may, however, be said that the most expert alienists and statisticians on both sides of the Atlantic are inclined to doubt whether insanity is really increasing at all, except on paper; owing largely to the fact that our hospitals and asylums for the care of the insane are better managed and more successful in their results, so that a large percentage of all classes of the insane, mild as well as unmanageable, are intrusted to them instead of being cared for by their own families. They are also inclined to hold that insanity is in no sense a special result of civilization, inasmuch as in every nation it is the lowest and most illiterate class of the population that contributes the highest percentage of its numbers to the insane asylums. That it is not American civilization in particular which is producing it, we may be sure, from the fact that our foreign-born population contributes from twenty to thirty-five per cent more in proportion to its numbers to our asylums than does our native-born population, and that the most highly civilized and most purely American classes in our republic contribute the smallest percentage.

A similar situation exists in regard to crime. Upon the face of the records, there is an apparent increase in crime both absolute and in proportion to the population. But while the subject is too wide to enter into here, when further analyzed it is found to consist chiefly in a great and disproportionate increase in minor offenses, especially among children and in arrests for drunkenness, or the violation of municipal laws. The percentage in frequency of all serious crimes has steadily and in many cases markedly diminished on both sides of the Atlantic with the single and somewhat unexpected exception of the crime of homicide. This, however, is not peculiar to America, as its relative increase is almost equally marked in several European countries, although nowhere reaching the disgraceful frequency which disfigures our records.

The presumption is that it is largely concerned with the wide diffusion and low price of pistols and revolvers and firearms that can be carried readily concealed about the person, turning fights which would ordinarily result in a broken head, or a few bruises and slashes, into fatal tragedies.

It must be remembered that crime is literally created by law, in the sense that it is made very largely by definition of what constitutes it: that, for instance, trivial offenses and escapades, such as robbing orchards and "smooching" watermelons, whose perpetrators were formerly punished, when caught, by a dog-bite or the application of a shingle or black strap, now in our huge cities are serious offenses against the integrity of fruit-stands and the sanctity of grocery stores, and get into the police courts and the publicity of the papers. Similarly, as the density of our population increases and our sanitary conscience awakens, trivial acts, like walking on the grass, or picking flowers, or spitting on the sidewalk, which in the open country are blameless and harmless, are in a park or city street serious offenses, punished with fine or imprisonment.

There is some slight cheer for us in the fact, first, that other nations are just as bad as we are, and, indeed, so far as our contrasts of this side of the Atlantic go, apparently worse; for the consoling statistics show that in our large cities, where our native-born population furnishes fifty-five per cent of the total, it contributes only forty-three per cent of the criminals as against fifty-six per cent from the foreign-born population. Strangely enough, in the gravest crime, supposed to be so peculiarly American and impulsive, — homicide,— the figures are most unexpectedly encouraging, as our native-born white population, forming eighty-five per cent, furnishes forty per cent, and our foreign-born population, sixteen per cent, of all homicides, or more than double its percentage.

Upon another count, statistics are apparently in favor of the pessimists, and that is the decline of our birth-rate. That this exists there can be no serious question, but whether it is a sign of racial degeneracy or not is an entirely different matter. The question is such a wide and wrathful one that it would be folly to attempt to enter into it here; but I would like briefly to suggest, first of all, that this sign of decay is again not peculiar to America, but is going on at present in every nation of Europe, even those that are most rapidly advancing in civilization and prestige, like England, Germany, and France.

Second, that it is not in any sense due to the decline of racial vigor or actual reproductive power, but solely the deliberate intelligence and conscientious determination upon the part of parents to limit the number of their children to that which they can properly and adequately feed, educate, and fit for life: that historically, instead of being a mark of a decaying race and failing civilization, it has always been an accompaniment of a rising nation and an improving physique, and probably always will be. It is not the size of a nation or man, but its efficiency, that counts, and the motto of intelligent eugenic parentage is "better children and fewer," and no amount of jeremiads or exhortations are going to alter this fact. It is a move in the interests of the child and of the future, instead of against them, and the twentieth century will never go back to the indiscriminate spawning of the eighteenth. If either mothers or children had been consulted, the change would have taken place long before.

Our high divorce-rate should be interpreted in the same light. It simply represents one of the triumphs of reason and humanity over tradition and prejudice. Why any one should not be permitted, under due safeguards, to correct the mistake which he or she may have made in one of the most serious steps of life, said permission being denied to him solely on the ground that the step is of such vast importance, is really difficult to conceive from a broad and rational point of view. Even in our most divorce-infested communities, the proportion of divorces to marriages is only one to eight, and if there be any other institution of human invention which shows only twelve per cent of failures, I should like to have it pointed out. So long as four fifths of our marriages remain permanent, we have little reason to concern ourselves with the divorce problem from a racial point of view. The new-found liberty may, of course, be abused, but careful students of the records hitherto agree that at least seventy-five per cent of the divorces so far secured were abundantly justified; and that the only pity was that the marriages which they dissolved were ever allowed to be contracted, and that such utterly unfit and undesirable individuals were permitted to reproduce their kind under the sanction of the law.

As to what the future may have in store for us, that would require the gift of prophecy to predict. There appears, however, no more biologic ground for us to dread it to-day than our forefathers had a century ago — in many respects, less. The only signs of danger are the rapid and enormous increase in our city-dwelling population as compared with those residing in the open country, the filling up and fencing off of the larger part of our richest and most desirable soil areas, and the increasing flood of European immigration of alleged less desirable character. We have slums and sweat-shops and social injustices such as our fathers never dreamed of in this clean, fresh, new country of theirs.

On the other hand, we have a sanitary science far

superior to theirs; a keener and a tenderer public conscience; a broader and a kindlier humanity, and a passion for justice and fairness and freedom which is in no way inferior to theirs. By the use of the new forces harnessed by civilization under the guidance of an aroused public conscience, we are converting our great cities into places as healthful and law-abiding as was the open country a century ago, and far more cheerful and desirable to live in. Though the best of our land be occupied, the new-born science of agriculture is so enormously increasing the returns of our labors that five acres to-day will support a family in greater comfort than five hundred would a century ago.

While the flow of alien immigrants becomes greater every year, until to-day we receive in two years' time an addition equal to the total population of the original thirteen colonies on their first Independence Day, yet its proportion to the total population of the country is no greater than it ever was before. Indeed, it has remained most singularly constant, as the earliest census in 1796 showed that fourteen per cent of our population was of foreign birth, while our most recent one in 1910 showed a little over twelve per cent of foreign birth.

While there is serious misgiving as to the quality of our modern immigration as compared with that of a century ago, and we do well to maintain a reasonable and rational barrier against the admission of criminals, paupers, and the physically and mentally defective, yet those who have studied the question most closely are inclined to the opinion that, all things considered, the general average is as good to-day as it ever was, with the exception of a brief period of about thirty years ago, and probably better than that of the early days of the Republic. We resent, and rightly, the tendency of any European nations to make America a dumping-ground for their paupers and criminals, but we are apt to forget that they actually did this unchecked and unhindered on quite a substantial scale in the early days of our colonization. While the leaders of our early colonists were of the very salt of the earth, many of their followers were — of anything but that description.

The records show that ten thousand criminals were transported from Old Bailey to America between 1717 and 1775. Contemporary historians estimate that there were twenty thousand transported convicts in Maryland in 1770, while Stith declares that "Virginia has come to be reputed another Siberia."

The court records of our earlier days are full of the difficulties and perplexities of our ancestors with the sturdy rogues who had been given their choice between America and the gallows.

It must, of course, be remembered that many of these so-called criminals were political offenders; others had been imprisoned for debt; others because they had offended some petty local tyrant and in the mass were a very different class from the habitual jail-birds or convicts of the present day. But even when all is admitted, our ancestors had troubles of their own in regard to the immigration problems which were quite as serious as ours are to-day, if not more so.

CHAPTER V

LO, THE POOR INDIAN

WE all have, in pensive moments, lamented the passing of the noble red man. Bards have melodiously chanted the melting away of the painted savage like snow before the sun of civilization. Even while we lamented, we have been perfectly willing to share the profits of said disappearance and melting; although, to a purely Pickwickian regret at his passing, we have added a gentle pang of self-reproach in ascribing its occurrence to the vices of our civilization.

Rum, gambling, and venereal diseases are universally accepted as the factors of our own introduction which have caused the ruin of this innocent child of nature. This explanation has such a soothing and soul-satisfying sound, it gives us such a secret sense of superior virtue in being able to resist the destructive temptations to which our red brother has succumbed, that it seems almost a pity to disturb our belief. Besides, the facts supporting it lie so obviously and flatly on the surface of things. The most casual visitor to an Indian reservation or a trader's post can see with his own eyes that poor "Lo" does get most abominably drunk upon the vilest of whiskey whenever he has the price, that he does gamble away the whole proceeds of a season's laborious trapping, or his entire quarter's income and rations, under the skillful manipulations of the white gambler and his female harpies.

But there is another side to the shield. These excesses are both morally and physically lamentably injurious, but the conviction is growing among careful students of the Indian that these influences are not in themselves sufficient to account for his decay, and that others more vital are at work.

In the first place, the Indian was not only thoroughly familiar with all these vices, but had been addicted to them for centuries before the first white man ever set foot upon American soil. Almost every tribe, except a few of the more stupid and degraded, had some form of intoxicant, upon which our firewater was an "improvement" only in the sense of its being more concentrated and enabling them to "get there" quicker. Like all savages, they had been gamblers from their boyhood for countless generations. It was their principal pastime around the lodge fire at night, and their greatest and most eagerly expected feasts and gatherings, at which all the clan and scores from neighboring tribes would come together, which began with dances, games, and races, would wind up in one gorgeous gambling spree, in which the warriors would stake not merely their ponies, their pelts, and their wampum, but their weapons, their clothing, and even their wives and families.

As to venereal disease, so far from the white settlers bringing it to them, it is now the opinion of the most careful students of the subject that it was actually brought to Europe from America by the sailors of Columbus's second voyage.

On the other hand, there were two things which we did introduce to the Indian, which were entirely new and untried. These were the infectious diseases of civilization, and habits of industry. The former we introduced to him in all innocence and, indeed, ignorance; the latter under the mistaken impression that they constituted a virtue. Both have proved deadly to a degree.

We never succeeded in making the Indian believe in industry, but we compelled him either to act as if he did or move farther west, and he usually moved. The modern industrial civilization of the Anglo-Saxon type, which proposes to labor with its hands and to make it uncomfortable for any one who does n't, has no place for the Indian in its organization.

But the weightiest factor in the decay of the aborigine is one which we have only come to appreciate properly in recent years.

Since we have begun to look into the matter carefully, we find ourselves facing a somewhat unexpected state of affairs. First of all, while accurate data are obviously out of the question, it is the opinion of the most careful students of the American Indian, like Mallory and Farrand, that it is doubtful whether his total population in the area of these United States has ever been very much greater than it is at present. Where the early explorers and pioneers reported attacks by thousands of plumed and painted warriors, swarming from every nook of the forest and from behind every rock on the hillside, the conservative modern historian reads hundreds. For "kings" he reads chiefs; for "nations," tribes, or even bands.

The aboriginal population of this country at the landing of the white man was astonishingly sparse and thinly scattered, and is estimated by Farrand at not to exceed 500,000 north of Mexico, where to-day the censuses of both Governments show more than 400,000, although this includes many mixed bloods. The second fact on which there is substantial agreement is that our worst campaigns against the Indian tribes—so far from rising to the dignity of even a partial extermination, — were little more than healthy gymnastic exercises for the noble savage; even when, as sometimes happened, women and children were included in the attack or perished of cold and starvation, as a result of defeat. However much at times we may have let our thirst for vengeance get the better of our humanity and our self-control, our wars against the Indians were Sunday-school picnics by comparison with the savage wars to the knife, and the knife to the hilt, which they were constantly waging against one another before our coming, and still continued until the combination of the white man became sufficiently far-reaching to put a stop to them. The Huron-Iroquois alone are believed to have been responsible for the extermination of some fifteen or twenty tribes and the depopulation of an area equal to a small empire. The deadly rifle of the white man has saved at least five times as many Indian lives as it ever took, by putting a stop to this perpetual intertribal warfare. Even the rapacity and the injustice which have often marred our commercial and economic relations with the Indian have been marked in the main by a rude fairness and humanity which he never even dreamed of practicing with his fellows.

We have taken his hunting-grounds, but we have given him valuable agricultural lands and rations in return; and the "pestilence-breeding swamps," which were so fiercely denounced by his sentimental friends, when the Northern Indians first began to be concentrated in a south-central reservation, have now been discovered to be the garden of the whole country (Oklahoma), and are eagerly crowded into by the white settlers.

We have frequently and abominably cheated and lied to the Indian in our land deals; but, like the gamblers of the mining-camps, we have generally left our victims a grubstake, and have made famine, instead of a yearly visitor to their wigwams, an almost unknown influence in their lives. In other words, our contact with the Indian, demoralizing as it may have been in many respects, has greatly diminished his mortality from death in battle and from famine. What, then, has been the element which has injured him most seriously in our contact with him? The infectious diseases of civilization, especially those which by centuries and generations of exposure and loss of virulence have come to be described as "the diseases of infancy." One thing is almost constant in the history of our contact with every tribe; at first, rapid diminution in numbers and vigor, usually attributed to the use of rum and to other vices of civilization; then a period of standstill, later followed in most cases by a slow but steady increase again in numbers. The influences which caused the sudden diminution, the stay in decline, and the adjustment and increase were chiefly the infectious diseases of civilization, and the slow acquisition of immunity to them.

Roughly speaking, I think it would be safe to say that for every Indian that has been killed by bullets, starvation, and alcohol, three have been killed by bacilli. As an experienced observer and explorer expresses it: "Many things have combined to bring the downfall of the liberty-loving aborigine, but no blow has been so acute as the warfare of the infectious diseases, and among these infections the most fatal results have been brought about by what we regard as the diseases of childhood."

Dr. Wilfred Grenfell has recently expressed a similar opinion in regard to the Eskimos. Both report attacks of measles, mumps, whooping-cough, and chicken-pox which swept off twenty, thirty, and even forty per cent of a tribe.

Pick up where you will almost any book of travel, of exploration, of study in the Indian country, and you will find it filled with stories of mysterious plagues, which swept down upon the villages and tribes and not merely decimated but almost exterminated them.

My earliest personal contact with the Indians in any considerable number was in the valley of the Columbia River in Oregon. And the first story that I heard from the old settlers about their diseases was of a mysterious plague which had swept down the lower reaches of the Columbia, just ahead of the vanguard of the white settlers. Not merely were whole clans and villages swept out of existence, but the valley was practically depopulated; so that, as one of the old patriarchs grimly remarked, "It made it a heap easier to settle it up quietly." So swift and so fatal had been its onslaught that villages would be found deserted save for the dried and decaying bodies of the dead. The canoes were rotting on the river bank above high-water mark. The curtains of the lodges were flapped and blown into shreds. The weapons and garments of the dead lay about them rusting and rotting. The salmon-nets were still standing in the river, worn to tatters and fringes by the current. Yet, from the best light that I was able to secure upon it, it appeared to have been nothing more than an epidemic of measles caught from the child of some pioneer or trapper and spreading like wildfire in the prairie grass. Even with some knowledge of the problems of immunity, the thing appeared to be incredible until I began to get reports at first hand of equally astounding modern instances.

For instance, a colleague of mine, who had been government physician to the Coast Survey and stationed in farthest Alaska in attendance upon the men engaged in the construction of lighthouses, told me of the coming of the 1889–90 epidemic of influenza or grippe into those fastnesses. Shortly after it had run its course among the white workmen, a couple of Indians, who had been bringing salmon and berries in from their summer village on one of the islands, ceased to turn up with their supplies. The workmen endured canned provisions in patience for a week or so, and then a couple of men were sent to stir the Indians up. When they landed at the village, they found every member of the tribe attacked by the disease and disabled, so that many of the sick were half-crazed with thirst for want of a single Indian well enough to wait upon them. Over one third of the seventy-odd inhabitants of the village died outright, and another third was so seriously ill that it took them months to recover.

It is now a familiar story from medical missionaries, army surgeons, and tropical physicians all over the world that the diseases which in civilized communities have so greatly declined in virulence as scarcely even to cause anxiety and which are described under the title of the "diseases of childhood," will smite the non-immunized aborigine with the fury of a pestilence. Everywhere that the white race has come in contact with the savage,— among the Maoris of New Zealand, the Blackfellows of Australia, the Papuans of Borneo, the Negritos of the Andaman Islands, the Eskimos of the Arctic Circle,— there is the same story of measles, influenza, chicken-pox, scarlet fever and mumps assuming among them the spread and the fatality of a plague.

As for the more serious infections to which civilization has not become immune, Virchow summed up our knowledge of them in one graphic statement with regard to smallpox, namely, that every known nation or tribe that had been exposed to smallpox within the past century and had not adopted vaccination, had been swept out of existence. "*Deleta ab variola*," "destroyed by smallpox."

And this is literally true. All the Oriental races above the lowest stages of civilization, and some, indeed, in stages little higher than savagery, habitually practice inoculation from a mild case, which, it will be remembered, was introduced into England itself by Lady Mary Wortley Montagu before the days of Jenner. All occidental races which are not in process of elimination rely upon vaccination.

The other diseases, to which we have acquired but little or incomplete immunity, such as pneumonia, bronchitis, dysentery, etc., fall with tremendous weight upon the aborigine. The mortality is at least double and sometimes quadruple that in the white race; but the contrast is not so vivid or so enormous as in the case of the milder infections.

The most striking illustration of this class is afforded by tuberculosis, at once the child and the deadliest enemy of modern civilization. When we woke with a shudder a few decades ago to find the fact staring us in the face in the boldest of figures that one seventh of our entire race die of tuberculosis of the lung alone, it was hard to imagine that the situation ever could have been worse. Yet our Indian wards furnish us with abundant ground for the belief that it was much worse, and that not so very long ago.

It was not until comparatively recent years that tuberculosis appeared to have gained much headway among the Indians. So long as they clung to their ancestral life in the open air, they had comparatively little opportunity to contract the disease, and if contracted, their natural method of life supplied them with a considerable part of the modern open-air treatment. But so soon as they began to be limited to a definite reservation and crowded into permanent villages, or, with well-meant but often deadly kindness, gathered into schools and missions, the disease quickly appeared among them and created fearful havoc. Particularly was this the case when they were induced and often coerced, by a well-meaning but not particularly intelligent Government, to give up their tepees and hogans and become civilized at one bound by living in those air-tight wooden boxes known as frame houses.

Absolutely the only thing that the Indian liked about these new quarters was that they could be made extremely warm at the expense of ventilation, which his tepees never could, and he naturally proceeded to work this advantage for all it was worth. The result was that within five or six years the agency physician would have been almost as glad to get the tribe out of their houses as the Government was to get them into them.

Although generally known among physicians that the reservation Indian suffered frightfully from tuberculosis, it was only within comparatively recent years that actual statistics covering the question began to be collected.

During a residence of six years on the Pacific Coast, I made careful inquiries of agency and other physicians, ranging from Alaska to Mexico and covering a

considerable part of the inter-mountain region and
the great Southwest. From almost every quarter
came accounts of enormous mortalities from tuberculosis, thirty, fifty, and even seventy per cent of the
total deaths being attributed to this cause: and this,
it will be remembered, in comparison with a rate in
the surrounding white communities of barely twelve
per cent. Some of these statements were, of course,
according to the inevitable tendency of the human
mind in studying new and surprising phenomena, a
trifle exaggerated. Estimates of fifty, sixty, or seventy
usually scaled down to about forty per cent on actual
statistical study. But there was a sufficiently appalling residue left even after the most careful allowance
for overstatement.

The most careful and admirably collected series of
statistics which have yet been published are those
of Dr. James A. Walker, of the Rosebud Agency of
Dakota. These covered ten years of careful personal
observation by Dr. Walker himself and are as absolutely reliable and dependable as statistics can well
be in this imperfect world. Starting out in a cautious
and conservative frame of mind, indeed, strongly
impressed with the quite correct belief that the actual
condition of affairs had usually been overstated and
exaggerated, Dr. Walker proved, as a matter of coldest and most inescapable fact, that of nearly five thousand Ogalalla Sioux, no less than forty-two per cent
of all who died — and their death-rate was a high
one — succumbed to tuberculosis.

It must be remembered, too, that these were not

a handful of wretched Piutes living from hand to mouth on roots and snakes, or of lazy Siwash squatting over their clam-beds and their rancid salmon, but as superb specimens of the noble savage as were ever imagined by Cooper. Tall, erect, fine-looking fellows, the best fighters that ever wore feathers in their hair, as scores of United States regiments can testify to their sorrow, averaging five feet nine and one-half inches in height and thirty-eight and three-quarter inches in chest-girth, — nearly two inches above the average of our boasted superior white race, — living in good houses, supplied with abundant rations of the best quality by a paternal Government, owning their own cattle, and with the finest hunting-range in the United States within easy distance, nothing could have been much more ideal than their physique and their surroundings — and yet these splendid children of Nature went down before the attack of tuberculosis like cattle before the rinderpest.

In the eleven agencies from which I was able to obtain exact figures, through the kindness of the Commissioner, the Honorable Francis Leupp, the average tuberculosis death-rate was between fifty and sixty per cent of all the deaths recorded. So that I think it would be perfectly safe to say that the death-rate of the Indian from tuberculosis, even under the most favorable conditions, is from four to six times that of the surrounding white population.

From the point of view of mere general vigor of physique, this state of affairs is difficult to account for. From that of the fearful susceptibility of an absolutely virgin tribe to a new and untried infection, it is perfectly harmonious and logical. A most graphic picture from life of just how tuberculosis affects a newly exposed tribe is given in a private letter courteously written to me by Dr. Paul Hutton, army surgeon at Fort Seward, Alaska.

Of 117 Indians examined by him in their houses and shacks in the villages surrounding the fort, no less than 24, or 20.6 per cent, had a well-advanced pulmonary tuberculosis, 12 per cent more in an early stage, and 16.2 per cent had tuberculous diseases in other organs and regions, making a total of 48 per cent who were tuberculous.

Now as to the future of the tribe. These 117 adults had had 312 children, of which 172 (or 55 per cent) are dead, with indications of tuberculosis as a cause in the vast majority of cases.

As we have no ground whatever for assuming that our primitive ancestors, when first exposed to the disease, had any higher degree of natural resisting powers than have the more vigorous specimens of our Indian tribes, we have, I think, fairly good ground for the belief that, destructive and deadly as tuberculosis still is, it has undergone considerable diminution in virulence in the past one thousand or fifteen hundred years. It is, of course, well known that a marked decline in its death-rate has occurred within the statistical period, though that, of course, dates back only about seventy years. Within this time, however, there has been a diminution of nearly fifty per cent in the actual death-rate from consumption, and the process is steadily going on. Most of this, of course, is probably due to our greater knowledge of the disease and more intelligent methods of fighting it, but a considerable share is undoubtedly due to the immense improvements in food, housing, and general sanitation that have been made, and the gradually increasing resistance which the race has developed.

An interesting straw pointing in this same direction is that, as between civilized races, those which have been longest and most constantly exposed to tuberculosis and other city and slum infections possess a decidedly higher resisting power to the disease than those who have lived in the open.

One of the many interesting features about the brilliant and successful Jewish race is that its death-rate from tuberculosis is only about one fourth that of the surrounding community. In the most crowded wards of New York and Chicago, for instance, the Jewish population has a death-rate from tuberculosis of about one hundred and fifty per hundred thousand living. Its Gentile neighbors in the same wards, in the same streets, have a death-rate of from four hundred and fifty to five hundred and fifty per hundred thousand living. Throughout the country at large the contrast is almost as striking. The general average death-rate from tuberculosis, according to the United States census for 1890, was about one hundred and sixty per hundred thousand living. That of the Jews, especially collected and compiled by Dr. John Billings, was only twenty-two per hundred thousand living.

This, of course, brings us to the question, How is this immunity on the part of the race or mitigation in the virulence of the disease brought about? The answer, of course, must be purely speculative and a mere expression of probabilities. But it would appear that two chief groups of factors are at work. One of these is the tolerably obvious one of the dying or serious crippling under the attack of, let us say, measles, a hundred generations ago, of those who were most susceptible. Consequently, this type would leave either no descendants at all or a smaller number of descendants than those who had a higher resisting power. Each successive generation would, therefore, contain a larger and larger number of the descendants of those who are most highly immune to the disease. A smaller number in each successive generation would be attacked, and those who did develop the disease would resist it better and exhibit it in a milder form. Of late years it has been suggested by one of our most thoughtful and brilliant students of bacteriology, Dr. Theobald Smith, that side by side with this there tends to go on a process of lessening of virulence and poisonousness on the part of the infectious germs.

The one thing which any germ must require, if it is going to survive, is to provide for its escape from the body of one victim to another. Therefore, any strain of any germ which is so virulent as to kill its host or victim before it has had this opportunity to transfer itself to another, will tend to become extinct. The milder strains of the germ, which allow their victim to live until he can excrete them in his sputum or other excreta for a sufficiently long time to be fairly safe of transferring them to another individual, will be likely to survive and dominate the situation.

Many of our disease germs quite closely resemble bacilli which are harmless, normal inhabitants of our food-tubes, skin, or surroundings. It is quite possible that we have literally bred our own disease germs, as society has often made its own criminals in the slum and the stews.

The outlook for the educated Indian seems even worse. In the last report of the medical officer of one school to the Indian Bureau of Canada, the careers of whose two hundred and fifty graduates had been closely followed for seven years, no less than seventy-five (thirty per cent) were already dead of tuberculosis.

This may partially account for the oft-lamented slight permanent results of our efforts to educate the Indian.

CHAPTER VI

CENTENARIANS

"THAT thy days may be long in the land" was a prophecy which meets one of the most universal longings of the human heart. Whatever the pessimists — celestial or terrestrial — may say to the contrary, man has ever found life no "vale of tears," but a red-blooded, vigorous, joyous thing, full of fight and of sunshine, and asks nothing better than it should last as long as possible. Hence the universal desire to live to "a good old age." No matter how plainly he may read his title clear to mansions in the skies, he is seldom in a hurry to step in and take possession any sooner than Fate decrees. There are few things of which we are prouder than that we "come of a long-lived stock," that a majority of our ancestors lived to an advanced age, and that, therefore, we have a reasonable basis for hoping to achieve the same desirable triumph. Yet the average age of the race is only about thirty-five years, and a century ago was well below that. This simply leads us to cherish more warmly the belief that we shall be one of the fortunate exceptions, and to dwell with especial delight upon and make much of those individuals who have accomplished an extraordinary span of years, and defied the King of Terrors for not merely the classic "threescore years and ten," but for eighty, ninety, a hundred or

more years, both as worthy of special congratulation
and envy on their own account, and still more as cheering illustrations of what may be accomplished. Not
a few enthusiasts have been so stimulated by a contemplation of the recorded instances of the attainment of a great age in the human species as to declare
that these represent the normal individual, and that
the man who dies under a hundred is to be regarded
as having met a premature end. Hence, the subject
of centenarians has ever been a favorite in the popular
mind, and each recorded birthday of these long-lived
survivors is heralded far and wide in popular comment
and in the public press.

As is to be expected, these stories do not shrink in
the telling. After they have been bruited abroad for
a certain number of years, some amateur or professional reporter hears of the legend, writes it down, and
it passes into literature. A more extraordinary collection of marvels than the alleged records of centenarians it would be hard to imagine. Though probably
most of us could count upon the fingers of one hand
the number of individuals whom we have actually
known to pass ninety-five years of age, out of a life-
long acquaintance covering at least from five to fifteen
thousand individuals, your chronicler of the marvelous
in the line of longevity does n't hesitate to accept
ale-house stories and old wives' tales, placing "Gran'-
ther So-and-So" or "Gammer Such-and-Such" at
one hundred and ten, one hundred and twenty-five,
and even one hundred and sixty-five years of age, and
he is even ready to credit such rank and palpable

absurdities as men of two hundred, two hundred and fifty, and two hundred and seventy-five years of age.

The reliability of the story which a centenarian will tell about his own age is aptly illustrated by an episode which came under my observation in southern California. The incident was related to me by one of the attorneys engaged in the case.

A water-right suit was on trial in one of the local courts. It was necessary to introduce evidence bearing upon the rights conceded to a piece of property upon the stream in question during the days of the Spanish occupation.

For this purpose a very aged Mexican was brought forward as a witness to testify in regard to the rights and usages of the water at the period in question. When this testimony — which was given through an interpreter — was completed, the attorney who had called him told the interpreter to ask the old man his age, in order to show that his memory could reasonably be expected to date back that far. The old man promptly returned, "I am one hundred and seventeen years old." Old as he was, he did n't look of such an advanced age as that, and the attorney glanced apprehensively at the opposing counsel. But cross-examination was waived, and the court adjourned for lunch.

During the lunch hour the lawyer called the interpreter and said to him: "Manuel, are you quite sure that old Pedro gave his age correctly there on the stand? Do you think he really understood what was asked of him? He does n't need to be that old."

"Well," said the interpreter, "I will ask him."

In a few minutes back he came.

"You are right. Pedro says that he *did n't* properly understand the question and was confused with the excitement of being in court and would like to correct his mistake."

Accordingly, as soon as court reconvened, the attorney addressed the court: "Your Honor, I should like again to place upon the stand for a few moments the witness, Pedro X, to correct an unintentional misstatement of his in regard to his age."

Opposing counsel had no objection, and Pedro was placed upon the stand.

The interpreter said: "Pedro, just before the court adjourned you stated that you were one hundred and seventeen years old. Was that correct?"

"No, Señor," said Pedro. "I got confused and made a mistake."

"Then, will you kindly tell the court your real age?"

"*Si*, Señor. I am *two* hundred and seventeen years old!"

It is now frankly admitted by statisticians and historians that most of the so-called classic instances of extreme old age must be regarded as little better than legendary. Take, for instance, the famous case of Thomas Parr, — "Old Parr," who has figured as the leading example and star illustration in all essays on How to Live to be a Hundred Years Old. He was gravely recorded in all standard encyclopædias and works of reference as having attained the age of one hundred and fifty-two years, and up to twenty years ago no suspicion even was breathed as to the substantial accuracy of this astonishing persistence. He was accepted as not merely, as in Mrs. Partington's phrase, "a centurion," but a centurion and a half!

The later editions, however, now briefly state that it is exceedingly doubtful whether the tradition of "Old Parr's" one hundred and fifty-two years rests upon any valid basis. Its origin was a popular pamphlet, whose frankly catch-penny and marvel-mongering character is well illustrated by its title, "An Olde, Olde, Olde, Very Olde Man." Parr was the illiterate servant of a country gentleman, and not a scrap of valid evidence as to the actual date of his birth is discoverable.

One after another the other celebrated examples of history have come to share the fate of "Old Parr."

His almost equally famous twin, Henry Jenkins, who has been cited a hundred times as having reached the extraordinary age of one hundred and sixty-nine years, is found on investigation to be an equally mythical character, so far as any actual proof of his real age is concerned. The only evidence is the popular report of a country town and the gossip of village-taverns.

Forty years ago an intelligent physician, named Thoms, published a book on centenarians in which, after careful investigation of the evidence in all the historic cases, he came to the startling conclusion that up to that date there were on record only *five* persons of whom there was reasonably valid evidence to show that they had passed one hundred years.

Sir George Cornewall Lewis goes so far as to declare that there is no authentic instance on record of any human being having ever reached the century mark.

All authorities are agreed that of the one class of human beings whose births and deaths are sure of accurate and indisputable record, the royal families of Europe, not one member has ever reached one hundred years. The same is true of three hundred popes; indeed, of these only five passed eighty years, and in twelve hundred years only six kings have reached fourscore years. No English insurance company in the past hundred and forty years has paid a death-claim to any beneficiary over ninety-six years old.

Thus the historical instances are rapidly falling into disbelief, and no modern instances reported in the papers have yet stood the test of investigation. The vast majority of them are reported as occurring in negroes, Indians, or those born in ignorant peasant communities on the Continent of Europe, or in remote rural districts of the United States, where no accurate records are kept. And the age of those who can present evidence making it probable that they have passed the century mark never exceeds it more than two or three years. A human being over one hundred and ten years of age may be regarded as practically as pure a fairy tale as one over nine feet in height.

Our love of the marvelous, combined with our desire both to be tall and to live to be old, has led us into an attitude of absurd credulity in regard to the existence of both of these extremes. Centenarians and seven-footers both occur, but they are very, very much rarer than is popularly supposed. The majority of those investigated are found to fall far below instead of exceeding these two comparatively moderate heights and ages, and the number who exceed either seven feet or one hundred years in any marked degree is exceedingly small.

"But," says some one at once, "granting that it is possible that exaggeration has crept into these ancient records, and that in an uncritical age, where little distinction was made between legend and history, this sort of method as to old age and stature may have grown up. What of the centenarians of to-day? One can hardly pick up a paper without finding the record of the celebration, amid his or her rejoicing family and fellow townsmen, of one or more venerable individuals of their one hundred and second, one hundred and tenth, or even one hundred and fifteenth, one hundred and twenty-fifth, or one hundred and thirty-third birthday."

It was precisely the study of these modern instances that first made us skeptical of the genuineness of the historic ones. It must be premised in advance that it is impossible to dogmatize or make positive statements upon this subject, and nothing of that sort will be attempted here. Its inherent difficulties are something enormous.

In the first place, the vast majority of ages recorded, even in official statistics like census reports and in legal documents, are merely based upon the statement and belief of the individual concerned. Not in one case in fifty is any further evidence sought. So that mere statements of the occurrence of a certain number of centenarians in a given country, State, or city, per ten thousand or one hundred thousand of the population, is of no scientific weight or value whatever until each individual instance has been investigated and the accuracy of the statement of the age been proved or disproved by evidence, such as would be valid in a court of law.

The second difficulty is that the majority of us, if we were suddenly called upon to prove our precise age, would have great difficulty in producing valid evidence which would determine that fact, apart from the word of our parents or relatives or acquaintances of the previous generation.

Last and most important of all, we have absolutely no reliable physical data upon which we can base an estimate of age in the human subject who has accomplished the eruption of the second or permanent teeth. A man or woman of fifty-five or sixty years of age may be of any age from forty-five to a hundred and forty-five for anything that can be determined by the most careful physical examination during life, or even after death.

Thus we are absolutely thrown back upon documentary evidence, such as would be valid in a court of law, in establishing a claim to an estate, for instance, in determining the actual age of an individual, no matter how venerable or decrepit he may appear, or how many years his hair may have been gray, what historical personages or facts he may claim to recall, or however imposing a flock of grandchildren and great-grandchildren he may be able to muster. In regard to this last, it is well to bear in mind that in the period and in the class of society from which even most modern centenarians spring, the age at which marriage was customary was very much earlier than that which now obtains. No small percentage of our grandmothers, for instance, were married at sixteen years of age, and of our grandfathers at eighteen. And those ages would form a fair average for the laboring and farming classes up to within thirty or forty years ago. Hence it is obvious that a man might become a father at nineteen, a grandfather at thirty-eight, a great-grandfather at fifty-seven, and a great-great-grand-father at seventy-six. And this by allowing descent to be always in the male line. While a woman, through her female descendants, could become a great-great-grandmother at sixty-eight. So that even the hugest legion of descendants is not necessarily a proof of more than a very moderate longevity.

Now for the actual evidence in cases that come within modern times, remembering, of course, that it is impossible to prove a negative, that these "olde, olde, olde, very olde" people may be even older than they claim, but that the burden of proof is upon them, and that proof must be sufficient to carry weight in an ordinary court of law.

The first thing that strikes us is that the overwhelming majority of centenarians reported within the past one hundred years in this country are either negroes, Indians, or immigrants born as peasants in some remote country district of Europe: in other words, in those classes in which exact records of dates of birth and even of identity are either impossible or most difficult to secure. This, by the way, has no new character. It has stamped the centenarian in all ages. In fact, most of the purveyors of the marvelous in this realm have innocently accepted it as a proof of the short life and heavy penalty paid for success and distinction by the great ones of the world. It is only the poor and lowly who, on account of their more peaceful and blameless lives, can attain these good old ages. As one of the most recent collections, Gould & Pyles's "Anomalies and Curiosities of Medicine," naïvely remarks: "Longevity is always most common in the middle and lower classes, where accurate records of births are seldom kept." And further, that "even the parish registers are apt to be monopolized by the gentry, and inferior lives are not considered worth recording."

Now this explanation may, of course, be correct, but it is entirely opposed to everything that we know in regard to both the mortality and the morbidity of those classes. Take our own negroes and Indians, for instance, — the former with a death-rate from fifty to seventy-five per cent greater than that of the white man, and the latter more than double. Does it seem reasonable that, after dying at from one and one half times to twice the rate of the white populations up to say fifty years of age, they should suddenly acquire a charmed life, and live on to ages ranging from twenty to fifty years greater than those ever known to be attained by civilized races or classes of whose birth there is accurate record?

In our United States Census the highest number of centenarians is reported from rural, illiterate States with large negro or Indian populations, while the progressive, highly civilized States with a well-educated native white population report the lowest. Arizona, for instance, reports twenty-one per one hundred thousand, Mississippi twenty, Alabama, Florida, Georgia, each fifteen, while Massachusetts, Connecticut, New York, Pennsylvania, Iowa, and six other such States report only one, and the record is far more perfect and complete in the latter States.

A precisely similar state of affairs obtains upon the Continent of Europe. Those countries, like Great Britain, France, and Germany, which have a fairly accurate system of registration and a minimum number of illiterate and ignorant peasants in their population, show in their official records the lowest number of centenarians per one hundred thousand living, while those such as Russia, Hungary, and Turkey show the highest, with the Balkan States at the top of the pyramid!

It was in the remote mountain villages of the Caucasus, it will be recalled, that Metchnikoff found his swarms of very, very old people, who had achieved such triumphs of longevity upon the now famous sour milk.

Now, what are the actual data upon which these negro and Indian claims of extraordinarily advanced age are based? As regards the negroes, we know in the first place perfectly well that few of those now alive and over fifty-five years of age have any accurate record of the date of their birth, and many of them not even of the place of their birth, or of their parentage, since up to a little more than forty years ago they were held as chattels and human beasts of burden, and recorded as such. Their claims to antiquity are usually based upon some such flimsy and unreliable things as remembering or having been in the household of some one of the earlier Presidents of the United States, preferably "Marse George Washington." And scarcely one of them will bear the test of even the barest and most superficial investigation.

As regards the Indian centenarians, the situation is even more nebulous and uncertain. In the first place, few of the Indian tribes, except those that have become civilized and settled down upon farms, have any accurate method whatever of recording dates and years. It is the exception even to find an Indian who knows who his grandfather was. And his ignorance of everything preceding the lifetime of his own father is almost absolute. When an Indian attempts to fix the date of a particular event, he will be obliged to do so by its relation to some incident that has occurred since the coming of the white settlers and has become a matter of civilized record. Or, failing this, he will describe it as the "year of the great flood," "the moon following the salmon famine," "the winter of the deep snow," "the fall of the great slaughter of bison." Secondly, when he does attempt to commit himself to a statement as to the precise number of years, you must first be careful to elicit what he means by a "year." Comparatively few of the tribes were good enough astronomers to have conceived the idea of a year, so as to utilize it in recording the passage of time, even by such primitive methods as notches in a stick or stones in a circle. Many of the tribes counted *two years* and others four to each calendar year, while, as every reader of his Cooper knows, the favorite unit of time with the Indians was the "moon."

Of recorded instances of centenarians among the Indians, the very number itself staggers credulity. One exploring expedition reports the discovery in a single Peruvian village of *over a hundred* inhabitants who could boast the age of one hundred years! Scores of them will be recorded for a single California tribe. And yet every scrap of credible and reliable evidence that we have as to actual vital conditions shows that the average longevity of all these Indian tribes is barely half to two thirds that of the white races. The simple fact of the matter is that the average Indian man or Indian woman — particularly the latter — after she has lost her teeth, anywhere from forty years of age on, will so utterly collapse and shrivel into a shapeless bag of skin and bones that the casual observer would be ready to believe her to be any age which might be claimed.

Two instances of Indian "Methuselahs" happened to come more or less directly under my own observation, and I simply give the findings for what they are worth, though personally regarding them as typical of all these claims. One of them was that of a very aged woman, the last survivor of a one-time flourishing tribe, whose face was simply one mass of wrinkles, out of which a pair of beady black eyes glistened, who, after being dramatically "played up" in one of the local papers as a remarkable instance of savage longevity, and reported to have remembered the first coming of the white man to the Pacific Coast, over a hundred years ago, and hence to be at least one hundred and ten to one hundred and twelve years of age, became an object of great curiosity to tourists. The extreme incoherence of even the newspaper reports of the good lady's recollections excited my suspicions, and I proceeded to make inquiries, with the result of finding three well-known citizens of that community who had been among the earlier permanent settlers, and who distinctly recalled the old woman as a young and buxom girl, certainly not to exceed twenty-five years of age, and, in their judgment, nearer seventeen or eighteen, barely forty-five years before, thus making seventy the extreme possible limit of her age. Their estimate was that she was about sixty-five.

Another celebrated old lady of the Umatilla Reservation gave me the pleasure of a personal interview. She was crouched in a shapeless heap on the dirty floor of a cabin, behind the stove, with the dogs and children sprawling about her. Her hands were like bunches of lean, brown tree-roots. Her back and neck muscles were so weak that her head drooped forward upon her chest, her chin resting upon her knees, and it was only with difficulty that she could lift it, so that we could see her face. One glimpse at it was enough, so far as appearances were concerned. I was ready to believe her not merely one hundred and fifteen, but two hundred and fifteen. For some reason the old dame was out of sorts and refused to talk at the time of our visit. But a friend of mine awaited a more favorable opportunity, and by means of an interpreter had a conversation with her.

Her sole claim to be one hundred and fifteen rested upon the statement that when she was a young girl of about fourteen or fifteen years of age she remembered the coming of Lewis and Clark into the Oregon country, which occurred exactly ninety-nine years before. What the conversation through an interpreter actually developed was that, when she was a very young girl, she recalled two white men riding into a village of the Cayuse Indians, of which her father was head man, and conversing for some time with the men of the clan. She had absolutely no recollection of the name of either of the men, had never heard her father say who they were. The sole point that identified these two unknown white men with Lewis and Clark was that one of them rode a white horse, and the other was tall and had flowing blond hair. And upon this broad and substantial basis was founded an identification of the great explorers which has found its way into some of the local histories. More than this, the two white men, according to the best of her recollection, were alone, whereas Lewis and Clark were accompanied by a large and well-armed party, and never at any time were both separated from it at once. In other words, the frequency of centenarians among Indians and negroes is simply the product of our ignorance and lack of accurate information.

Finally, as to the modern instances in white Americans, which, if one were to believe the newspapers, occur almost every day, these again have the age-long preference for the foreign-born, the ignorant and the inhabitants of remote country districts where no accurate records of any sort are kept. The precise date of birth of the average European peasant, or even of one of the poorer classes of the less thickly settled districts of our own farming country, is difficult to establish for two reasons. First, in a very considerable percentage of cases it has not been recorded at all in any official records, or even in the renowned "Family Bible." Second, and even more puzzling, is that, as is well known, in a given country neighborhood in Europe, the family names of the peasantry inhabiting a district are apt to be exceedingly few in number, and alike. Certain parishes, even in England, will have all their laboring population, something like two thirds of their total number, divided among three great family names. A similar state of affairs obtains in Scotland, and even in Scotch and Irish settlements in this country.

One case came under my own observation which illustrates so beautifully how centenarians get to be one hundred years old that I think it is worth a brief description.

Seven years ago I was attracted by a report with large headlines, in several newspapers, of the celebration of her one hundred and nineteenth birthday by an aged woman in a town in the Middle West. Naturally, the event was made much of, the town decorated in honor of the occasion, and a formal address and presentation of valuable books to the good dame were carried out. A full and detailed life history also was published in the county, stating that she had been born in Georgia, recalled as a young wife, her father going to fight in the War of 1812, had been three times married, the last time at seventy-six years of age, had a daughter nearly eighty and a son of eighty-five, had a record of her birth in the family Bible, and had resided in the town where she then lived for nearly fifty years.

This certainly sounded authentic, but I fortunately happened to be acquainted with two gentlemen who lived in that town, and I determined to get their account of the matter. Both of them were men of good education and standing, and I knew I could rely upon the truth of their statements absolutely. One was a well-to-do business man and the other a lawyer of unusually cautious and critical type of mind, with a keen appreciation of the value of evidence.

The first one said that Mrs. X had a family Bible containing the date of her birth, that he had no reason to doubt the newspaper account of her age, and that the good lady herself firmly believed that she was one hundred and nineteen years old, and her mind was clear.

My lawyer friend, in his letter, said that he had sifted the matter thoroughly, and this was the net result. He had visited the old lady and thought she looked the age; but —

The family Bible was not to be found. Her "recollection of the War of 1812" simmered down to a memory of seeing her father start out to fight Indians, and instead of being a young married woman she was only a child of eight or nine, thus making her, even if the date were accurate, one hundred and three instead of one hundred and nineteen. The only date in her life that could be positively proved was that of her arrival in the town fifty-two years before.

Four old settlers united in declaring that Mrs. X at that time, instead of being seventy-six years old, *appeared and claimed to be about forty or forty-five*. One said that Mrs. X had always claimed to be the same age as her mother, and the latter, if still living, would be ninety-six. Another, aged eighty-seven, stated that forty years ago the "centurion" had told him she was just ten years older than he was.

None would admit that she could possibly be one hundred, and most regarded her as about ninety-five or ninety-six. Finally, none of the older settlers could recall any claims to such advanced age on her part, or even reports of them, until about eight or nine years ago, and the story was ultimately traced almost directly to a "josh" of the town joker on a "drummer from Chicago," to the effect the old lady was one hundred and ten.

The drummer was taken to see her, and was convinced by her appearance. The story spread, and the town began to take a pride in its centenarian. Said town joker was still living, and, though not openly admitting it, strongly hinted that he had had a part in developing the tradition.

One of the most amusing features of the records of centenarians is the eager credulity with which most of those who study them have besought them for their "secret" — the means or method by which they succeeded in living so long.

The fact of the matter simply is that the centenarian has eaten just exactly the food and drunk the drink and lived the life common and habitual in the rank or community in which he happened to be born, and as this is usually the lowest and poorest, his habits have been those of the day-laborer and the peasant the world over. To attempt to draw any conclusions from them would be about as absurd as anything that can be imagined; first, because we have absolutely no evidence that these habits have any connection with such degree of longevity as may have been attained; second, because the degree of longevity itself is open to the most serious doubt in the great majority of cases.

Last, it is a little difficult to conceive why any intelligent individual in this twentieth century should have the slightest desire to live to be one hundred. The record of the last ten to twenty-five years of these apparently very old people, whatever may have been their real age, is invariably one of eating, dozing, mumbling a little in the sun, and sleeping — mere animal, nay, vegetable existence — or, more accurately, *persistence*. The only feature about it which would appear to contain any sort of satisfaction or enjoyment is such celebrity and notoriety as they may attract on account of their great age. Explain it as we may, the discouraging fact stares us in the face that not a single human being has been proved to pass or attain the age of one hundred years who had any celebrity or reputation outside of his own town or country, save merely for the fact of age.

What is the use of living to be one hundred, if your life has been one hundred years blank? A majority of these alleged centenarians are found in almshouses. The only man of international, or even national, reputation, who is accepted by statisticians as having passed the century mark, was Chevreul, the chemist. Of all the numerous collections of men of genius that have been made, while their average life is long, well above that of the rest of the community, many of them living to be seventy-five, eighty, eighty-five, and ninety years of age, not one save this exception passed the one hundredth year. It is better to do one thing that the world thinks worth remembering and die at thirty than to *exist* one hundred or even a hundred and fifty years. So that, frankly, there does n't appear to be very much rationality or profit in any of the more or less visionary schemes so far advised for making the average span of human life a hundred years or more.

The length of the life of an individual is determined by the interests of the race. And when we have lived that period which is best adapted to doing our share of the active work, bringing into existence the new generation, and giving them a good start in the race, Nature cares little what becomes of us, nor should we ourselves be very much concerned.

To do our work, to enjoy a fair period of rest and contemplation of the results, then to depart as swiftly and painlessly as possible, this seems the really rational ambition, and not a mere clinging to profitless persistence on the planet. This, so far as we can determine, is actually the tendency of the course of civilization thus far. While the average age at death is rising, and the average longevity of the race increasing, this is more by the diminishing of infant mortality and the suppression of the diseases which find their victims in youth and young adult life, enabling each individual born to live out his fair share of days, rather than by increasing the actual length of life of those who survive to middle age.

In fact, such statistics as are available indicate that it is doubtful whether the percentage of those in the community who pass seventy-five or eighty years of age has in any substantial degree increased. This, I frankly confess, seems to me as it should be. We have increased the period of growth, of development, of adolescence, the period of vigor, of happiness and of effectiveness. We have enabled and are enabling a larger and larger percentage of men to live their life and do their work before being cut down by the hand of time.

Why should we endeavor, or desire, to prolong the twilight of life, which at best is little more than a holding at even level of the balance between comfort and discomfort?

CHAPTER VII

WOMEN IN PUBLIC LIFE

WE are always approaching a crisis — and surviving it. We have waxed fat and flourishing on a diet of crises, in fact, these thousands of years past. Balancing upon the brink of catastrophes is just the exercise we need to keep us in health; and if ever we should get out of sight of an impending calamity, we had better get a telescope and proceed to hunt one up for the good of our livers — lest we grow fat and scant of breath. To run risks of death twenty times a day is precisely what keeps us alive.

Just now it is the health and nervous system and moral tone of the modern woman that are causing concern to the souls of the serious prophets of the century — prophets, that is, who take themselves seriously, as prophets always do, and imagine that their denunciations and predictions will have more effect upon the tides of human life than Mrs. Partington's broom had upon those of the Atlantic. "Woman is becoming a public character," they all wail in chorus; "and the fierce light of publicity will fade and wither all her womanliness and the sweet virtues of the hearthstone, while her peace and balance of mind and vigor of health will be shattered in its storms."

That a striking and almost revolutionary change

in the work and place of woman has taken place within the last thirty-five years is obvious to the dullest eye — just like the change that has taken place in the working habits and surroundings of man since the discovery of steam and electric power. The vast majority of men no longer perform their entire day's work and round of tasks within rifle-shot or shouting distance of their hearthstone, or in a workshop which is a room in the house, or its annex or lower story.

Home has become for the man of to-day, we are told, merely a place in which to eat and sleep; indeed, according to some cynics, a place to go to after all the other places are shut. And now it looks as if a full half of womankind were about to follow man's example in finding their work outside of the home. The cry is not unnaturally raised — that is, considering the nature of prophets — that the new state of affairs is going to take woman entirely outside of the home; and the only point upon which the Jeremiahs are unable to agree is as to which will be more injured by the change — the home or the woman.

It never appears to have occurred to these moralists to reflect — if, indeed, some moralists have anything to reflect with —that the removal of man and his work from the home has not only been not injurious but markedly beneficial to the latter.

Never were homes half so commodious, so well lighted and ventilated, so beautifully equipped and furnished, so well heated, so sanitary, so comfortable and attractive as they are to-day. The farther a man gets away from his home in the daytime the more he appreciates it. It becomes a luxury to him, and he is far more ready to lavish time and thought and money upon its adornment and improvement.

There is probably nothing, since the days of the fortress and the walled town, that the home has suffered from so severely as from being a place of work. The primitive farmer's home, for instance, was little better than a second story of the cow-stable — an annex to the barn; a link in the sacred circle of the pigpen, the chicken-roost, and the manure-heap — as it is frankly to-day among the peasantry of Europe. Even in some of our own country districts it has not yet escaped from the bondage of being an appendage to the barnyard as completely as might be desired.

Then, when the shop was born, it always appropriated the best room or series of rooms in the house, leaving only a few boxes behind it or lofts above it for the family to live in; while that the whole house should be filled with the odor of leather, or cheeses, or hides, or groceries, or the noise of the saw and the hammer, or of the anvil, or the steam of the dye vats, or the heat of the baker's oven, was considered a necessary and natural part of the home feeling. No poet has ever yet rhapsodized over the dear old scents and smells of home. Some of them might carry our memories back more vividly than delightfully nowadays. We talk enthusiastically about encouraging cottage industries and occupations for earning money at home, and thus keeping all the family together under the sacred influences of the rooftree; but we forget that the loom or the work-table occupies the best room in

the house and the best window in that room, and that
the worst possible thing for the harmony and domestic
affections of a family is to be incessantly soaked and
saturated in each other's company all day long, without possibility of escape, six days out of the week.

A colleague of mine, who in his younger days had
an extensive practice among the Jews of the lower
East Side of New York, tells me that they have a
quaint phrase which is significant of much in this
regard. When they first come over to this country,
and with toil and suffering accumulate capital enough
to start a tiny business, the shop, of course, occupies
the main front room and the family lives upstairs
and at the back; but as soon as they have reached a
certain standard of success and prosperity, they take
a full-sized modern shop in a better street; and the
family, instead of meekly roosting above it, moves
up into Harlem, to — as they quaintly express it —
"live separate" in all the glory of a steam-heated flat.

Nothing strikes the American in Europe quite so
forcibly as the stuffy, ill-ventilated, ill-smelling, and
undesirably situated living-rooms and even houses
which people in comfortable circumstances will occupy
because the latter are mere appendages of "the business." Few things have done more for the comfort,
health, and happiness of the home than the modern
ability to "live separate." Talk about the home being in danger in this twentieth century! The home
of the vast majority of men scarcely began to have
an independent existence of its own until about seventy years ago. Until then it was practically a bunk-

house attached to a barn or a shop for all below the aristocracy.

Even some aristocratic homes are not yet entirely emancipated from this slavery to "business" — such as the doctor's and the minister's.

Our acres of villas and square miles of suburbs are cheering proofs of the emancipation and new lease of life of the home. Their architecture may be monotonous and superficial, their furniture too plushy, their upholstery too vivid; but they are an immense improvement upon anything that ever preceded them from the point of view of both health and comfort; and they signify this much unmistakably — that man is no longer content to live and house his family in any old hole or corner which happens to be near his business.

A town may or may not have fine business streets and a great wholesale district; but what it stands or falls by to the eye of the sanitarian and the biological engineer is the extent and attractiveness of its new spick-and-span residential suburbs — whether of cottages, tenements or mansions. Call them birdboxes, or barracks, or mushrooms, or gingerbread and claptrap, — what you will, — they are the cheering and dominant feature of the architecture of the new century. Never were there half so many real homes in the world before. The home decaying? It's just beginning to flourish! They may not all be in the perfection of good taste yet, but they will be in fifty years' time. Taste can hardly be expected to flourish in cellars and hovels and rookeries. You must have light enough to see colors before you can judge whether the ornamentation is well chosen or not.

At the same time, far from the manners and tempers of men having become harsher and fiercer and more unscrupulous by their removal from the sweet influence of home, there has been a most noticeable increase in kindliness, in sympathy, and in intolerance of cruelty and injustice. The past seventy years have been emphatically the age of intelligent philanthropy, of the abolishment of slavery, of the legal protection of woman, of education for all, of the relief of disease and suffering.

Why, then, should we fear that the migration of the work and the daily activities of half or even more of our adult women should have any injurious or demoralizing effect upon either the woman or the home? Perhaps it will be answered at once that a man in the house always was an awkward, inconvenient sort of creature, of very little real use and dreadfully in the way — so that it was no loss to get rid of him; but that woman is the very genius of the place, the main support of all its activities and the only priestess who can keep the fire burning at its shrine.

There is merit in the first part of the suggestion. Few things promote harmony and affection between the women of the family and their menfolk, and *vice versa*, more than a regular daily vacation from each other's company. As to the latter part of the objection, there are other considerations to be borne in mind. One is that, though in the nature of the case, from the natural division of labor between the sexes, the bulk of the work of the home has always been performed by woman and always will be, yet to-day a large and constantly increasing share of the work of the home is done outside of it.

In more primitive times — in fact, until less than a hundred years ago — the range of home activities was nearly three times what it is to-day. Nearly all the clothing of the family, for instance, was manufactured upon the premises; the wool and flax were carded and spun and woven and dyed and cut and sewn into garments; the socks were knitted; all the articles of underwear were made by hand; soap was boiled and candles cast in moulds; butter and cheese were manufactured on a large scale, not only for home consumption, but also for the market; herbs were gathered and medicines brewed from them; meats were salted and stored; fruits and vegetables dried and preserved — in fact, every household of any size required the continual and constant labor of from two to five grown women in order to keep itself in good running order.

Now, however, two fifths to two thirds of all these domestic activities are being done by machinery in factories, in shops and in stores; and, as a natural result, woman is following her work out of the home into the places where it is now being done. Why should the work be either more physically injurious or morally degrading to her in one place than in the other? And why should the home suffer from the removal of half or two thirds of these women workers any more than it did from the removal of the men?

Certain kinds of work, such as the care of children, the preparation and serving of food, and the care of living- and sleeping-rooms, are still carried on in the home or in some modified form of it. The actual labor, however, of even these has been greatly lightened by both machinery and modern methods, so that they do not absorb or require the energies of more than half, or possibly not more than a third, of the women who were previously employed at home.

To assume that this change of place of work will make the woman who does her housework in a factory or shop think any the less of her home on this account, or lose interest in it, or cease to appreciate its value and importance, seems to me not merely illogical but unreasonable. On the contrary, home becomes, instead of chiefly a place of hard, monotonous, and wearing work, a place of rest, of enjoyment, and recuperation.

It is a ludicrous mistake to suppose, for instance, that the farmer loves his home more than the clerk does his simply because he spends a larger share of his time in it. Not even the fact that he spends more of his nights at home is any sign of his preference for it, but merely that it is too much trouble to hitch up the team and wash up and get away from it.

The average farmer of fifty years ago grudged every penny that was spent upon the house or its furniture, in decoration and repairs. The average city dweller delights to spend money, within the limits of his purse, upon his home, and enjoys making it as attractive and convenient as possible, because it is to him purely a place of rest, of refreshment, and of enjoyment. Why should not employment in factories, shops, and stores have the same effect upon the feelings of the working-woman? As a matter of fact, it has had precisely that effect already; and you will find few women prouder and more keenly appreciative of and devoted to their homes, and their embellishment and improvement, than most working-girls and working-women.

The fact that the "home-loving" and "home-keeping" women of former generations, whose disappearance is now lamented by the pessimists, spent nine tenths of their working hours in their homes, was no proof whatever of love of home; nor, indeed, did it tend to foster that feeling. Their much-boasted home-staying was simply due to the fact that they could not escape, being chained by a never-ceasing round of duties, — prisoners under their own roof, — and that, when a momentary lull in the routine did occur, they were too tired to take advantage of it, and, after fifteen or twenty years of the performance, too stupid!

It is one of the most convincing and triumphant proofs of the strength and stability of woman's mental powers that successive generations of that delightful form of semi-solitary confinement at hard labor known as home life has not made her a candidate for the insane asylum! Man would have gone raving crazy or blown up the institution with dynamite long ago! To chain a woman to her home by the ankle can scarcely be regarded as a promising or hopeful method of promoting in her an affection for it or an intelligent and competent interest in its management and improvement. Slave labor or serf labor has always proved the dearest and least efficient labor in the world. To set woman free from the bondage of home is to give her the first reasonable opportunity of developing an affection for and an intelligent interest in it.

To put it very crudely, since from one half to two thirds of the work formerly done in the home has now been transferred to factories, shops, and public agencies, a like proportion of women have followed it or are preparing to follow it. They are engaged, in fact, in what are quaintly and suggestively termed by the mountaineers of Georgia and the Carolinas "public works," by which they mean, not government improvements, but sawmills, factories, mines, and so forth. Incidentally, it may be remarked that the first and most striking fact of the engaging in these public works by the mountaineers has been a great improvement in the furnishing, decoration, and conveniences of their homes, the money which they have earned in this way having been first applied to repainting or making additions to their houses and to equipping them with cook stoves, rocking-chairs, cottage organs, and other modern conveniences. Similarly, all over the country to-day, the homes maintained by working-women, either for other members of their families or for their own comfort and pleasure, will be found to compare most favorably in attractiveness, convenience, and comfort with those supported on the same income where the women of the family spend all their time at home.

There need be little fear that this partial physical

removal from the home atmosphere will diminish the working-woman's interest in her home, for the simple reason that a home is a thing self-existent and self-supporting. The need for a home of some sort is as universal and irresistible as the attraction of gravitation. Even though there be, in the bitter language of the pessimist, —

> Nothing to breathe but air;
> Nothing to eat but food;
> Nothing to wear but clothes
> To keep us from going nude!
> Nowhere to go but out!
> Nowhere to come but back!

yet there must be some place to come back to, some point in space to engulf one's food, somewhere to rest, somewhere to go when all the other places are shut. To have a home of some sort is as necessary as breathing. The much eulogized "old-fashioned home" may be disappearing, but that is because something better is taking its place.

Nothing but the rosy mist that hovers over the past — "the light that never was on sea or land" — makes us fondly believe that the old-fashioned home was superior to the modern one. As a matter of cold, historical fact, it was not half so good. Outside of the homes of the wealthy, there is scarcely a house to-day over a hundred years old that is really fit to live in from a modern, civilized point of view; indeed, which would not be actually condemned as a nuisance on sanitary grounds by an up-to-date board of health.

The houses of a century or more ago were badly lighted, worse ventilated, utterly incapable of being properly heated; cold, damp, and most inconvenient in their arrangements — because, for the most part, they were constructed either for purposes entirely unconnected with residential uses, such as farm buildings, shops, businesses, or by mere males who had absolutely no proper conception of how a house should be built so as best to promote its comfortable and convenient operation as a home. Rooms were strung out one behind the other or piled up in successive tiers, according to the plans of the architect or the exigencies of the situation or the material, and then afterward assigned to their various domestic uses in such makeshift fashion as might best be feasible.

The shop or workrooms were given first choice of location; the rooms which were most likely to be entered by strangers — and consequently least used by the family — second; bedrooms, third; and kitchens and dining-rooms, last of all. Yet, from a biological and rational point of view, the kitchen and dining-room are precisely the two most important rooms in the house, the ones which should be given the best light and air, and at least second choice for position in the whole house, and upon whose arrangement and equipment should be expended the best intelligence and the most careful thought of both architect and family.

Now that women are earning real money and can contribute hard cash toward the support and maintenance of the home, they are entitled to and are gaining a proper voice and share of control in its building arrangements and equipment; and, in consequence, houses to-day are being built which are really fit for civilized human beings to live in, from the point of view of sanitation and comfort, for the first time in history.

Yet there are still too many houses that are built too much upon the principle of the cottage erected by a former colleague of mine during his wife's absence in Europe. He was an eccentric and somewhat impulsive fellow, and he suddenly decided that it would be a delightful surprise for his wife to build her a new house during her absence. The work was pushed with all speed and the bungalow was finished and ready for occupancy before the date of her return; but when he proudly showed his delighted wife through the new home on the day of her arrival, it was discovered that he had forgotten the kitchen — and it had to be added as an annex, or leanto at the back of the house!

There is not the slightest danger of the home suffering on account of woman being given a larger voice in its construction and management, or placed in a position to build and equip it herself if she chooses.

Nor is there any great reason to fear that this transference of woman's activities to fields outside the home will have any more injurious effect upon her than upon the home. The work is the same work she has always done, only carried out in a more effective and intelligent manner; and though, in the beginning, the wholesale methods employed, so to speak, the crowding together of large numbers of operatives in buildings designed solely for the welfare of the business, without much regard for theirs, produced some undesirable and unwholesome conditions, yet these are rapidly diminishing and disappearing under intelligent and humane management and legislation.

It is doubtful whether, at their worst, they were ever more undesirable or injurious to health than the conditions under which those women had been working in their own homes. Certainly no class of women factory-hands, operatives, or shopgirls are worked so hard and for such long hours, poor pay, poor food, and poor accommodations as are the average domestic servants. In any case, these unfavorable conditions are not an essential and inherent part of the new methods; indeed, it has now been proved by abundant experiments that for the turning-out of the largest amount of work of the best quality, with least waste of material and loss of time, the most careful provisions for the health, comfort, and safety of the workers are not merely advisable but absolutely necessary.

Thanks partly to their own increasing intelligence and partly to the pressure of an awakened public opinion, as expressed in legislative enactments, the better class of manufacturers, merchants, and other firms employing large numbers of women are so arranging and improving their places of work, shortening their hours, and providing for their comfort and even recreation, that the condition of the average working-woman of to-day, outside the home, is already far superior to her average condition in the home fifty years ago, as is shown by the grim but convincing testimony of mortality and morbidity statistics. The general death-rate of women employed in gainful occupations is from fifteen to thirty per cent lower than that of the average of women employed in their own homes; while among women working for wages, the lowest death-rate is among those employed as clerks, stenographers, and teachers, and the highest among those engaged as domestic servants.

So far from the health of women being wrecked and their nervous systems being shattered by the strain of factory, shop, and office work, the records both of such firms as provide medical attention during sickness for their employees and of friendly and other societies insuring against sickness show that the health of working-women, as measured by the number of days of disability in the year on account of sickness, ranges from fifteen to twenty per cent better than that of the average women in their own homes; while, again, those employed in clerical and commercial pursuits have a smaller amount of sickness than those engaged as domestic servants.

It is only fair to say, of course, that allowance must be made in these comparisons for the fact that a larger percentage of the women engaged in outside industries are either young or at the more vigorous ages and conditions of life, while all ages and conditions are, of course, employed in homes; and that working-women, when no longer able on account of sickness or advancing years to hold their positions in public works, will drop back into homes as domestic servants or as semi-pensioners and are, in consequence, at death reported under this heading. However, it may be fairly and safely taken as indicating that the new methods of life and work are not in themselves injurious even in their crudest and least civilized forms, and that there is certainly no valid basis for predicting any physical deterioration of woman from this cause in the future.

One of the most vivid apprehensions of the prophets of misfortune appears to be that women are either losing or will lose their graces, their attractiveness, and their charm — or, as the phrase is, "become unsexed" — by this new relation to and contact with the outside world; but whoever seriously dreads this knows little of biology, or of woman. It has taken at least five million years to make woman female and man male — for the primitive creature was bisexual; and he who imagines that such a trifle as a change in methods of education or a few years of freer contact with the world is going to wipe out those differences is singularly lacking in a sense of proportion — to say nothing of humor.

If there be any serious likelihood of woman's losing her charm, her sexual attractiveness, her delightful spontaneity, her delicious incalculableness, and becoming transformed into a stupid, rational being whose actions are controlled by the laws of cause and effect and whose conduct can be predicted with the dull and uninteresting certainty of the machinelike male creature, then let the sun be turned into darkness and the moon into blood as speedily as possible, for life will no longer be worth living! A woman may work in the

home or outside the home at whatever she pleases or
sees fit. She may educate herself as she will, may dress
as she pleases, may preach, vote, practice medicine —
and yet remain a woman. She could not be anything
else if she tried, and she does not try. Nothing that
woman has done or assumed so far, in coming out into
the world and meeting it on its own terms, has in the
slightest degree diminished her attractiveness to the
opposite sex; in fact, certain coeducational colleges,
and other institutions of learning, with admirable
advertising judgment, even if with doubtful taste,
frankly call attention in their announcements and
prospectuses to the large percentage of their students
who become mutually engaged during their college
course and marry at, after, or even before, commence-
ment.

Nor would it be possible to discover the slightest
prejudice on the part of the young men of the day
against selecting as their life-partners girls who are or
have been engaged in some public capacity as teachers,
stenographers, or saleswomen. Indeed, harmless and
honorable love-making is as brisk in the department
store and in the factory as it is in the well-conducted
coeducational college or the ballroom. We ought never
to let ourselves forget that the trade or occupation
was made for man or woman, not man or woman for
the trade; and that we are men first, last, and all the
time, and linen drapers, blacksmiths, or preachers
second and temporarily only.

We are terribly in dread that women will become
masculinized by doing man's work; but we forget

entirely that most of this man's work was originally woman's work, and that men have now for generations been doing woman's work without any sign of deterioration in courage, aggressiveness, or other so-called masculine traits.

We never dream of being apprehensive lest men who are engaged in the manufacture of linen and cotton and woolen goods, which, from the days of the distaff and the spindle, has been woman's work, are in any danger of losing their manliness. Nor are the "jolly millers" who occupy their entire energies in the grinding of corn and the bolting of flour, which was originally and is yet in the Orient the exclusive prerogative of the women, regarded as an effeminate or ladylike class of creatures. Even where men make and fit garments, or manufacture laces or stockings or underwear, or even ribbons and women's hats, we dread no deterioration in the fiber of their manhood.

It is true that at one time the mere fighting man affected to despise the "linen draper bold," the "greasy burgess," and we still have echoes of that attitude in the old saw that "it takes nine tailors to make a man"; but that snobbishness died a natural death centuries ago — ever since, in fact, these gentlemen of the sword and spur shattered themselves upon the square of pikes or were scattered like chaff before the charge of the train-bands of these same burgesses and greasy varlets.

To paraphrase the famous lyric: —

> The trade is but the guinea's stamp,
> The man's the gowd for a' that!

Can we imagine for a moment that such a trumpery trifle as a trade or an occupation is going to have the slightest vital effect upon that all-conquering, unchangeable and utterly unmanageable mystery that we call woman?

The one bugbear of those who are uneasy as to the diversion of women's interests and work from the home which has the greatest show of rational basis is that it may result in robbing the home of the quota of women who are fitted to carry out its central and so indispensable activities which cannot well be performed elsewhere — the bearing and rearing of children and providing of food and shelter. Even this dread has little valid basis, for the reason that, as has already been suggested, a large majority of the women who are going outside the home to work are going to earn money for the home and perform former household duties. So that the actual number of women engaged in or needed for these essential and indispensable home duties is not and never has been more than from a half to a third of the entire number of women.

Only about seventy per cent of the adult women of a community are married at any one time, and of the seventy per cent not more than half are actually engaged in the process of child-rearing or the direct personal conduct of the commissariat department of the home. So far as any estimate can be made in regard to such a widely varying and perpetually changing problem, it would appear probable that it would not require the entire time of more than a third of all women to carry out satisfactorily the duties which

are fundamental to and inseparable from the home, —
that is, child-rearing and housekeeping in its narrower
sense, — especially if these women be given the benefit of modern sanitary conditions, of efficient education, and of labor-saving devices and scientific methods.

Or, to put it in another way, it would only require
about one third of the entire time of the women of
the community to carry out, by modern and rational
methods, these most important duties. There is no
more reason why a woman should be compelled to
devote and mortgage all her life to housekeeping than
there is that a man should devote his entire time to
the business of housebuilding, house-repairing, gar-
dening, and paying rent — though the latter occupation will always seem to absorb a respectable share
of his activities.

In other words, it is no longer necessary that, because a woman becomes a housekeeper and a mother,
she must on that account give up all hope and ambition of being anything else; and our methods of reasoning upon this subject are singularly primitive —
not to say savage. There was a time, ages ago, when
the duties of race continuance and child-rearing absorbed the whole life of woman. She was married
when little more than a child, bore her annual crop
of children every spring, and lost two thirds of them
by famine and exposure every winter; and, as a natural
consequence, at thirty she was an old woman, a shapeless roll of fat or bag of skin and bones, as the case
might be — little better than an object of charity for
her few remaining years. No wonder the race made

slow progress when its children were borne by children who never had a proper chance to grow up!

We have outgrown that barbaric and brainless method of spawning, and modern woman declines to assume the grave responsibilities of the new life until her own has been properly rounded out and matured, and she is able to make an intelligent selection, for herself, of the father of her children. She is reluctant to marry — and rightly — until twenty-three, twenty-five, twenty-seven years of age — a period when her savage great-great-grandmother was beginning to feel the approach of decrepitude! When she does mate, she is not swamped under an annually rising flood of children — indeed, regards it as immoral to bring into the world more children than will allow her to devote to and expend upon every one her best and most thoughtful intelligence, her clearest and serenest judgment, and her fullest and sunniest powers of body and mind.

The famous Old Woman Who Lived in a Shoe was by no means the only mother of earlier times "who had so many children she did n't know what to do," or whose methods of discipline and training were, in consequence, of the same primitive and indiscriminate character. "To spank them all soundly and put them to bed" was the solution of many a domestic problem in the olden time. The woman who is a mother and nothing else can never discharge her maternal duties properly.

The assumption of the noble duties and dignities of wifehood and motherhood, so far from serving as a bar to a woman's further mental, moral, and physical development, or as an excuse for abandoning all further effort or ambition in those directions, renders it, on the contrary, urgently obligatory to develop and broaden and perfect herself and all her powers in every possible way so as to fit herself to be the guide, teacher, and companion of her children — to say nothing of her husband.

Moreover, the markedly increased and increasing span of life under modern scientific and sanitary conditions has given woman a second girlhood after the period of child-bearing is over — the richest, ripest, and happiest period of her life, when she is in the full maturity of her powers of both body and mind, and begins to see the results of her work and to exercise her greatest influence over both public and private affairs.

Women no longer begin to grow old and drop out of the current of life at forty; already they have postponed the period when they cease to have any more birthdays to sixty, and there is no limit in sight. Yet, less than a century ago, Jane Austen, in her delightful "Sense and Sensibility," makes one of her "old-maid" heroines remark, with axiomatic finality: "Of course, mamma, a woman of twenty-six can never hope either to feel or to inspire affection again!"

The tremendous and imposing duty of child-rearing, which is thrown with such a delighted and satisfied air of "Now I've got you!" across the forward path of modern woman, can be perfectly and adequately performed without absorbing more than about a third of her lifetime and only a little over half of her total energies during that third. Indeed, it will be best performed if it is not allowed to absorb more than this percentage of her total life and energy. And there will be a period of from five to ten years between adolescence and the beginning of race continuance in which noble and useful apprentice work can be done in the world outside the home; and another period of from fifteen to twenty-five years after its duties are over in which active and most efficient expert service can be rendered to the community before the decline of her powers sets in.

Nor is there any need for the woman who intends to find her career in marriage to keep herself, as it were, in a glass case or wrapped up in cotton-wool, in a species of chrysalis-like suspended animation, through all her girlhood and young-womanhood until she marries. On the contrary, I believe that the best interests and happiness of both a young woman herself and of her future husband and children, whatever her social position, from the lowest to the highest, will be best served by her taking some definite salaried work of her own outside the home after her seventeenth or eighteenth year.

A few years of teaching or business or clerical training is as admirable and valuable a preparation for life for the girl as it is for the boy, even if only upon the principle suggested by Oliver Wendell Holmes when he declared that young ministers ought to have "a sort of mild course in iniquity" between graduation from the theological seminary and their acceptance of a call.

There is not the slightest question, on biological grounds, but that the rearing of children is the highest and most vital and important duty of both a man's and a woman's life — that no life, in fact, can reach its highest development and happiness without it. So important is it, and so absolutely necessary not only to racial but to individual welfare and happiness, that there is very little danger of its falling into neglect by relieving woman of the absolute, and, in many cases degrading, necessity of choosing it as her sole means of livelihood and existence. It is not fair or just that a girl should be compelled, at the beginning of her individual life, to choose once and for all between marriage and any or every other form of occupation and interest, any more than a man should.

A boy is not expected to decide whether he will become a husband and father or a lawyer, a business man, a carpenter, or a farmer; he can be both, and better in each capacity for being a success in the other. It is like the story of the romantic and imaginative young lady who had recently become engaged and endeavored to test the devotion of her fiance by propounding, with soulful gaze under the crescent moon, the question: "Henry, if you had to choose between me and a million dollars, which would you take?" To which the resourceful Henry replied: "Why, I'd take the million, of course; then you'd be easy!"

The man or woman who has made a thorough success of his or her individual life need have little fear of failure in becoming a successful father or mother.

It is, of course, true that, in the division of physiological labor between the sexes, the mother must devote a larger share of her time and attention to the process of child-rearing during a certain period of her life than the father; but this is partially counterbalanced by the fact that the father's period of care and stress both begins earlier and lasts longer than that of the mother.

For, of course, all the efforts and struggles of a young man to establish himself in business and make his place in the world are in a large measure for the purpose of securing an income and a position that will enable him to have the luxury of a home and the dignity of a family. And the period at which boys and girls begin to lessen their demands upon the mother's care and time — the beginning of the boarding-school and college age — is precisely the time when their demands upon the gray matter and exchequer of the father are heaviest, and continue so until they are finally settled in life for themselves.

On the other hand, too, it must be frankly admitted that the average father, though his intentions are good and his performance fairly creditable, ought to devote a great deal more of himself, his personal services, and his time to the companionship, education, and care of his own children during their growing period. He salves his conscience with the reflection, "Oh, well, their mother understands that sort of thing so much better than I do!" — but he has unquestionably been shirking his duty in this regard and leaving a weight of responsibility for family care and management and discipline, which he should have carried upon his own shoulders, upon the all too willing ones of the mother.

One of the social reforms most urgently demanded is that the hours and methods of modern business — that Juggernaut of family life — shall be so readjusted that all fathers, from the day-laborer to the millionaire, shall have the opportunity of devoting at least a fifth of their waking hours to the companionship and care of their own children. It would be the most profitable investment of time possible to both the state and the business world, for it would result in a vastly improved type of children — and fathers.

From a biological point of view, it is self-evident that, not only will the proper and adequate rearing of children and care of her household not prevent a modern woman from entering public life and taking part in a wide range of activities outside the home, but, on the contrary, it will absolutely demand that she should do so. Just in proportion as the work of the home has been transferred to the world outside, so the interests and welfare of the home are affected by and bound up with conditions in the external world.

It is idle and worse than useless, for instance, for a mother to bear and rear healthy, intelligent children if, the moment they pass from under her care, they are worked ten or twelve hours a day in overcrowded, unsanitary death-traps called factories; or if, before they pass from under her care, they are obliged to spend the best part of their waking hours shut up in gloomy, ill-ventilated barracks called schoolhouses.

Similarly, though in an earlier day she could supervise the growth and preparation of almost every article of food that appeared upon her table, and know that it was sound and wholesome, to-day nine tenths of the food of the family comes from all over the surrounding country and from every part of the habitable globe. The mother who wishes properly to protect the health of her children must actively take part in the agencies and movements which are engaged in the proper inspection and testing of food-supplies; in the securing of clean milk and pure water, and the scrupulous cleanliness of shops and streets. A large share of the activities of municipal public life and so-called politics has become simply good house-keeping on a large scale — and is even more emphatically woman's business than it is man's.

Any sanitarian or public-health officer of experience will cheerfully testify that the strongest force in the community for the protection of the public health is the influence and work of the women, especially of the at one time much scoffed at and good-naturedly ridiculed women's clubs. Why on earth woman should not be given exactly the same voice as man in determining how the food, water, and other vital interests of her children should be kept pure and wholesome, and in personally seeing that they are so kept, is a question to which, from a biological point of view, there is no answer!

The same wholesome tendency is also showing itself in state and national politics. War and the currency and taxes are no longer the sole issues in the realm of politics. Questions can no longer be settled solely with eloquence and with clubs. Politicians are actually beginning to discuss questions which there is some prospect of their being able to understand and upon which definite and rational conclusions can be reached by the collection of facts and the use of scientific methods, instead of determining everything by its accordance with ancient Republican principles or true Democratic doctrine.

And upon these new issues in politics woman is at least as well posted and as well equipped to judge as man; and, indeed, she could n't very well know less about the currency and the tariff, for instance, than the average male voter does now. "Such an excess of stupidity is not in nature," as Dr. Johnson pithily remarked. Woman in public life will simply be exercising on a larger scale and in a wider field those same noble qualities which have made her worshiped in the home, and extending over the welfare of the entire community that watchful care and that wise protection which she has always exercised over her children.

If the atmosphere of public life is so rank and impure that it will sully her moral purity to breathe it, then, in Heaven's name, it is time that she enter it to throw open the windows and let in the sunlight! Objections of this description are simply tantamount to a confession that man, in his own special and exclusive sphere, has not yet succeeded in properly civilizing himself. The mere fact that standards and methods of public life are and in the past have been male standards is no valid argument whatever that they should always remain so; in fact, they may be just the contrary. Bernard Shaw wittily says one of the reasons why he most strongly approves of the entrance of women into politics is that "they have no business habits of mind and thought." They have never got into the habit of worshiping property and disregarding human life and suffering or learned to accept the creed expressed in the phrase, "Business is Business!" — a sentiment fit only for pirates!

When woman is once set at liberty, freely and voluntarily to choose wifehood and motherhood as her highest triumph, her proudest accomplishment and her greatest happiness — not merely driven to it as a means of livelihood; when, in order to fulfill this lofty aim, she is free and encouraged to develop to the highest possible degree all her powers of mind and body and soul; to enter into every field, both public and private, that is necessary for the perfect carrying out of her mission; to choose, in the fullness of her womanhood and her judgment, her husband without pressure or interference and to be faithful to him as long as he remains worthy and no longer; then, and not until then, shall we discover and realize the full possibilities of development and perfection of the human race.

CHAPTER VIII

THE HARDY NERVES OF WOMAN

THERE is no question about it — woman is different. That is half the secret of her charm. She is one of those delightful subjects we can discuss, concuss, and rediscuss from every imaginable point of view, *ad infinitum*, world without end, without ever coming to any final conclusion, because woman is not final herself.

She is always changing, always improving, forever eluding the grasp of the crude male intelligence by never doing just what it expects her to do — the net result being that she usually arrives at her predestined goal before the perplexed and blinking man in the case finds out what she is really driving at.

Then, of course, he consoles himself by denouncing her as illogical, and endeavors to cover his defeat with some such cynical philosophy as that of Chimmie Fadden: "You never kin tell what a woman is goin' to do until it 's too late to do you any good to know." This is the principal function of philosophy everywhere — explanation of failure.

Every cynical proverb about woman, invented by man, is a salve or a plaster for some sore spot on his self-esteem. If he calls her untrustworthy, that simply means some member of her sex has played him for a sucker — and landed him. When he declares her illogical, it means that her rules of thought and conduct are different from his, and usually, in some particular instance, have worked better and, in the language of the day, "beat him to it."

In fact, the element that has most hopelessly clouded all discussions of the differences between the sexes, next to man's injured self-esteem, is the fixed obsession that the differences are mere variations upward or downward on one and the same scale, or on a series of different scales — that woman is necessarily, where she differs from man, either weaker or stronger, higher or lower; though, as a matter of fact, she may be both at the same time. That is one of her privileges, of which no law will ever rob her.

Woman's ability can be safely said to be different from man's. Her point of view is other than his. But when we attempt to declare women greater or less, higher or lower, we leave the realm of science or accurate knowledge and plunge into that of conjecture and prophecy. Consoling as it would be to our masculine pride, it is utterly impossible for us to longer hold the simple and picturesque creed of the poet: —

Woman is the lesser man, and her passions matched with mine
Are as moonlight unto sunlight and as water unto wine.

Nowhere is the confusing effect of this weaker-or-stronger, higher-or-lower delusion more clearly shown than in the general impression as to the differences between the nerves or nervous make-ups of men and of women. Up to half a century ago the verdict of science was perfectly clear and confident: Woman was unmistakably the inferior sex, mentally and cerebrally. She had a smaller and lighter brain, a less richly convoluted cerebral cortex; her sympathetic nervous system dominated her cerebro-spinal system; her conduct was determined chiefly by emotion; she had little power of concentration and continuity. And as for her reasoning powers —!

Most of this — all the confidence — has already gone the way of the dodo; partly because much of our science in those days was no better founded, and partly because man up to that time had a practical monopoly of anatomy, physiology, and biology, and the case was argued and the verdict of science delivered by an unconsciously prejudiced and biased judge, jury, and bar. In other words, it was itself an illustration of the extent to which man's cerebro-spinal system is dominated by his sympathetic system.

The lighter-smaller-brain-weight-of-woman prop fell out from under the pagoda a couple of decades ago, when it was discovered that, in proportion to her body weight, woman's brain is heavier than man's. In other words, on a purely anatomical basis the inferior sex is brainier than the superior. The less-complex-cerebral-convolutions pillar bore up nobly for a few years longer, until it was found that the richest and wriggliest of these brain-surface wrinkles of thought were to be found in those paragons of intellect, the Eskimos — and incidentally also some of the heaviest average brain weights.

More disconcerting still, careful studies of the cortex — "bark" — or surface of the brains of great men, many of whom have been willing them for a quarter of a century past as a legacy to science for purposes of such study, have led us to the perplexing conclusion that though, broadly speaking, the brains of men of great ability are above the average in size and richness of convolutions, there are so many striking exceptions in both directions that we shall have to look further and deeper for the physical basis of intellectual power.

These convolutions which have been so much discussed are simply folds or heavy wrinkles on the surface of the cerebrum, or brain; and their purpose is roughly that of increasing the amount of gray matter, which grows chiefly on the surface, just as the wrinkles and folds of the skin of a merino sheep enable it to bear more wool — though, of course, the analogy between wits and wool goes no further than this.

So far as any conclusion can be expressed, it now seems that the intellectual power of the brain depends not so much on its bulk or on the acreage of its gray matter as on the way in which its different parts are linked together by connecting fibers for team-work, so to speak, and on the complexity of its internal organization.

So far as the alleged domination of woman's intellect by her instincts and of her cerebro-spinal system by her sympathetic nervous system is concerned, the less man says the better. Exact and dispassionate study of the mechanism and control of the human gas-motor in the cold, dry light of science has led us already to the somewhat humiliating conclusion that some seventy-five per cent of all the vital actions of even the dwellers on the most exalted mountain-peaks of intellect are controlled by this lowly and despised sympathetic nervous system. So that any possible difference in the degree of dominance between men and women can be little more than a fraction of a per cent.

This sympathetic nervous system, which in the form of a slender, double-knotted chain of nerve stuff runs down the whole length of the interior of the body on each side of the front of the spinal column, controls our whole "innards" — in the good old rustic phrase — and is literally " the works" of the body machine. It is the real power behind the throne, which controls the digestion, all the secretions of all our glands, our respiration, our sleep, in fact, eight tenths of the things we do, as we say, without thinking about them — automatically.

The other and much the larger parts of our nervous system — the brain and spinal cord, with the five senses and their respective nerves — attract much more attention and admiration, because they are on the surface and receive impressions from the outside and return responses to them; but the kind of responses they return depends much more fundamentally and vitally on the verdict, so to speak, of the sympathetic nervous system than on anything else.

We can get along quite fairly well after the loss of half of our senses; after the destruction of large areas of our brain tissue; after the paralysis of whole groups of our spinal nerves; but let more than the very smallest portion of the sympathetic nervous system be destroyed or diseased, and it spells serious disaster for the entire body.

One of the most interesting recent developments in our study of the nervous system is the remarkable influence exerted on the brain by an obscure group of the children of the sympathetic nervous system — the so-called ductless glands, the thyroid, parathyroid, thymus, adrenal, and pituitary. These glands appear to control the toxicity (poisonousness) and wholesomeness of the blood; and it is beginning to be suspected that many forms of nervous and mental disturbances are more dependent on the quality and kind of blood on which the nerve cells are fed, and with which they are bathed, than on any structural or organic defect in the cells themselves.

Indeed, some advanced morpho-pathologists go so far as to declare that man's make-up and powers are the result of the interworking and balance between the secretions of his various ductless glands. In short, a man is what his ductless glands make him! One form of idiocy — cretinism — already can be changed into comparative rationality by feeding with the dried thyroid gland of the sheep. To paraphrase Shakespeare's famous phrase: —

> We are such stuff as ductless glands are made of,
> And our little life is rounded by a sheep!

The adrenal gland controls the heart, circulation, and oxidation processes in the blood; and its extract,

adrenalin or epinephrin, is already one of our most
powerful remedies in diseases and disturbances of the
heart and blood vessels, and in asthma.

Enlargement with overaction of the thyroid gland
in the neck produces exophthalmic goiter, or Graves's
disease, — a serious and often fatal general toxæmia,
with very rapid heart, shortness of breath, and pro-
trusion of the eyeballs. Shrinkage of the same gland
produces a puffy and bloated condition, with drowsi-
ness and stupidity, called myxœdema.

Overgrowth of the pituitary gland at the base of
the brain causes giantism in childhood, and in later
life a strange disease called acromegaly, in which the
hands, feet, and jaws enlarge enormously and the
mind slowly decays. Shriveling is associated with
dwarf stature; so this gland appears in some weird
way to control the height of the body.

Small and apparently insignificant as most of these
glands are, the influence they exercise in the body is
marvelous, and we are but beginning to glimpse their
powers. Some of our most promising possibilities of
control, both over disease and mental and nervous
defects, appear to lie in this direction. The influence
of these glands over fatigue and other forms of self-
poisoning, as well as infections from without, is profound; and when we thoroughly grasp the action of
the ductless glands, we may find our hands on the
levers which control the entire body.

The one count on which the verdict of science as
to the differences between the nerves of woman and
of man appears to be, in part at least, sustained, is

that as to power of continuous concentration. This is not to say for a moment that a woman is less persistent than a man — good Heavens, no! — but merely that the two sexes have different ways of hanging on to their purposes. Did you ever try to change a woman's mind after she had once made it up?

The general impression is that woman's nerves are less stable and more sensitive than man's; that she is more easily deflected from her course by irrelevant considerations and stimuli; that she is more emotional — that is, blows up in a tantrum or dissolves in tears more easily than the tougher-fibered, more stolid male. Yet the very same sagacious and experienced judges of human nature who would assert all these self-evident truths, with most judicial ponderousness, will a moment later ruefully admit that, in spite of all this susceptibility to tearful and emotional excitements, all this weathercock fickleness, and pleased-with-a-rattle, tickled-with-a-straw mental make-up of the unreasoning sex, nevertheless, when a man or a woman deliberately sets out to get his or her own way about a particular point, it is the woman who will get it at least eight times out of ten. She can be easily deflected from her purpose, it is true; but for how long?

The same sort of paradoxical difference is amusingly illustrated in the helpless but admiring perplexity of the modern business man over the fact that, though his wife is all nerves,— upset by the least little thing, aggravated to the verge of distraction by any hitch or complication in her social or household affairs, —

she is really nervously and physically stronger than he is; can outlast him at various forms of mild dissipation, can stand loss of sleep and irregular hours of eating better; is cooler and clearer-headed in serious trouble; stands the wear and tear of life better, and looks younger for her years than he does for his.

Nevertheless, it does seem that there is a considerable degree, at least, of average difference between the nerves of men and of women in this respect — that is, the readiness with which they break continuity of action under strain.

From a physiological point of view, another statement is almost equally true, and in the same broad sense, with the admission of many exceptions, and that is, that where a woman sticks to her job as a man does to his she pays a heavier physical penalty than he does in the long run. A woman will get through with an extraordinary amount of work in proportion to her body-weight and muscular horse-power — quite as much as a man; but she will not do it in the same way or within the same hours.

So far as any explanation for this fairly constant difference between the nervous systems of men and women can be offered, — and that only with the greatest diffidence and expecting to be instantly confronted with a hundred striking and individual instances to the contrary, — it would appear to depend on a difference in what, in neurological language, is called the height of the threshold.

The term "threshold," or "threshold of consciousness" — "*Treppe*" of the Germans, whose genius

for picturesque nomenclature invented the term —
has come to mean that level to which stimuli and
external impressions must pile up before they can, so
to speak, overflow into consciousness. In the nature
of the case, the height of the threshold of consciousness is anything but a fixed term; in fact, it varies
enormously, both with different individuals and in the
same individual under different times and circumstances.

What appears to be one of the differences between
the nervous make-up of men and of women is that
man's threshold either is naturally higher or he pos-
sesses the power of making it so when occasion seems
to demand. In other words, he appears to have to a
higher degree the power of, as we say, closing his eyes
and ears to all irrelevant distractions and irritations —
or, perhaps, to put it more accurately, for a longer
period at a stretch — than woman has.

How much of this is the result of training from bitter, necessary, lifelong experience, and how much of
it innate, is a question; but the main point to be borne
in mind is that it has no necessary connection whatever with what might be termed the total nerve power
or the ultimate result in the sense of attainment of
their aim by the two sexes.

One of the first things the psychologists discovered
about this threshold of consciousness was that, in the
majority of cases, the influence which would most frequently and certainly lower it, so as to diminish the
power of continuous concentration, was fatigue or
any form of disturbance to health.

Yet everybody knows, including the man himself, that even the coldest-blooded, clearest-headed, most relentlessly persistent business man is, as we express it, not himself at driving a bargain or deciding an important executive question when he is completely tired out, or suffering from acute indigestion, or coming down with a fever — even so slight a fever as that of a common cold.

So obvious, in fact, is this result that the majority of our successful men of affairs, our commercial geniuses, have quite unconsciously fallen into the habit of either shortening their working hours markedly or else refusing to make important decisions or to discuss big questions except at such times of the day when they are fully rested and fit, and all there.

A most interesting light has been thrown on this relation by our recent studies of fatigue, which have shown clearly that the all-too-familiar tired feeling is due to the piling-up in our blood, to a point where they can literally poison our nerve centers, of those waste products of our bodily and mental activity, the smoke and ashes of our body-motor, pompously termed autotoxins.

Getting rested is getting rid of or neutralizing these fatigue toxins. The fatigue and mental disability of illness are of exactly the same character — the poisoning of our nerve centers by either the introduction of outside poisons, like alcohol, lead, or opium, or of the toxins of disease germs bred in the body. The difference is, that in this form of fatigue the getting rested — which we call recovery — is a much slower process, because it takes the body a considerable length of time to manufacture the antitoxins required to neutralize these poisons and to deal with them so that they can be excreted by the body sewers.

From this point of view, the difference between the powers or habits of persistence and concentration in men and women would appear to be at least largely influenced by the fact that woman has not acquired so high or rapid a power of detoxicating or neutralizing her fatigue poisons as man has.

In other words, she lives nearer the line of saturation and so keeps her threshold of consciousness more or less consciously lower. According to this view, — to use a Hibernicism, — the difference between the nervous systems of men and of women lies in their ductless glands.

"But," one might reply, "this makes woman a hopelessly trivial and inefficient creature, congenitally incapable of prolonged concentration and of that persistence which are necessary to win success." By no manner of means does it, for there is another point of view to the toxic theory of fatigue that is of great importance in this respect — and that is its protective office.

The neutral and instinctive effect of feeling tired is to make us stop working before harm is done; and we are beginning to regard the sensation of fatigue as our most valuable danger signal and one of the greatest defenses of our health and efficiency. The individual who yields fairly promptly to the sensation of fatigue or switches off to that new distraction which his lowered threshold makes him keenly conscious of, both cools the hot-box of his body machinery before any serious grinding out is done and insures a quick recovery and early ability to resume his task.

In short, the secret of successful work, and particularly of steady increase in capacity, is frequent, brief intervals either of actual rest or of change of occupation, with a shortening of hours to such a degree as may allow abundance of time for the complete detoxication of the blood and recharging of the body battery that occur during sleep and play. The individual who works like this will, other things being equal, outwork and outwear the one who overtires himself persistently and without regard to the sensation of fatigue until it becomes absolutely overwhelming.

This view would appear to accord with the results of experience in several ways. Wherever records are accurately kept, though woman is physically smaller, weaker, and less aggressive than man; has a less vigorous digestion; is more easily upset by all sorts of unfavorable influences; is much more frequently indisposed and slightly ill, and lives, for the most part, under conditions as to fresh air and exercise that are much less wholesome than man's, — yet in the long run she outlives him; has a lower death-rate at almost every age of life; has fewer serious illnesses; is less liable to all of the great infections, and shows a better recovery rate when she does contract them than big, powerful, self-assertive man.

As Byron once cynically remarked, "It takes a good constitution to be dissipated." The cause of woman's superior endurance appears to be that her lowered threshold causes her to give up and go to bed at the first brush of discomfort; and this saves her from undue persistence in unwholesome habits of living or from prolonged exposure to serious infections or other sources of danger.

To paraphrase the famous old saw, "A headache in time saves nine breakdowns."

A fresh illustration of woman's extraordinary toughness and survival power is furnished by the much-heralded and lamented increase in the death-rate after the age of forty-five, which is declared to be one of the menaces of modern civilization. Though the average longevity — length of life — has been greatly increased and the average age at death has risen in the last thirty years from about thirty-three to fifty-one, this improvement has been chiefly effected by the saving of lives of babies and children from dirty milk and the acute infections, as well as boys and girls from the great plagues of young adult life, such as typhoid and tuberculosis.

Naturally this preserves a much larger number of individuals to live to, say, the age of forty-five. And, as we must all die sometime, we begin to drop off somewhat more rapidly after this point has been reached — that is to say, the stupid and helpless creature, man, does. Woman, however, is far too shrewd for that. While man's mortality, after falling off markedly up to forty-five years, begins after that period to increase distinctly, woman's death-rate, on the other hand, continues to decrease until fifty-five years of age,

beating man ten years; then yields to the force of circumstances only to the extent of about one tenth of
the increase man shows between fifty-five and sixty-
five; and after seventy proceeds to decrease again.

Incidentally, it may be remarked that the total
increase of mortality after forty-five in man is only
about six per cent; besides which the race need not
worry much about what happens to the individual
after fifty-five or sixty, provided he has done his share
of the world's work. But women pass men three laps
to the mile, for their increase of death-rate after the
age of fifty-five is barely one per cent, or one sixth
of man's.

The other fact, which appears to fall in line with the
lower-and-higher-threshold theory, is that when man
does break down or give way, or allows himself to be
distracted, the result is much more serious and permanent than in the case of woman. A woman, for
instance, may be literally utterly worn out, ready to
drop, tired to the verge of the tomb, — not merely
every day, but three or four times daily, — and yet,
after half an hour's nap or ten minutes' collapse on
the lounge, or a cup of tea, or a whirl at the piano,
or a gloat over her laces and ribbons, come back with
redoubled vigor and get through a huge amount of
work in a day.

A woman may be sick and yet remain a comparatively reasonable being and be fairly good company;
but a sick man is a sight to make angels weep — the
most awful combination imaginable of a child with a
cut finger and a bear with a sore ear. Small wonder

that downright old Dr. Johnson once snapped out, "Your sick man, sir, is always a scoundrel!"

To put it roughly, the actual amount of time and energy lost in deflections from the course in hot-boxes and breakdowns is pretty much the same in men and women in the life's work — only women take theirs by the teaspoonful and men by the quart at a gulp.

Of course this is only true of the average man and the average woman, who, as has been truthfully remarked, exist only on paper. There are bushels and "lashin's" of men who have about as much concentration of purpose as a butterfly and as high a threshold against the overflow of their irascibility or self-pity as a poodle dog — men who will whimper for sympathy at every scratch and go up in the air if you point your finger at them. And, as every doctor of experience can feelingly testify, for apprehensiveness that rises to the pitch of genius in invalidism, there is nothing quite equal to a thoroughly fussy, nervous man.

There are also almost as many cases of true hysteria among men as among women — though, in the loose sense of a tendency to tantrums and undue excitability over trifles, it is somewhat more common in women, on account of their lower threshold.

That the difference between the sexes is due to a mere variation in the forms of expression and amount of emotional response at a given time is also supported by the fact that, as soon as we come to the grave and serious forms of genuine nervous disease or defect, including insanity in all its phases, the percentile occurrence in the two sexes is almost exactly the same. The number of insane women in a thousand of the population is almost identical with that of men, in all classes, races, and climes; and the same is true of hereditary defects, such as imbecility, feebleminded-ness, and pauperism.

Here, again, are the same curious differences be-tween the sexes in their responses to particular or individual stimuli, and of somewhat the same sort. To put it roughly, men are more prone to mania and excitement — women to melancholia and depression. Men are subject to certain forms of both nervous dis-ease and insanity — as, for instance, locomotor ataxia, paresis, and the alcoholic neuroses and insanities — from which women are almost exempt. So marked is this difference that of certain serious forms of ner-vous and mental disease we can say positively that they will probably be inherited by the sons of the patient, but not by his daughters, and *vice versa;* though the daughters who show no signs of the defect may transmit it to their sons.

A familiar illustration is the bleeding tendency, in the victims of which the blood, so to speak, seems to be unable to clot; so that they may bleed to death from a mere scratch on the gums or a cut on the finger. This appears only in males and has been traced as far as eight generations, transmitted through daugh-ters, nieces, granddaughters, and great-granddaugh-ters without a single female member of the family being affected; while our studies of inebriety incline us to regard the inborn weakness that leads to this addiction as transmitted almost exclusively to males.

It is interesting to notice in passing that even here woman gets, in the main, the best of it. Though there are plenty of grave nerve defects inherited by both sexes, and a number that are inherited by man alone, there is scarcely one to which females only are liable. In spite of individual variations of this sort, the total net result, as to death both from various forms of nervous disease and from insanity, is almost absolutely identical in both sexes. Where there is any difference, it is usually in favor of women. The records both of hospitals and of asylums indicate that, if anything, woman's nervous system is tougher and more enduring than man's.

Oddly enough, there does not appear to be much adequate basis for the frequently offered explanation of the differences between masculine and feminine nerves, to the effect that the latter are more sensitive. This is true apparently only in the sense already described — that their threshold of resistance to the piling-up of stimuli is somewhat lower; but not in the sense in which it is usually meant — that they are capable of response to weaker or more delicate stimuli than the grosser male nerves.

It came with a real shock of surprise — now some twenty years ago, when we actually came to test out by careful experiment the range of sensitiveness and susceptibility of human nerves — that even the most sensitive and delicate of women, who would be upset by the least thing, had neither the range nor the accuracy of nerve perception of crude, insensitive man. One after another the results were written down — that woman's sense of smell was less delicate and less capable of distinguishing accurately between different odors, or varying strengths of the same odor, than man's.

This is one of the reasons for the puzzling, oft-quoted, and rather humiliating fact that men make the best cooks; and that, though there are at least fifty women to every man engaged in this business, at least nine tenths of the artistic accomplishments and *chefs-d'œuvre* of the gastronomic art are achieved by men; not because they have better intellects or more powerful brains, — perish the thought! — but because they are better able to judge when a thing tastes right. In fact, woman's cookery is kept as good as it is only by the fact that she has to satisfy the exacting demands of the more critical male taste.

All the professional tasters — not merely of wines, but also of teas and coffees — are men, not women. Perhaps it would be fairer to say that what woman fails in is the ability to realize how certain flavors will taste to man; but this does not alter the fact that there is a whole gamut of delicate gustatory sensations, which man is capable of enjoying, which woman would readily sacrifice for the crass sugariness of angel food or chocolate ice-cream.

Woman cannot see so far as man or discriminate so accurately between the different shades and tones that fall on her retina. She has one point of superiority over man here, in that she is less susceptible to outright color-blindness; but in accurate discrimination between the finer shades of color man is distinctly her superior. The real reason why the patient, model husband suffers such agonies in the classic feat of trying to match samples or ribbons is that he really gets them right, but his wife does not know it and consequently cannot see it.

This is probably one of the reasons why, in spite of the fact that almost every girl above the poverty line has been given a wishy-washy course in water-colors or in hand-painting on china, — while scarcely one boy in five ever gets that privilege, — at least ninety-nine per cent of the great artists, both portrait and landscape, are men.

The hearing of men and women is more nearly equal, though in both range and discrimination man is slightly in advance again.

In the last and possibly the most fundamental sense of all, however, — that of touch, — are found, strange to relate, the most striking differences between the sexes. This is, of course, totally contrary to the popular impression, for the delicate, tapering fingers, the thin, translucent skin, and the graceful lines and gestures of women would certainly lead us to expect that they would have a greater delicacy and sensitiveness of touch to correspond.

The facts, as ascertained by careful tests, are exactly the reverse — particularly in that form of so-called touch sometimes known as the muscular sense or pressure sense, which gives us information as to the size, shape, and weight of bodies handled. Here woman's perceptions and discriminations are little better than infantile; and it is to this peculiarity that she probably owes her well-known difficulty in learning the use of tools, the control of machinery, and the mechanical arts generally, and not because she has not a mechanical brain or an inventive genius.

It is probable that in some of these respects — notably the last — training and education will do much to wipe out the difference between the sexes.

So far as the criteria at our disposal or tests hitherto applied go, woman's intellect is just as good as man's; but she does differ from masculine standards in both the range and the discrimination of her sense perceptions. Putting it crudely, it is not that she does not reason accurately and generalize ably, but that her material is faulty, because it has not been adequately reported to her by her sense receptors — not that she is illogical, but that her premises are imperfect.

It is in the lower rather than in the higher part of her nervous system that she appears to differ most from man; but, of course, the training of the senses is the true field of education, as the schools of to-day are just beginning to find out. And, when boys and girls are both given mental training that will fit them for this life, instead of for the next, there can be little doubt that many of these differences in sense perception will greatly diminish if not completely disappear.

The most discouraging feature of the attempts to educate women, even so far as they have gone, is that we have taken the old, traditional, classic idea of what was a proper education for boys, lifted it over bodily and imposed it on girls.

It is not in the least logical or fair to taunt woman — as is often done — with her failure to score an adequate proportion of the great successes in public life and other fields of the world's work, because the methods of activity, the rules of the game, have been laid down exclusively by men and for men.

As is nearly always the case in action based on too narrow a point of view, the resulting methods — if they deserve the name of methods at all rather than that of customs — have not by any means been those best adapted to bring out the highest powers of men themselves; while they have been almost prohibitive for women. Yet, in spite of them, she has held her own, won her own way, and made the hand that rocks the cradle rule the world.

CHAPTER IX

MAN'S darling ambition is the discovery of the new. His most frequent feat is the rediscovery of the old. Two great discoveries in the economics of human efficiency have been reserved for the twentieth century: that women work, and that they may injure their health thereby. It is to be presumed that previous to this discovery they spent their days in idleness, and that this idleness enabled them to acquire such high potencies of health that they never fell sick and seldom died. Idleness is notoriously healthful. At the same time that a satellite star was discovered circling round this great central planet, another truth was discovered, bearing on this same subject, namely, that when a woman works she takes the bread out of the mouth of some man who has other women depending upon him for support; which renders inevitable the distressing conclusion that the more a woman works the more harm she does to her sex as a whole. This leaves her in the embarrassing position of the cat in the well in the nursery arithmetic problem, which fell back eighteen inches every time it climbed up a foot — to say nothing of the damage to its claws and temper in the process.

Thus woman as a producer is put in an absolutely unique and anomalous position in the economic, or, indeed, the physical, world. But then woman is notoriously an exception to every rule, obeys none, and is the most illogical of all creatures — except some of the men who undertake to discuss her affairs and settle her problems for her.

It is, of course, to be presumed that man as a whole, who nobly supported woman as a whole before her suicidal attempts at self-support, never required any equivalent in the form of labor for such support; and that his self-assumed burden of her support is in no way lessened by the subtraction of that percentage of the sex that insists on supporting itself.

It would be sheer presumption for a mere doctor to attempt to pronounce upon the economic aspects of the problem — for doctors are so unpractical. But upon the hygienic side there are facts and factors of much weight that are not usually recognized at their full value in discussions of the subject. The first of these is that the real question to be considered is not whether employment in industrial occupations is in itself beneficial or detrimental to the health of women engaging in it, whether their hours and surroundings are ideally hygienic, but how such employment and conditions compare with the work that women did and the conditions under which they lived before engaging in industrial employment, and to which they would be compelled to return if they should withdraw from it. It may be, and unfortunately often is, true that in the factory, the shop, and the office, hours are too long and work too exhausting, wages too low, and hygienic conditions abominable; and these injustices should be remedied and are being remedied year by year. But the real problem is, How do these compare with the hours, wages, and conditions in the homes in which these women would otherwise be compelled to live and to work?

He would certainly be a rash man who would assert that the hours of any factory or sweatshop were longer than those of housework, or that the wages were lower. The only questions open for discussion are whether industrial work is more exhausting and the hygienic surroundings more favorable. As for length of hours, the old distich sums it up: —

> Man's work is from sun to sun,
> But woman's work is never done.

For almost every man or boy who has to rise in the gray dawn of the winter morning to report for work in the factory or shop at 6 or 7 A.M., some woman has to rise an hour or more earlier in order to prepare his breakfast. And at whatever hour he plods wearily home in the dusk of evening to his supper, some woman has to go on working an hour longer to clear up the table and wash the dishes.

Most factories have got down to the ten-hour day and many to the eight, and all are rapidly approaching this standard; but the average household day, whether for housekeeper or for domestic, still runs from fourteen to sixteen hours. It is true that the average rate of work is slower and that there are many lowerings of tension and occasional complete intermissions, even periods of rest, during the day, but the sense of tension, of obligation, is never entirely relieved. The feeling that the day's work will not be done until the clock strikes eight, or nine, or ten, and the realization, every day in the week and every week in the year, that it will inevitably begin again at daylight on the following morning are always present. The work may be light or it may be heavy, it may be enjoyable and interesting, or dull and wearisome to the last degree, but it will constitute a first mortgage on all a woman's time from the moment that she wakes up in the morning until she lies down at night. And the monotony, and what is worse — to coin a word — the "result-lessness," of it! Buying food with which to dirty pots, pans, and kettles in the cooking and serving of food, and cleaning pots, pans, and kettles in order that they may be ready to get dirty again; washing the breakfast dishes that they may be ready for dinner, and dinner dishes for use at supper, and the supper dishes for breakfast again — the only change being that gradually dishes enough are broken and a new set is bought. Dusting and sweeping and scrubbing and mending from dawn till dark, with the net result that you are still alive and clothed at the end of the year and none of the family is dead, or sick, or in rags.

If any man thinks that domestic labor is light work and housekeeping a nice, easy job, just let him trade places with his wife for a week — a month of it would drive him crazy or send him to a sanitarium.

Much has been truthfully said of the deadly monotony of factory work, of shop work, and of office hours, but at least this work comes to an end at a definite hour each day and at a definite time on Saturday afternoon of each week. It results, usually, in a visible and definite output of manufactured product, or business of some sort accomplished, and the wages, however scanty and hard-earned, are placed in the hand in a solid palpable lump at the end of each week or month, which at least gives the recipient the pleasing illusion that she can spend them as she wishes.

So far, then, as the hours and the general mental tension are concerned, there appears no good reason to anticipate that industrial occupations will prove any more dangerous to the health of women than those to which they have been accustomed from time immemorial. If anything, the probabilities would appear to be that they would be rather less so.

The next vital question is whether the conditions under which the work is done are more favorable in the home than in the factory or shop. This may be considered roughly under three heads: the actual muscular and bodily strain involved, and the possibility of cramping or unfavorable posture; the amount and character of the food upon which the work is done; and the surroundings under which it is done as regards ventilation, light, purity of air, and so forth. Heterodox as it may sound, my observations have distinctly inclined me to the conclusion that all these conditions are, on the whole, more favorable in the office, shop, and factory than they are in the house or home in which this class of industrial workers has been, or would be, compelled to live and work. I am aware that it will seem a little less than blasphemy to intimate that conditions in that last earthly refuge of paradise, the home, can be as unhygienic and as unfavorable as in the shop or the factory, and in the ideal home, of course, they are not. But, alas, ideal conditions are always rare on this mundane sphere, and any one who, as a physician, health officer, or social worker, has had practical experience in visiting and inspecting the sanitary conditions of the homes, not merely of the poor, but of the average worker as well, knows that the factory and the shop are far from having a monopoly of poor light, poor ventilation, smells, dust, and lack of sanitary conveniences. In the homes of the working-classes — which form from sixty to seventy per cent of our population — ventilation is a lost art, or rather an art that has never been acquired.

Not merely in nine tenths of these homes, but in at least seven tenths of the thirty per cent of middle-class homes in these United States, a window is merely a transparent piece of the wall through which light is to be admitted, but never air, save during the summer months. This may seem like an extreme statement, but in the course of our Fresh-Air Crusade a few months ago, one enthusiast, who had occasion to go through the streets of one of the well-to-do residence portions of a large city at about 5.30 A.M., reported that, out of some two hundred and fifty houses counted, less than twenty had a single window open in their fronts and such sides as were visible from the street. The burglar dread accounts for some of this, of course, but the fact remains.

Any circulation of air that occurs in such homes

comes through unintentional chinks and cracks around windows and doors, the porousness of brick or other building materials, and from the opening and shutting of doors. On an average, one window in a bedroom and two in a living-room are considered abundant, and if reading, writing, or sewing is to be done, it usually must be taken near these windows in order to get light enough for the purpose. The rooms are continually occupied both day and night, and throughout the cooler and cold months of the year the vast majority of them never have all of the air they contain blown out and replaced with fresh air, because, at almost every hour of the day or night, they contain inmates who would bitterly object to the draft.

In the average house, flat, or suite of rooms, all the cooking is done on the premises, and from motives of convenience in access to supplies, getting in coal, disposal of waste and so forth, the kitchen is usually on the ground or basement floor, where every odor of food or cookery, following the invariable law of heated air, rises and circulates comfortably through the entire establishment whenever the door is left open. And wherever economy of heat is a consideration, which is the case in two thirds of all working-homes, the kitchen is made the central and most accessible part of the house for the sake of the warmth derived from its stove or range. In at least two thirds of the average homes, washing and other cleansing of garments is done under the same roof. And in small houses and the two- or three-room homes of tenement dwellers, the whole establishment becomes a combination of clothesbag and wash-kitchen — a receptacle for pro-gressively accumulating soiled clothing six days of the week and for the steam of its stewing on the seventh.

On the other hand, many as are its drawbacks and defects, the commercial establishment — be it factory, shop, or office — has also certain offsets from a sani-tary point of view. In the first place, like all commer-cial and public buildings, it is usually constructed upon larger and more liberal lines, with less pinching regard for economy of space. This is partly due to a desire to present a good appearance and make a favorable impression upon the public and upon prospective customers; partly to a recognition of the need of elbow-room and an adequate space for the carrying-out of operations and the storing of products. When it comes to a question of light, the average workroom, office, shop, or factory has distinctly more window space in proportion to its floor than the average living-room. One reason for this is that it is physically necessary that there should be light enough to do work as nearly as possible in every portion of the room; another is a natural pride of appearance and the same recognition of the advertising value of display that operates in the direction of large rooms and high ceil-ings. The most crowded, worst-lighted, and worst-ventilated factories and workrooms are the sweat-shops that are housed in living-rooms and private dwellings.

As regards ventilation, when it comes to the actual opening of these large, handsome windows, shops, factories, and offices have little to boast of over private houses; many of them, in fact, are so arranged that only a single pane out of thirty or forty can be opened for the admission of air. On the other hand, by the greater height of their ceilings, the much more frequent opening and shutting of doors to permit the ingress and egress of customers, or the raising of hatches to allow of the passage of raw materials or manufactured goods, there is apt to be in proportion to the individuals present a larger circulation of air *per capita* than in the average home, living-room, or bedroom. The store, the salesroom, and the office make no intrinsic addition to the impurity of the air to compare with that made by the kitchen, the wash-boiler, and the cellar in the private house; and only the factory or the workshop equals or exceeds the home in this respect.

A certain group of factories and workshops add markedly to the impurities and the unwholesomeness of the air, especially those that throw quantities of dust or lint into circulation, — as do certain of the woolen and other textile factories, — or those that give off poisonous or otherwise injurious vapors and fumes, such as match factories, pottery works where lead is used, certain dye works, and so forth. But these do not form a very large percentage of the places where women are employed.

The greed of capital is, of course, unlimited, but people are beginning to discover — with the assistance, in a good many instances, of strikes on the part of the workers on the one hand, and factory-inspection laws, passed at the demand of the thoughtful element of the community, on the other — that a reasonable regard for the health and comfort of its employees is, in the long run, a good, paying investment. And though, of course, precise and accurate data are lacking, I think it would be fairly safe to say that the average progressive shop, store, office building, or factory of to-day, constructed for the purpose, compares favorably in point of light, ventilation, and purity of air with the average living-room of the average home of the class from which its workers are drawn. And it is only fair to say that some of the more broad-minded and progressive manufacturers and merchants provide surroundings for their workers which, in point of light, airiness, rest-rooms, lunch-rooms, and sanitary conveniences, are distinctly superior to those of the average private house. In fact, in view of the awakening of the public conscience in general, and of that of the average business man in particular, in regard to the sanitary and hygienic rights of those who, because of sex, age, or social condition, are less able to insist upon securing them for themselves, places of occupation and life that are either freely open to the eye of the public or regularly inspected by their appointed representatives are rapidly becoming among the most wholesome and sanitary places to be found indoors. If laws like those respecting the cubic space per individual, the amount of window space, the circulation of air *per capita* per hour, the freedom from smells, the restrictions as to age and length of continuous employment of the workers, which are now applied to stores, shops, and factories, were to be applied to private homes, it would work a sanitary revolution — if it did not produce a political one in the process!

But those who are convinced of the injurious effect of industrial employment for women will rejoin, even granting that the hours are shorter than in the home and the hygienic surroundings no worse, that such industrial work is very much heavier and the strain upon the physical powers of the worker greater and more injurious. This is a point upon which it is even more difficult to make actual comparisons than the others. But so far as data at our disposal go, I think it is doubtful whether we have adequate ground for such a statement. On the one hand, there is no question but that the labor that is carried out in the factory is carried out at a greater tension, a higher rate of speed, and under a sterner stimulus of competition than in the home, with the possibility of a lower wage or loss of position if the worker falls behind in the race.

On the other hand, with certain exceptions that have now been almost abolished by our admirable labor legislation, the great majority of the tasks done by woman in the store, the shop, or the factory do not severely tax her muscular strength, or call for any violent or straining effort. Many of them involve rather rapid and repeated light movements of the hand and arm; they can be carried out sitting, and after a time almost without mental effort, or even consciousness. Their principal drawback, in fact, is their deadly monotony, the fact that they call into play only a few small groups of muscles and nerves and a fraction of the total activities of the body, and that in some cases they involve a somewhat cramped or unwholesome position of the chest or abdomen — interfering with proper breathing or circulation — or the strain of continual standing.

Though the tasks themselves are monotonous, they are usually carried out in the company of a number of others, and their very automatic and mechanical character permits of a certain amount of relief in the form of conversation and gossip. Even though the product of their fingers, or of the machines that they tend, be turned out at the rate of hundreds or thousands per day, and all exactly alike, yet the counting-up of the numbers, the coming of other workers to supply new materials or take away the finished product, the excitement of competition, — if this be kept within healthful limits, — and the certainty that it will end at a definite time each morning and afternoon and be rewarded by a definite wage, help to make the hours and the days pass more tolerably than might, at first sight, be supposed. In fact, as will be considered later, one of the strongest reasons usually urged by girls and women to explain their preference for industrial occupation is that it is less monotonous and wearing, and gives far wider social opportunities for acquaintance and for keeping in touch with what is going on, with definite hours for rest and recreation. Though the strong tendency of modern women toward industrial occupation may be denounced as an unsocial one as regards the home, it is exactly the reverse of this as regards the broader interests and activities of communal life.

The very publicity of industrial occupations for women has become a safeguard. The conscience of the community has revolted, not only at the length of hours and bad ventilation, but also at the spectacle of the employment of woman at tasks that are obviously injurious to her physically, or even degrading mentally, such as work in mines and brickyards and foundries and garbage-dumps and slaughter-houses. Thanks to the enlightened activities of organized philanthropy, laws have been passed in all but a few benighted States of our Union, either severely limiting or absolutely prohibiting the employment of women at such tasks.

In fact, paradoxical and bitterly ironic as it may sound, the home and the farm have become now practically the only places where women can be habitually and persistently overworked, overstrained, and underfed, without the interference of law. Though a large part of housework and farmwork is wholesome and healthful exercise, we cannot afford to forget that such work habitually imposes tasks upon women and young, growing girls which are as severely overtaxing and injurious to their physical powers as anything which they would now be allowed to undertake in the factory or the shop. Though factory occupations have fewer remissions and are pursued for more minutes and hours at a stretch than any in the home, yet there are very few of them that, in severity of strain, would exceed many everyday and familiar household tasks, such as scrubbing floors, washing clothing, beating carpets, carrying heavy trays, scuttles of coal or buckets of water up and down flights of stairs, moving furniture, lifting washtubs. The burning heat, the stifling air, the heavy odors, the incessant activity and tension, both mentally and bodily, of baking-day are as severe a strain upon the back, the eyes, the nerves, and the general strength as almost anything that has been invented in industrial occupations outside of a blast-furnace. There are few industrial or other public occupations in which young girls are permitted to engage that are half as exhausting, as straining, as badly fed and housed, and as demoralizing physically, mentally, and morally as the position of scullery maid in many a large house, or of general servant in a small one — to say nothing of the "slavey" in a lodging-house. Even in the very bosom of the family and in the exercise of the most sacred duties of kinship and protection, the unfortunate twelve-year-old — oldest of a family of six — may have half the joy and freedom crushed out of her own young life and have her slender spinal column bent into a permanent curve by being loaded down with a perpetual weight of twenty pounds of baby, which she drags about continually, as a prisoner his ball and chain.

When we further recall that previous to the general introduction of steam and machinery, and in many of the rural districts even at the present day, woman was habitually employed, not merely in the most difficult and disagreeable tasks of the house, but in those of the farm, the garden, and the field as well, — milking, churning, digging, hoeing, harvesting, reaping, and even assisting to drag the plough, — one cannot help feeling a trifle skeptical about the ruinous effects upon her health that are certain to be produced by the physical strain of modern industrial occupations. If it comes to industrial competition between the sexes, man has good cause for uneasiness!

Though it may possibly be admitted as at least open to question that modern industrial conditions compare favorably with home employment in respect to length of hours, wages, hygienic surroundings, and physical strain, there rises an almost unanimous chorus of condemnation of the new departure when it comes to the question of how well or badly woman is fed or feeds herself under the new conditions. On all hands is chanted the jeremiad that the modern working-woman is forgetting or utterly failing to learn how to cook, and thereby not merely imperiling future generations and households, but undermining her own health in the process. It is assumed as almost axiomatic that the woman in the home is far better and more wholesomely fed than she who goes forth to labor in the store or factory and who attempts to stay her hunger with the deceptive and commercialized products of the restaurant, the lunch-counter, and the delicatessen shop. Such universal agreement must have a certain amount of basis in fact; but in practical experience there are a number of hard facts and basic tendencies of human nature that go far to upset the popular belief that woman is best and most naturally fed when working in the home.

In the first place, while it is highly desirable from the point of view of the continuance of the race that there should be cooks, it is notorious that cooks for the most part have poor appetites, especially for the products of their own skill. The average woman who works in the home, whether as a member of the family or as a paid domestic, usually regards the dinner as the most exhausting and disagreeable task of her day. By the time it is placed upon the table she is so exhausted with the labor of cooking it, so disgusted with the smell of it, so fatigued by the incidental cooking of her own face and nerves which has accompanied the preparation of the food, that the last thing that she looks forward to with any pleasure is eating it. Woman will cook for others, but she will not cook for herself. If it were not for the hungry men and boys, whose everlasting appetites she has to supply, the vast majority of women living and working in the home would never get enough to eat. In fact, where women live alone, or only with other women, they are exceedingly apt to get along on "pick-ups" like bread and butter, jelly, pickles, purchased confectionery, and tea, to save the labor of cooking. A woman working in the home often eats less really nourishing, adequate food during the day, on account of exhaustion, lack of appetite for her own cookery, and willingness to give the best of what is placed upon the table to the so-called workers of the family, than the six-dollar-a-week shopgirl who boards round at lunch-counters and delicatessen shops. In fact, it not infrequently happens that one of the first effects of industrial occupation upon women and girls is distinctly to increase their appetites and to put a keener edge upon the enjoyment of their meals.

Furthermore, these meals, now coming at fixed and regular hours instead of after everybody else has finished, and being taken in places designed for the purpose, — which, whatever their drawbacks, are distinctly more appetizing and attractive than a partial clearing among the dirty dishes on the corner of a dining-room or kitchen table, — become a much more important function and one that is positively looked forward to instead of being merely tolerated as a tiresome custom, as is often the case with the busy housewife or the domestic servant.

When woman first begins to work for herself and to pay for her food in hard cash out of her own pocket, there can be no doubt that her first tendency is to economize unduly and to endeavor to satisfy her appetite at the lowest possible expense, without much regard to the nutritive value or the sustaining power of the food. But a very short practical experience brings her sharply to the conviction that, after all, she is physically merely a machine for doing a certain amount of work, and that her ability for doing that work depends absolutely upon the amount of fuel with which she is supplied. No food, no strength; no strength, no wages, — these, of experience, are the factors in the brutal but convincing logic. So that it is not long, if her wages are anything like humanly adequate, before she begins to demand good food and enough of it, just as does her male fellow worker.

The nutrition of woman in the home is perpetually interfered with by her unselfish preference of the tastes and interests of her husband and children; her fatigue and general lack of appetite at the time meals are served; and her unwillingness to go to the trouble of cooking and serving a regular meal for herself if she is alone at home. If she be employed in the house of another, she has to contend with this same exhaustion at meal-times, this saturation of all her senses with the odor of the food, this same unwillingness to make additional work by preparing food for herself; while she has the additional handicap of being very often obliged to eat simply what is left, and in many cases, I am grieved to say, is expected to subsist chiefly upon bread, potatoes, scraps, and weak tea. I have never known women — or, for the matter of that, human beings — worse fed, anywhere, than the servants in some of our large hotels and in some highly respectable private houses. Certain it is that women who have once been accustomed to working for wages in commercial occupations most strenuously object to any contract that includes board as part of their remuneration. All things considered, women engaged in industrial occupations are quite as well fed as those in the same social position and financial position living at home; indeed, in my experience, they are better fed.

This brings us to the final and most important consideration of all: What does the physical condition of the women engaged in industrial occupations actually show as to the effect of this employment upon their health? The data upon which to base a reply are still scattered and inadequate, the comparison for obvious reasons is a difficult one to make; but so far as they go they unanimously support the conclusion to which our comparison of conditions has been leading us: that such occupations have not been injurious, but positively beneficial.

To take some of the simplest and most available data first: The death-rate and disease-rate among women engaged in gainful occupations, as furnished by our census reports and the investigations of the Bureau of Labor and Commerce, show, somewhat to our surprise, that the general death-rate among women engaged in domestic service is much higher than that of those employed in any other occupation. For instance, the death-rate among domestic servants is 17.1 per thousand; that among women employed in mills, laundries, and factories, 5.1 per thousand; that among women employed in stores and offices, 5.6 per thousand; while that among women engaged in the professions and higher clerical occupations is only 2.7 per thousand. A similar contrast is shown in the data collected by some of our large life insurance companies, particularly those engaged in industrial insurance. In practically every instance among women employed in gainful occupations those who are engaged in what have been regarded as the normal and most healthful occupations show the highest death-rate and the lowest expectation of life.

Of course, there are other considerations that must be taken into account in making these bald and rather crude contrasts between the different classes of women workers. For instance, it is usually the more aggressive, energetic, and vigorous girls and women who are inclined to strike out for themselves and push out into these relatively new fields of occupation and employment. Also, we must remember that the class of domestic servants is the great unskilled-labor market for women, in which practically any woman, however unskillful, stupid, or feeble, can manage to find some sort of employment; and that into it fall back those whose health or intelligence is not sufficient to enable them to stand the strain and competition of commercial employment. Domestic servants, as a class, being less energetic, and, as a rule, less intelligent, than the majority of women employed in commercial occupations, would, of course, be less careful of their health, less hygienic and sanitary in their habits, and less fitted to protect themselves from infection and disease. But when all these allowances have been made, the fact remains that two thirds of these two classes — the domestic servant and the industrial employee in the factory, shop, and the lower grades of office work — are recruited from the same class, and that those who have entered the newer and supposedly more trying fields of activity have certainly not in any physical respect fallen behind their less enterprising and more domestically inclined sisters.

Unfortunately, data relative to weights and measurements at given ages and percentages of disability from illness, such as would enable us to make contrasts between the two classes, are as yet lacking. It is to be hoped that they will be supplied in the near future.

But I have little hesitation in declaring, from my own personal experience in the clinic and in the hospital, and as sanitary inspector of private homes and of stores and manufacturing establishments where women are employed, that the average height, weight, and physical vigor of the women now employed in industrial occupations will be found to be distinctly above those of their sisters engaged in domestic service or living at home.

This would certainly seem to be indicated by the fact — as shown by the tables of the last United States Census — that the general death-rate per thousand of women engaged in gainful occupations was 8.6 per cent per thousand living, as compared with 16.3 per cent for the general average of all female deaths. As, however, this latter, of course, included infants and young children, much of this nearly one hundred per cent excess of mortality was due to this cause. But, taking the death-rates at various ages, the same relation holds. The death-rate between the ages of fifteen and twenty-four is 6.1 per thousand for all females; while that among women in gainful occupations at the same age ranges from 1.9 for stenographers and typewriters to 5.1 for hotel and boarding-house keepers and 5.3 for domestic servants. From twenty-five to forty-four a similar contrast holds. The death-rate for all females is 8.5, while that for females employed in gainful occupations ranges from 4.1 for stenographers and typewriters to 5.1 for cigarmakers and factory-workers, 6.3 for bookkeepers, clerks, and copyists, and 14.2 for servants.

From forty-five to sixty-four the contrast is even more striking. The average for women of all ages is 20.1 per thousand, while that of women employed in gainful occupations ranges from 12 per thousand for mill and factory operatives, 10 for dressmakers and seamstresses, 14 for bookkeepers, clerks, and copyists, with the appalling pitch of 53.4 for domestic servants.

In short, every gainful occupation in which woman is employed in the United States shows a lower mortality than that of the total number of females for the same age period, with the single exception of domestic servants. The contrast between the women who work outside of the home and those who work for wages inside the home is positively appalling. The general average for the two classes is 8.3 per thousand at all ages, and 17.1 per thousand for domestic servants!

The employment of women in commercial and public occupations is and has been subject to an enormous amount of abuse, and the various philanthropic agencies that have fought with energy and success against such abuse and exploitation are entitled to the greatest credit for the successful issue of their fight. No one who knows anything about the conditions of women workers and child workers in factories, mills, and shops would propose a moment's relaxation of the vigor of factory, women, and child-labor legislation. In fact, its standards ought to be steadily raised all along the line.

However, the most serious hygienic indictment against the employment of women in industrial occupations remains yet to be met, and that is its effect upon the vigor and stamina of future generations and upon the birth-rate. There can be no question that the general birth-rate is steadily decreasing all over the civilized world and that this decrease is more rapid and more noticeable in the classes of women that are or have been employed in public industrial occupations. But there are two important offsets to this admission which decidedly alter its bearing upon the future of the race. The first of these is most obvious and can be readily dismissed — namely, that it is an axiomatic statement on the order of the truth that no one body can occupy two different points in space at the same time, and that, therefore, a woman cannot successfully and satisfactorily both earn good wages in a factory and bear and rear children. The employment in factories of married women who have young children to rear is certainly most undesirable from every point of view — hygienic, economic, and moral.

The remedy is a comparatively simple one. Pay the husband a wage that will enable him adequately to support his wife and rear his children without having to demand the assistance of the wife and mother. Or, as is already being proposed in France and Germany, pay the widowed mother a certain pension for staying at home and taking care of her children. It is gradually dawning, though very, very slowly, upon the minds of our legislators and economists that the one thing no community can possibly afford to do is to allow its children to grow up stunted, deformed, or kept below their full level of normal possibilities by neglect, starvation, disease, or overwork. And that the most remunerative occupation that the community can devise for a mother is the care of her children. She will earn at least three times her factory wages at it.

A large majority of the women employed in industrial occupations marry with the intention of leaving that occupation when they do so. Nor am I able to find any adequate basis for the belief that they are less competent or capable housekeepers, wives, or mothers for their industrial experience. On the contrary, so far as their industrial experience has broadened and sharpened their intelligence, has given them a wider knowledge of the world and a more intelligent interest in general affairs, has broadened their horizon and blunted their spites and their prejudices, it has made them capable of more intelligent and more effective wifehood and motherhood and home-making.

So far from public employment driving women away from marriage, one of the strongest inducements to many girls and young women to enter these occupations is that it frees them from what they believe and practically find to be a social stigma, by taking them out of the class of personal domestic servants — the class whose labor is conducted under conditions more nearly resembling the slave labor of more than a century ago than any other form. And the principal value of this improved social position to them is that it will enable them to make a more desirable and advantageous marriage — an ambition that is as honorable and praiseworthy as any that can be imagined.

As to the lower birth-rate of women who are or have been employed in public occupations, that is only a part of the great movement toward what might be termed intelligent parenthood, which is swaying every class of society and every nation in the civilized world. The same accusation used to be brought against the college woman, and the woman with the higher education and the new woman generally. But the point of these criticisms has been very largely dulled now that time enough has elapsed to show that of the smaller number of children borne by the intelligent and thoughtful mother a far larger percentage survives to reach maturity; and that this percentage is of a height, weight, and physical and intellectual vigor distinctly superior to that of the average of the larger family of less adequately supported and carefully trained children. In other words, a high birth-rate always meant and still means, wherever it occurs, an enormous infant mortality, a lower general average of height, weight, and physical and mental vigor at maturity, a higher disease-rate and death-rate at all ages. Therefore, modern civilized nations, with their distinctly falling birth-rates, are — with the exception of France — actually increasing in population, in mental and physical vigor, and in influence upon the world at a more rapid rate than ever before.

CHAPTER X

THE HEALTH OF THE EMPLOYEE

THIS is an age which, above all other things, prides itself on being practical. Its first instinctive question about any proposal is, Will it pay? Everything must be demonstrated in cold percentages of profit on investment. It does not connote a particularly lofty ethical standard, perhaps, but it is one with which every reformer is bound to reckon. In some lines of advancement its demand is exceedingly hard to comply with, and in them progress is distressingly slow.

In other fields, profit and progress can be shown to go hand in hand with a weight and vividness of proof convincing to the dullest intellect, even that of the pillar of society. This, fortunately, is one of them.

One of the instinctive mental habits of that interesting and very common type known as "the successful man" is to divide all men into two classes — the practical and the theoretical. In the final analysis this means those who make money, regardless of the means used, and those who don't. For the opinions of the former he has the profoundest respect; for those of the latter, an equally profound contempt. Occasionally, much to his surprise, the views of the theorist turn out to be more "practical" than those of the practical man, namely, they will increase his profits. Then they are adopted into his scheme of the universe (without thanks) and cease to be theoretical. Thus is progress accomplished.

Nowhere is this more strikingly true than in the history of the relation of the employer to the health and comfort of the employee. Historically, of course, the original primitive relation of the two classes was that of master, or owner, and slave, or owned. Therefore, it was perfectly obvious to the crude and pitiless logic of the primitive successful man that the less he spent upon the keep and comfort of his employees, the more profit he would make out of their labor. And this was the primeval law of the labor market-place, which still runs. However, even before the laborer became a free man, the master began to discover his mistake in the slow and painful school of experience — slow, that is, for the master; painful for the laborer. Men, it was discovered, were almost like horses: if well fed and kindly treated, you could get more work out of them. So the red law of the market-place has gradually been softened of its ferocity, age after age, until now the theorist, the dreamer, who called himself a humanitarian and would not bow to the absolute inspiration of the sacred formula of success, "Business is Business," has been triumphantly vindicated by the logic of events.

No more convincing demonstration of the profitableness of humaneness could be asked than the state of affairs all over the civilized world to-day. For the past forty years the health, comfort, and general con-

dition of the laborer have been steadily improved —
partly by the foresightedness of the more intelligent
class of employers, whose results have proved an object-
lesson to the duller class, and partly by the grim pressure exercised upon the unwilling through laws born
of the increase of popular intelligence and the awakening of the public conscience. Turn where we will, we
find the vast majority of the evidence unanimously
indorsing the same surprising conclusion — that although the laborer is getting more for his labor, in
every sense of the term, than ever before, the profits
of the employer have increased instead of diminished.
Only the merest outline of the overwhelming mass of
evidence can be given here.

First of all, taking the rate of wages as a rough but
fairly reliable index of the ability of the laborer to
provide himself with the necessaries and the health-
giving comforts of life, it is, of course, notorious that
all over the world the higher the rate of wages the
lower the actual percentage of cost chargeable to labor
in the article produced. The United States, which
pays the highest wages, has the lowest percentage of
labor-cost in the goods produced. England, with the
next highest wages, charges a higher percentage of
the cost of production to labor. Germany, with still
lower wages, has a still higher debt to labor in the total
cost, and so on down the scale. Underpaid labor is
everywhere the dearest, partly because it is unintel-
ligent, but also because it is inefficient from strain and
fatigue, subject to large deductions of time on account
of illness, is apt to be drunken and dissipated on ac-

count of the discomfort in which it lives, and is exceedingly wasteful of material.

Next, as another rough index, is the length of hours of labor. Here, again, the amount of time which the laborer has at his own disposal furnishes a rough but reliable indication of his ability to secure sufficient rest, recreation, and general development, and of his balance, resisting power, and efficiency. Precisely contrary to what one might expect upon *a priori* grounds, it is now abundantly proved the world over that the shorter the hours of labor, the larger percentage of profit to the employer per workman. The hours of labor have been steadily reduced from fourteen and sixteen for agricultural, and ten and twelve for factory, down to eight and nine, and, in every instance, the reduction has resulted in profit to the employer instead of loss. The most striking and spectacular development of the past fifty years has been the growth of colossal fortunes. But it would also be equally true to describe it as an age of increasing wages and decreasing hours of toil for the laborer. Even if we do not regard the two facts as cause and effect, they certainly cannot be said to be in any way incompatible.

These two methods — increasing the wages and reducing the hours of toil — are not only the fairest, but have proved far the most effective, means of improving the condition and comfort of the worker. They have also the merit, in his eyes, of having been chiefly won upon the field of battle by his unions and other labor organizations.

There are, however, a number of paternal methods

by which both the efficiency and comfort of the laborer and his profitableness to his employer have been increased. Earliest and most common have been the various methods of providing him with reasonably commodious and sanitary dwellings, with gardens and a good water-supply, sewers, bathrooms, and other sanitary necessities. The effect of this, in the main, has been exceedingly good from the point of view of both the laborer and the employer, giving the former conditions under which he can live in such a manner as to retain his own self-respect and bring up his children with a fair, fighting chance in the world. To the employer they have yielded a steadier and more reliable class of labor and a body of workmen who have a higher degree of daily efficiency than those who are overcrowded, or poisoned by bad water or sewer-gas. They diminish the amount of drunkenness and dissipation by providing rational occupation and intelligent recreation for leisure hours. They diminish the number of accidents, both to machinery and to employees, and, where tactfully managed, inspire a spirit of loyalty to the establishment which is actually worth something in cold cash on the credit side of the ledger.

I may be pardoned, perhaps, for speaking rather positively upon these points; but in the earlier days of my practice many of my patients were workingmen employed in factories, and their families, and the difference between the feeling of the men toward those companies that housed them like cattle and those that treated them as human beings was most perceptible, and repeatedly resulted in benefit to the humane company.

It is true that a number of apparent failures of these commercial Utopias has been reported; but they are small in total percentage, and usually due to the fact that the company either were actually endeavoring so to utilize their control of the model tenements and gardens, which they supplied to their employees, as to put the latter absolutely at their mercy, not only as to wages, but as to the roofs over their heads; or that the men were led to imagine that such was or would be the ultimate aim of the company, and chose the risks of independence in much less healthful and desirable quarters in preference to those of dependence and comparative luxury.

Sometimes, the failure has been, in part, at least, due to the fact that the workmen, either through lack of intelligence or a natural impatience with what they believed to be an interference with their liberties, rebelled against even the sanitary restrictions and rules which the company rightly enforced. Any one who has been a health officer will readily understand that that kind of revolt is by no means limited to the wage-earning classes. A workingman is naturally and properly exceedingly sensitive about any procedures which he thinks tend to infringe upon his independence and his personal liberty. But as employers and employees come to recognize both the strength and the justice of each other's cause, and to treat one another through their organizations more as equals and as man to man, these causes of friction will tend to disappear. In fact, they are rapidly disappearing, and, in spite of the pathetic tales told by deeply grieved capitalists about the ingratitude and unappreciativeness of the laboring-classes, the experiment of providing comfortable homes and good sanitary surroundings for the workmen has been a decided success so far.

Another interesting field of endeavor has been that of providing proper ventilation for work and factory rooms, proper sanitary accommodations, and measures for the comfort of the employees, such as lunch rooms, rest rooms, and baths. These have been provided partly spontaneously and partly under the pressure of law; but in the overwhelming majority of instances, with one and the same result: great benefit to both classes involved.

This has been strikingly shown in those occupations in which there is a direct risk to the health of the employees, as, for instance, in lead factories and match factories. In the first of these, careful study by the companies' physicians revealed the unexpected fact that far the greater part of the conveyance of lead into the system of the laborers was not, as had generally been supposed, by inhaling the fumes or dust in the atmosphere. Painters' colic, for instance, was shown to be entirely due to the men eating their lunches with *unwashed hands*, and often actually in the workroom. As soon as lunch-rooms were provided in the factories and in the big paint-shops, with lavatories attached, and employees were strictly forbidden to carry food in any form into the workrooms, and were compelled to scrub and wash their hands thoroughly before eating in the separate rooms provided, attacks of lead poisoning, with its exceedingly serious and often fatal results, which were regarded as a necessary rule in the occupation, became the exception. When the regulation was carried to the extent of cautioning and watching the employees against putting their fingers up to their mouths while at work, or putting objects into their mouths while in the dangerous rooms, lead colic practically disappeared.

Similarly, phosphorus poisoning, or the much-dreaded "phossy jaw," which decimated the workers in the match factories, while still due to the inhaling of the fumes in the "dipping" stage of the process, was found to be *able to attack only such jaws as contained ulcerated or decaying teeth.* A dentist was appointed, who inspected every work-girl before she was admitted to the factory. At first, all with defective teeth were absolutely excluded; but, later, all that was found to be necessary was properly to treat and heal the teeth and gums, put the tissues of the mouth into good condition and keep them so, and then the worker could be allowed to resume her place. Every match factory now which uses the yellow phosphorus has a dentist in regular attendance for every so many of its employees, and their teeth are inspected and kept in absolutely perfect condition. The salary of the dentist is paid ten times over by the savings in suits for damages and loss of the services of the workers just when they are becoming expert.

Some ten or fifteen years ago, a prominent firm of scientific manufacturers, whose name is honored all over the scientific and the philanthropic world, offered a prize for an essay, based upon a study of the best methods of improving the hygiene and protecting the health and safety of laborers in factories. This resulted in some rather unexpected findings. First of all, it was clearly demonstrated that methods like ventilation and lighting of the rooms added so much to the efficiency of the work done and to the lessening of waste through spoiled raw materials as abundantly to pay for themselves. Secondly, that lunch-rooms, rest-rooms, and proper sanitary appliances, by increasing the efficiency and improving the morals of the employees, very soon yielded a good profit on the expense of their installation. Last, and perhaps least expected, that proper provisions for the escape of the employees in the way of broad staircases, abundant exits, and easily descended fire-escapes distinctly diminished the risks of damage by fire. How any danger could be diminished simply by providing a way of escape from it certainly appears paradoxical at first sight, but the solution is really very simple. Supposing an explosion to occur, or a fire to start, the employees, knowing that their way of retreat is perfectly clear and safe, will, in the first place, not develop any panic, and, in the second, will remain at their posts to the last minute, fighting the fire. This has been shown in a number of striking instances of the putting-out of what would certainly have become large and serious conflagrations by the energetic and courageous action of the employees in the room in which the explosion or blaze occurred.

A similar condition was found to result from the employment of guards and protectors of various sorts upon machines, to prevent, so far as might be, the risk of bodily accidents and injury. So long as the employee had to be — so to speak — constantly watching the machine with one eye to see that he did n't lose a finger, and his work with the other, the work naturally suffered, both in amount and quality. When he felt reasonably secure and easy in his mind, he could devote his entire attention to carrying out the work in hand with the highest degree of perfection and dispatch.

Last of all, a study has been made of the incidence of accidents in connection with machinery in the factories. A large number of factories have been put under observation, grouped according to the degree of dangerousness of the work; the number of employees has been taken, the number of accidents in a year, and the precise hours at which these occurred. From this, an ordinary graphic curve has been plotted, showing the number of accidents per thousand employees that occur at each hour of the working day. The results are surprisingly uniform. Starting with the hour of beginning work, from zero, there is a rapid rise for the first half-hour. This, of course, is readily accounted for by the hitches in the starting of the machinery, by the more dangerous manipulations which often have to be carried out to get the raw material properly introduced into the grasp of the machines, and by the condition of the workers at the time. By the end of the first hour the curve has fallen to what might

be called its normal level. After two hours it begins
to rise, and steadily runs upward from that point to
the time of the noon intermission. After the noon hour
the curve again gives a short upward rise, due again to
the risks of starting the machinery, falls to a level,
which, however, is slightly higher than that of the
morning, and after a short time, begins to rise again
and continues to do so steadily until the six-o'clock
whistle blows. In other words, we have, as in the handwriting upon the wall, simply an hourly record of
human fatigue and its cost in terms of limb and life.
The longer the hours of labor in the factory, the higher
the percentage of accidents, not merely in the total,
but per hour. More significant yet, the earlier in the
morning the day's work was begun, the more striking
was the initial rise. Men, women, and children stum-
bling into their workstalls in the chill, gray dawn, only
half awake — unrested, underfed — upon them the
red penalty falls!

Kipling has another of his wonderful flashes into
the very heart of things in one of his finest poems,
"The Sons of Martha," when he sings: —

They finger Death at their glove's end when they piece and repiece
      the living wires;
He rears against the gates they tend; they feed Him hungry behind
      their fires;
Early at dawn, ere men see clear, they stumble into His terrible
      stall,
And hale him forth like a haltered steer, and goad and turn him till
      evenfall.

It pays, oh, richly — not only in money, but in other
things which are almost as good — to treat employees

like men and women instead of like cattle! But that there should be a creature in human form, calling himself a man, and yet boasting that he must be shown this before he will grant such treatment, is enough to make one ashamed of one's species.

CHAPTER XI

WHAT is work for? To get something done which will either supply you directly with food, clothing, or shelter, or which some one else will think worth paying for, so that you can provide yourself with these things. When it has accomplished this purpose, plus ten per cent for a rainy-day fund, we ought to stop. But we pursue it as if it were an end in itself. Regular and continuous work is a comparatively modern bad habit; that is why it irks us so — we have n't yet got it adjusted to our constitutions.

We have been eating, sleeping, and breathing for several million years, and we do them by instinct and fairly well; we have been working steadily and drinking whiskey for only a few thousand years, and we do them, according to reason — and very badly. The noble savage never worked — he was a gentleman, and got drunk like one, three or four times a year! The barbarian looked upon work as a slave's job, while only civilized man is foolish enough to work six days out of the week and get drunk on Saturday night. The first men who worked regularly every day were slaves; and something of the "Slave Morality" of Nietzsche still hangs about the institution of work. The spirit of the slave-driver still sets our hours of work, which are all there are, with just sufficient intermission to allow the beast to rest and feed himself, so that he may continue to work on the morrow. The spirit that should set the hours of modern work should be, in how few hours can this work be done well?

It is interesting to study the gradual growth of the standards of hours of work. In primitive times work was done spasmodically, at irregular intervals under the stimulus of hunger, or the sight of easy booty, or prey, as in hunting or gathering wild fruits, nuts, or roots. When the first slave was caught and set to work, his master, owning him and consequently all of his time, proceeded to utilize it all, and whenever he did n't have any *real* work for him to do, he invented some. This standard of requirement still exists in some of the lowest and least specialized of our occupations, notably domestic service and hired-by-the-year farm laborers; and this is one of the reasons why these ranks in the army of workers are so unpopular and so hard to fill. Instead of their time belonging to themselves, except such hours of it as they contract to render to the employer, their time belongs to their employer, except such hours as they specifically reserve for themselves in the form of holidays and "Thursday nights out."

Naturally the work done in these classes is poor, stupid, wasteful, and inefficient — unprofitable alike to both employer and employed. As a Western philosopher has phrased it: "A man who will work for a dollar a day ain't worth it!" Of course, as a partial offset to their all-day-and-half-the-night hours, farmwork and housework both have periods in the day, or seasons in the year, of considerably lightening if not actual remission of toil.

When handicrafts sprang up and manual labor began to be organized in groups and crews, the slave was found too stupid and too little ambitious for this sort of work; so the worker was given a measure of freedom, but still with the old slave standard of selling practically all of his daylight time to his employer. Most of our industries began with a twelve- and even a fourteen-hour day, and some still remain in this backward and barbarous stage. Naturally this kind of day permits of little improvement in either the physique or the brains of the worker, and of little rise from one generation to the next. And the product of twelve-hour industries is, for the most part, all over the world, of low grade, poor quality, and small output *per capita per diem*. As the quality of the work improves and the worker is required to utilize, not merely his own muscles, but the great elemental forces in his task, the hours steadily shorten, until now the highest grade and most efficient work done everywhere in the world is done in an eight- or a nine-hour day.

Not only is the work done in the eight-hour day of higher quality, but the amount accomplished by each individual laborer is greater; and the percentage of labor-cost in the product is smaller than in the ten-hour and twelve-hour industries. The nations of the civilized world which have the shortest working day have the highest output *per capita*, the highest wages, the lowest percentage of labor-cost in the finished product, and the highest reputation for fine work and reliable goods. While, conversely, those that have the longest hours turn out the poorest, lowest-priced, and flimsiest products, pay the lowest wages, and have the lowest output per worker and the highest percentage of labor-cost.

In the old days the cost of making an article would run from thirty to fifty per cent of its price; in modern industries it seldom exceeds twenty per cent and often falls as low as five. It is the work that a man does with his *brains* that is really profitable, both to himself and to his employer; and good brain work requires that every other organ in the body should be kept in perfect condition, even if it takes sixteen or eighteen hours out of the twenty-four in sleep, feeding, and recreation to do this.

Is the time spent in tempering and grinding the axe, or cleaning or oiling the engine, wasted? Is the money spent upon new patents and improved machinery ill-spent? We pour out millions of dollars every year to improve and increase the output of our machinery. Would such investments and careful thought for the improvement of human machines, our own as well as others, be a less profitable investment?

Of course, no amount of the most intelligent training and conditioning, with food, recreation, and rest, will turn a hack-worker into a great executive, or a duffer into a genius; but whatever a man's possibilities and powers, from very lowest to highest, he will develop them most nearly to their utmost and turn out his highest possible output of hard, effective work by devoting one third of his day to sleep, one third to recreation and bathing, and one third to work. Plato divided the education of youth into two great branches — music and gymnastics, with literature as a branch of music. For gymnastics read work, and you have the ideal division for the lifelong education of the grown man. The most important and valuable product of any industry is the type of man or woman that it turns out!

What is true of men in the class, or group, is equally true of you as an individual. What wins the prize, and more so to-day than in any age preceding, is not a large output of mediocre work, but a small amount of high-class work done with finish and judgment. Your brain is the apex of a pyramid, of which your body is the base; it is a blazing spark between the carbons of the arc-light which calls for all the voltage of the dynamo behind it to keep it going. To burn clearly and steadily for eight hours, it must spend sixteen every day storing its batteries. Indeed, for the very highest and most brilliant quality of executive, inventive, creative work, eighteen and even twenty hours a day of charging may be required.

Paradoxical as it sounds, if you are not turning out enough work, or of good enough quality to suit you, shorten your hours and see what you get. Consider the lilies — they *do* toil harder, and grow faster, than you do, only they don't groan and sweat over it — and remember how many fine, high, and beautiful things can be *grown* into naturally, wholesomely, happily. Some of the best things in life are those that cost nothing, only the taking!

One of the most significant and hopeful things in this twentieth century is that our workshops and factories are becoming clean and light and beautiful. Just as our earliest houses were caves, so the earliest workshops were mere holes and corners at the back of a living-room, or the side of a warehouse, or up in some stifling attic — anywhere where space could be had to stand a bench or a loom, and where the wind and rain were excluded. They were for the work, not for the worker! Even up to a few score years ago a shop or factory was expected, as a matter of course, to be a grimy, crowded, stuffy, littered-up sort of place, just as it was taken as a matter of course that a workman's clothing should be dirty and stained and ragged. Then it was gradually discovered that fine work could not be done in a bad light, that delicate fabrics would be soiled and injured by dirt, dust, and unwashed fingers; and that soot, dirt, and litter of all sorts meant waste of fuel or material.

When machinery was introduced, more light had to be let into the workroom in order to catch the first sign of friction, or breaking down, as well as from the fact that nothing will be kept clean unless it is well lighted. Darkness and dirt are inseparable — like the Siamese twins. Soon shops and factories became so light and airy and clean that visitors and customers were invited to come and view them; and still further improvements were introduced as a matter of advertising display. Then it dawned on the managers that the human machines also did better work when they were kept well lighted and aired, that they lost less time through absence on account of illness, and turned out larger amounts of a better quality of work.

Finally the community began to take a hand in the game, and to insist, by legislative enactments, that those employers who had not progressed and kept up with the procession should provide healthful surroundings for their workmen as well as for their products.

The same sort of change has taken place upon the selling side of commerce. Any little hole or corner, with a door opening on the street and a show window, or gloomy barracks of a warehouse, was a good enough place for a shop. All that was needed was sufficient shelfroom and counters to pile goods on. But it was soon discovered that half the secret of selling goods was attractive display, and that this called for space and light and air; that customers must be kept comfortable and in good humor if they were to buy well. This meant good ventilation and decorations, finally, rest-rooms and lunch-rooms. Incidentally, it was found that the sellers were almost as much benefited by these improvements as the customers; that they put more energy, courtesy, and imagination into their work.

Many of our great shops and department stores are now literal palaces. Light, spacious, beautifully planned and decorated, well ventilated, — considering the large number under one roof, — and equipped for both customers and employees with rest-rooms, lunch-rooms, concert halls, play places, and gymnasia.

Hygience and Good Business go hand in hand. Science is nothing but *glorified common sense.* If you want to get the most and best possible work out of a man or a woman, you must keep them as healthy, as comfortable, and as happy as possible while they are doing it. And it is just as true if that man or woman happens to be yourself!

There is no valid reason why a work-place should not be made healthful, and, with a few exceptions in special occupations, reasonably comfortable. It will pay you well to spend time and thought, and money, if need be, in order to make it so, whether for yourself or for others. Poor light, whether from too few windows, or through dirty window panes, means poor work, either from direct inability to see clearly, or from the blurring that comes from early fatigue, peering, and straining in half-light. Dirt and dust are bad for your papers and account books, for the bearings of your machinery, for the finish of highly polished surfaces, and for delicate fabrics. The most delicate fabrics and exquisitely adjusted bearings known are to be found in the lining of your human lung and the joints of your body machine.

Bad air is simply a narcotic poison which dulls every sense, fags every muscle, and slows down every nerve message. See that your work-place, whether it be kitchen, or sewing-room, or desk, or factory, or shop, has plenty of light, as much sunshine as possible, freedom from dust and foul air, and that you don't stay in it too many hours a day, and you have done the best thing possible, not merely for yourself, but also for your Priceless Product, whether that be schemes of empire, or sausages, or soap, or sealing-wax!

Almost any occupation is healthful that is well enough paid. Making Good Money is an important step on the road to Wellville. If your pay is sufficient to enable you to feed yourself well and control your hours so as to get plenty of sleep and fresh air, so that you can drive your work instead of having it drive you, you can resist the severest strains and all but a few of the most unwholesome and abnormal surroundings.

Your body has not been practicing the trick of adjusting itself to its environment for five million years for nothing. There is a shrewd old Spanish proverb, "Threatened men live long"; and it is not those occupations which are followed in momentary peril of killing and death, and are marked "Extra Hazardous," such as diving, blasting, working in air caissons or mines, which have the highest death-rate, or the lowest longevity. These occupations have frankly recognized the danger, admitted the tremendous strain, shortened the hours, and raised the wages accordingly; and those who pursue them are strong and vigorous and live to a good old age in spite of risking their lives daily. This is, in part, due to a half-conscious, natural selection which takes place in the final choice of all occupations. Naturally, most of these "Extra-Hazardous" tasks could only be accomplished and persisted in by strong, vigorous, clear-headed men; and men of this type become preponderant in their ranks.

A similar selection takes place adversely in many occupations of the unskilled labor class, where neither training, intelligence, nor special vigor of either mind or body are required, and become filled up by weak or mentally inferior men, because smart, vigorous workers will not stay in them on account of the low wages. These consequently have the highest death-rates and lowest longevity of all classes of occupations. Both of these groups, however, are small detachments at the extreme wings of the great army of workers in which we are all enlisted. Eight tenths of all men and women of reasonable vigor and health can succeed sufficiently well to earn a fair living in three fourths of the different occupations and avenues open to them, providing that these latter are intelligently managed and conditioned.

So that the problem before us in the choice of a lifework is not of a risk between absolute failure and triumphant success, or between a total breakdown and wearing-out before our time and a vocation which is all roses and sunshine, but of a choice between two different grades of almost certain moderate success, providing that we study our own aptitudes and preferences intelligently and insist upon surrounding ourselves with reasonable conditions for work. We may be "standing at the parting of the ways," as the copybooks inform us, when we make our choice of a lifework, but both ways, and in fact five out of any six, lead to the same place so far as reasonable success is concerned.

Given vigor and intelligence, you can earn a moderate living wholesomely and happily in almost any occupation, providing that all parties concerned use their brains about it. At the same time there is little question that there are distinct differences between the ways in which perfectly healthy men and women will accomplish work and fit themselves to the surroundings of different occupations. What is a perpetual source of worry and hindrance to one will run off from another like the proverbial water from the duck's back; and what one individual does only by conscientious effort and laborious strain, another will find only an enjoyable exercise of his powers.

So a little preliminary experimenting in boyhood as to both aptitudes and likings for the work itself, and degree of ability to resist confinement, high temperatures, dusty air, or other inevitable surroundings, is most helpful in the choice of a life-work. Here is a point at which the school and the shop might combine to great advantage, and every boy, or girl, over fifteen be given an opportunity to take the practical part of his chemistry in some great commercial laboratory or factory, of his physics in some workshop, of his arithmetic in some counting-house or store, of his biology, botany, and nature-study on some farm; both as a means of giving him a rounded education and symmetrical experience, and as a means of enabling him to choose his life-work intelligently.

Broadly considered, however, every decent profession and occupation which is fit to be tolerated in a civilized community can be made wholesome and healthful if all parties concerned put their heads together — the employer, the employed, and the community. The interest of the community is the keenest and deepest of all, for to run with unoiled bearings and ill-fitting cogs soon means a machine on the scrap heap; and the community has to provide the scrap heap and support the widow and children. Every trade should pay for its own breakages, — human as well as other, — and the best way to pay for them is to avoid making them.

An occupation is not necessarily unhealthful because it has to be carried on indoors. The advantages of all outdoors for a workshop are, of course, obvious; but like everything else, it has certain balancing drawbacks. The death-rate among farm-laborers, for instance, is not so much below that of indoor workers as is usually supposed, nor is their average longevity so much higher. Farm-laborers, for instance, have the lowest death-rate and highest longevity of all unskilled laborers, or of those usually paid by the day; but they have little advantage in either respect over the better-paid class of artisans, craftsmen, and factory-workers; and are surpassed on both counts by railroad employees, miners, and clerks; and while farmers themselves are among the healthiest and longest-lived of the non-wage-earning workers, they are beaten in both respects by bankers, clergymen, government officials, and merchants. The work of the outdoor man is apt to be exceedingly heavy and straining, and not a little of it has to be done under the broiling sun of midsummer, or in mud and storm and snow. His hours are very long, his food coarse, and, though usually abundant, often poorly cooked, and at certain times of the year, monotonous and inadequate. So that, even though the tendency of modern life toward indoor occupations should continue, there is no ground for uneasiness as to the future vigor of the race on that account.

There are a few occupations which are inherently unwholesome, such as making soap out of garbage or putrid grease; collecting carrion to be converted into fertilizer or gelatine; but these are almost equally unwholesome for the users of their product, and for the surrounding neighborhood, and should be either reformed or abolished, on sanitary grounds.

Any decent, civilized occupation can be made perfectly wholesome, and, indeed, invigorating, for all parties concerned in it, providing that good enough wages are paid to permit of good food, good housing, and clothing; that the hours are short enough to allow for adequate rest and recreation; and that the conditions under which it is carried out are such as are best for the product, both commercial and human.

Work in strict moderation is health. It is necessary to life, but it is not life. We should not make life subservient to work, but work subservient to life. The most important, the most valuable product of any industry is the type of man and woman that it turns out. Work is far from being the biggest and most important thing in the world. Indeed, it is only vital, important, and valuable in so far as it is the means of growth, either for the individual or for the community. Yet we are unconsciously coming to regard work as more important than life; and the moment that any proposal is made to regulate or restrain it in the interests of the worker, the cry is raised, as of one aghast at sacrilege, that we are "interfering with BUSINESS!"

The real purpose of work is to build up the State and develop men, and not to build up industries or rear monuments for kings and conquerors. It is neither the amount nor the intensity of the work that counts, but the ends to which it is devoted. We can easily see, at this distance of historical perspective, how much better it would have been for Egypt if the colossal labor wasted in building the pyramids had been expended in building a dam across the Nile. But hundreds of thousands of us to-day are building monuments of industry pyramids; of wealth to ourselves, or to others, as useless as the pyramids, as cumbrous as Cleopatra's Needle, while neglecting the labors which would give bread to this generation and new life to generations yet to come. For the sake of living, we let industry crush out and destroy the things that make life really worth living, — health, happiness, and honor.

Those people and races who profit most by their industry are not those who work hardest and most incessantly, but those who aim and plan their work most intelligently. The man who works hardest and most incessantly is everywhere and always has been the peasant and the day laborer. A large part of our work, from a broad and rational point of view, is little better than busy foolishness. All good work should be educational, should make for growth as well as profit to yourself, and above all should be enjoyable. The best work that we do is done in the spirit of play, because we love it and are bound to make it win.

We speak of education and play as something confined to the schoolroom, but our whole life's work should be one continuous college course, and could be made so if the community would turn its brains to the matter in a broad-minded, considerate way for a few months. If we would stop to consider our toil and toilers as Solomon bade us "consider the lilies of the field," we should see some astonishing things — and make some surprising changes. Scarcely a century ago we fought Nature with our bare hands, and wrested our living from the soil, the sea, and the burrowed rocks, with such feeble hand-weapons as the hoe, the spade, the pickaxe, and the hammer. Now we have yoked the steam demon to our plough and our chariot and our loom; we have chained the lightning and we have harnessed the snows of the mountain and the rush of the torrents to our service. We have enlisted half the forces of Nature on our side, and yet — we strain the muscles and bow the back and plough the weary furrow, from the first clear light of morning until the dusk of evening, and even far into the night, just as if we still fought single-handed. Our working day is still constructed upon a farmhand basis. One hundred years ago, the net efficiency, the actual horse-power of the average worker was less than one fifth what it is to-day. Yet we work far more than a fifth as many hours a day, and are far short of making five times as good a living. We have enlisted the stars in our service, but we have n't lifted ourselves as far toward them, as a result, as we should. While we accomplish at least three times as much, we have shortened our working hours barely one fifth and raised our standard of living scarcely one fourth. Yet we have piled up enough of that dead man's labor called capital, to enable us to take full charge of all our new heritage of power if it were only intelligently applied to the purpose. The wealth of the United States, for instance, is estimated at $150,000,000,000, or $1500 *per capita*, $7500 for each family of five. But what good does it do most of us, when one per cent of our citizens own fifty per cent of our wealth and the other ninety-nine per cent — admire the way they spend it.

The trouble is that we have never seriously considered the problem from a broad, racial point of view. If we were to be asked why we go to work at such and such an hour, and keep on until such and such a time, we could only give the cuckoo-like answer: "Because everybody else does." We have never asked ourselves the question, In how many or in how few hours a day can the largest amount of most efficient work be turned out with the greatest amount of benefit to the worker? There are few things we do so senselessly as work. To put in all the hours of daylight and steal one or two from the night at each end, no matter how stupidly and slavishly, ourselves, and to demand the same tale of bricks from those we have hired — that is the spirit of our boasted "modern" industry.

We know better than to work an ox, or a horse, or even a loom, or a locomotive, on such principles, but we will, and do, so work ourselves and our fellows. The thing that would most increase the efficiency of your work would be an extra hour in bed in the morning and from one to two hours of play between closing-time and nightfall. Such unconscious, and often most unwilling, experiments as have been made in this direction, yield the same result with a positively astonishing unanimity. Every time that the hours of labor have been shortened in a given industry, the actual output per worker *per diem* has increased, and especially if the change was accompanied by an increased wage. Those countries of the civilized world, and those trades which have the longest hours, have, nine times out of ten, the lowest wages and the smallest output per worker. The best-paid and most intelligent labor is, in the long run, the cheapest, whether it be your own or that of your employee. Only recently, for instance, the mills in a certain industry in this country cut down their schedule from six days a week to four and a half, in order to limit production, on account of the high price of raw material. Within a month, to their surprise and almost dismay, they found that they were turning out just as much product as when working on full time.

The more snap and energy, yes, and cheerfulness, you and your workers have to put into your work, the more and better quality of work they will turn out. We know that we cannot afford to reap profit from the labor of our children, at the price of stunting and impairing their efficiency for life; that it is the most ruinous of blood money which is wrung from the wearied bodies of mothers, either of the present or future generations. But we still treat ourselves and our fellows without any reasonable consideration or common sense in this regard. Work and hustle, hustle and work! Never let up from daylight until dark, until you land either on Easy Street (when you work harder still), or else on the scrap heap!

Sit down and consider the problem of your life-work seriously, and when you have done it, go to your associates, your employees, and your neighbors and ask them to consider it with you. All that is needed is team-work and mutual agreement. Early closing, for instance, is now almost universal in our great cities; and yet our merchants make better profits than ever before. Any given community could add ten per cent to its efficiency, and twenty per cent to its health, lower its death-rate, and raise its income by getting together and mutually agreeing to begin work in all lines an hour later in the morning and quit an hour earlier in the evening. All the goods that the community requires can be sold, all its necessary work can be done, just as well in eight hours *per diem* as in ten. If Mrs. A would agree not to start shopping before nine o'clock and to get all her shopping done before five, Mr. B and all his clerks could shorten their day's work in exactly the same proportion and both accomplish just as much.

No work is profitable, however well paid, if it undermines your health. No work is profitable, whatever its wage, which does not increase your efficiency for to-morrow, and for next week, and for every week after that until you are sixty.

The final degree in the great University of Life should not be taken until a course of threescore years has been completed, and every year should, and can be, made to count toward its honors.

CHAPTER XII

DO not blame God for the fly, for man made him — outside of Egypt, at least.

Somewhere in the beginning, of course, he "jest growed," like Topsy, but we have made him what he is, our pet and our pestilence.

Musca domestica is his name, and *domestica* will he live and die. If you cut off the *domestica*, there won't be any *musca*. Go where you will, into the desert, the mountains, the untrodden plains, the rule holds everywhere — no settlers, no flies.

Hunters, voyagers, rangers of the Western mountains and plains, carried with them as their staff of life jerked beef or venison, the *carne sec* of Spanish America yet, cured by cutting fresh meat into strips and hanging it in the sun until dried, with neither salt nor smoke.

Hang up a batch of meat to-day in that same country and climate, now that it has become civilized, and within twenty-four hours it is a swarming mass of maggots laid by our domestic animal, the fly.

Flies live off of and on us and our filth, just as the bees in our hives do on our flowers. No filth, no flies.

One favor Nature has granted us, one weapon she has put into our hands: the eggs or "blow" of the fly do not explode into flies, but turn first into maggots, and these take fourteen days to hatch.

Household waste or manure, therefore, may be permitted to accumulate for a week or ten days about our premises without breeding any flies, if it is hauled away and got rid of promptly and certainly at the end of that time.

If the manure heap cannot be carted away, or the privy vault emptied as frequently as this, sprinkle the former with crude petroleum or one of the "black oils" made out of the wastes of oil refineries, or with a weak solution of arsenic, or a strong one of chloride of lime, or borax, or copperas. Treat the privy vault in the same way, or even take a handful of paris green or white arsenic and sprinkle it well over the sides of the vault and its contents once a month.

Or, if you prefer not to poison the manure, build a tight box or chamber with bottom and sides of matched flooring for its reception, and fit this with a swinging screened door through which the manure can be thrown into it. Thus put where no flies can get at it, and if the sides and floor of the box are tight, and the manure be kept wet down, such few maggots as are hatched will smother from lack of air.

The greatest danger is from horse manure, and next from hog manure, last of all from cow manure on account of the wetness and sogginess of the latter smothering the larvæ.

All garbage and household waste, of course, should be cleared away daily, or at least every other day, in summer time, and, to make assurance doubly sure, sprinkle the place where your garbage can stands and the ground about and under your kitchen stoop, and about your barns and in your chicken runs and houses, with one of those black oil or copperas solutions.

A few tablespoonfuls in a bucket of water is strong enough. If you carry out this campaign thoroughly, you will need no screens against flies, nor — if your neighbors join with you, — against mosquitoes either.

But, as an extra precaution, keep all food, particularly milk, in screened rooms or safes, and have screens upon your kitchen windows and door.

The fly is strictly domestic in more senses than one, and seldom travels a few hundred yards from his birthplace unless carried.

Clean up your own flies, and your neighbors' brood won't trouble you much, unless they are born within a hundred yards of your back door.

When Emerson said that a fly is as untamable as a hyena, he had little idea that it was also a thousand times as dangerous. A hyena will devour you only after you are dead, while a fly preys on you while you are alive and fills you and your food with the seeds of disease and death.

A man's foes are they of his own household. We shudder at the thought of the man-eating tiger of the jungles, or the death-dealing cobra of the tropics, the original fiery serpent whose burning bite is a passport to the hereafter.

But the real devouring beast of prey who, with his cousin, the mosquito, has slain more human beings than all the wolves and lions and tigers and snakes put together, is the little, harmless, buzzing fly upon the window pane.

His familiar trail of specks is the real Handwriting on the Wall foretelling pestilence and death. He is the real viper whom we have cherished in the bosom of our family; bred and sheltered and nourished him to bite the hand that fed him.

That is why we hate him so. Our instincts are astonishingly sound and right at bottom. Weak-headed sentimentalists have urged us to spare him, and idiotically exalted unwillingness to "hurt a fly" to the very pinnacle of the virtues; but unregenerate human nature, in its heart of hearts, knows better and "swats" him with a ferociousness and vindictive joy every chance it gets.

Keep it up; organize your instincts into a campaign of extermination; treat the fly according to the policy of Custer, "One more Indian war, and then no more Indians."

Three fourths of the colics, the typhoids, the summer diarrheas and the sicknesses which we attribute to the summer heat, generally including even most cases of sunstroke, are due to the poisons spread by that busy bastard, sired by *Summer Heat* out of *Human Dirt*, the housefly.

Wipe out flies and mosquitoes, and three fourths of the terrors, dangers, and discomforts of the good old summer time will disappear. You will be able to sit out on the porch at night, and sleep late in the early morning in peace and comfort. The comfortless and pernicious habits of rural districts of both retiring and rising at unholy hours are closely connected with the plague of flies. As the bard of Hoboken has put it, —

> " Early to bed and early to rise,
> There is a reason; the answer is flies."

Flies are — what General Sherman said war was, and the way of salvation is already plain.

The fly is the most affectionate and devoted of our domestic animals. He simply cannot bear to be out of your sight.

He eats with you, sleeps with you, crawls all over you, wakes you up in the morning and watches over your slumbers at night, attends you in your last illness, and would accompany you to the grave if you would let him. He also sends you there far oftener than you think.

So closely attached is he that he can neither breathe nor live save in your house or barnyard, or upon your refuse and fertilizers.

He is a scavenger, sure enough, but his notion of garbage disposal is to eat as much of it as he can, and then smear the rest over his hairy legs and dirty feet, and shake it off into your pie and over your bread and butter and into the baby's milk.

You can do your own scavengering about one hundred and fifty per cent better, and if you would just CLEAN UP, he would be out of a job and literally have to get off the earth.

The Persian legend declares that flies are the perspiration of the Devil, but they have no such lofty lineage; they are born in a dung heap, and if the dung heap was not there, they would not be born.

No dung heaps or dirt piles — no flies. Screened or boxed-in dung heaps — no flies. Poisoned dung heaps — no flies.

You breed horses and pigs; horses and pigs make manure heaps; manure heaps and garbage dumps breed flies. Ergo, you breed flies, and can quit breeding them whenever you like. Any harm flies do to you is your own fault.

You can't hide dirt from a fly. He is a literal Eye of the Lord, in every place beholding the evil and the good, particularly the evil. He has as keen a nose for the odor of filth as a bird dog has for quails, and will follow a scent a hundred yards up the wind, if necessary, to find it; then, when he has found it, he gorges himself full of it, smears himself with it, like a small boy eating pie, clear up to the backs of his ears, and proceeds to tell the female of his species about it that she may come there and deposit her one hundred and fifty eggs. No race suicide for him.

No matter how deep the gully into which you may have heaved the mortal remains of your defunct feline; no matter how thick the underbrush or long the grass into which you have thrown the cleanings of your fish, scrapings of your dinner plates, or the dishwater from your kitchen, the fly will find them all. And when he has found them, he is far too unselfish to keep the treasure trove to himself, but comes hurrying joyously back to you laden with fragrant scraps and mementoes of the dear departed.

Dirt is like Banquo's ghost; it will not down in the summer time when there are flies about. Though he prefers nice, warm, moist, natural hotbeds, like manure heaps and garbage piles, for his nursery, he is neither proud nor exclusive, but will lay his little white eggs and hatch his velvety, maggoty young in any little pile of sweepings under the back stoop, or in the earth around a bone or crust carried under the house by the dog or cat.

There is a Scriptural proverb to the effect that you cannot prevent the birds from flying over your head, but you can keep them from building nests in your hair. You can do both with the fly. For, unless permitted to nest under your eaves, he will never grow up to fly over your — bald — head.

He literally grows upon us and our leavings and untidinesses, just as fleas grow on a dog. If you would spend half the energy that you waste in slapping at him or scratching his bites, one fourth of the psychic dynamic which you expend in profanity and objurgation, and one eighth of the money that you waste in putting in and repairing screens every year, you could, in the terse vernacular of our schoolboy days, "spit on him and rub him out," literally wipe him out of existence.

If you have no regular garbage collection, and have garbage and other refuse or offal, such as a dead bird or dead animal to dispose of, dig a pit or trench, soak it well with a mixture of kerosene or one of the black oils, two tablespoonfuls to a gallon of water, and sprinkle a layer of earth over it a couple of inches thick every day until the trench or pit is filled, then dig another one. The black oil and kerosene mixtures (or carbolic acid if you wish, though this is ten times as expensive and less than one fifth as strong a germicide) are best because, being volatile, they penetrate upward as well as downward and keep the air over the trench full of their vapor. This both repels flies and poisons them when they hover over it. If you prefer, however, to use a powder, you can take either chloride of lime or powdered copperas or a mixture of copperas and paris green or other form of arsenic, one part to one hundred, and keep the surface of the deposit sprinkled with a bloom of either of these.

After you have cleaned up every pile of dirt and poisoned every dirty or swampy-looking hollow, it is a good plan to keep a watering-can full of one of these petroleum mixtures or of a solution of chloride of lime or copperas, standing handy about the back premises, ready to catch up and sprinkle any spot that looks as if it might furnish any attraction for flies. If you will extend this sprinkling process with petroleum to your water butt, or lily pond, or duck pond, or any other accumulation of water, from the size of a tomato can up, that may be about your premises, you will get rid of mosquitoes, as well as flies, at the same time.

A fly is Nature's reminder that you have n't washed behind your ears properly. He is the angel of the resurrection of your garbage, the means by which your dirt and offal are, like curses, brought home to roost on your own doorstep.

To again paraphrase the bard of Hoboken, —

> " Often we sickens, and early we dies.
> There is a reason; the answer is flies."

No longer can we dismiss the fly with a contemptuous "shoo."

He is an Influence to be reckoned with. Black as his character is painted, we must concede him certain virtues. From a worldly point of view, he is a hustler from way back; perpetually on the job, and always delivers the goods.

He distributes samples of pestilence with a lavish hand, and the goods always match the samples, whether you have ordered them or not, and are marked D.O.D. — Death on Delivery.

From an unworldly point of view, he is a veritable means of grace, separating the sheep from the goats, the elect from the non-elect, developing in the former all the Christian virtues, including patience under affliction, an early death, and a glorious immortality. Among the non-elect he produces profanity, pugnacity and a long life of open rebellion against the decrees of All Wisdom, thus making their damnation doubly sure.

We may admire the fly for his industry, pertinacity, and business enterprise. We may even love him lukewarmly as one of God's creatures; but we had better wipe him gently but firmly out of existence, just the same. Flies, like Artemus Ward's Injuns, "is pizen wherever found."

He is the best traveling salesman known to humanity; carries a grip on each of his six legs and a trunk on his head. His line of samples is the most extensive and longest known, and will last you, not merely from this year to next, but from time to eternity.

He is more of a nurseryman and tree agent than

anything else, but does not despise other branches, and carries a number of side lines. He is the only such agent known whose seeds and cuttings and plants bear blossoms and fruit equal to the pictures in the catalogue, and sometimes superior to them, for they bloom, never fading, on the other side of Jordan, or rather translate you to bloom there.

Here are a few of the leading specialties that he handles, not so much to make a profit, but just to work up a trade.

BACILLUS TYPHOSUS (*Eberth*), hardy perennial, seldom known to winter-kill even in Alaska; heavy cropper; produces thirty-five thousand deaths annually in the United States alone. One fifth of all who grow it guaranteed never to grow any other. Blossoms, rose-colored, all over the abdomen and chest. Fruit, cherry red deepening to black, all through the intestines. No difficulty in disposing of any surplus to your neighbors; a splendid market variety for both city and country trade. Strong, well-rooted specimens, carefully selected from sewer mouths and privy vaults, now ready for delivery, F.O.F. — Free on Food. Special million rates. This is one of our best sellers.

No. 187, Fig. 14; see colored plate. *Cytoryctes variolæ*. Common or garden name, Variola, or smallpox germ.

Half hardy annual, formerly great favorite, now very rare. No up-to-date family garden should, however, be without it, as its superb and striking flowers of yellow umbilicated pustules on a crimson ground, once seen will never be forgotten; will not grow in vaccinated soil, but flourishes superbly everywhere else. Specimens we offer collected at great labor and expense by our special agents in pest-houses and Christian Science communities. Guaranteed to blossom in suitable soil inside of three weeks, and to form a most striking addition to any garden. Order early, as the stock is limited.

"No. 2341. BACILLUS SHIGÆ (Spirillum Obermeieri.)

"This interesting group of quick-flowering, tender annuals, especially adapted for kindergartens. Colors black and white, closely resembling crêpe and satin with plumes on the hearse. Wonderfully free bloomers, very attractive; every child ready to take them. Crop for 1907, 40,000 dead babies, value $8,000,000 as guaranteed by the United States Census. No trouble at all to grow; all that is needed is a baby, a little dirt, plenty of carelessness, and flies will do the rest. Best sprouted in milk for a few hours before sown.

"These interesting schizemycetes were long recognized only when in bloom, and then given a variety of popular and vulgar names such as summer diarrhea, summer sickness, cholera infantum, cholera morbus, etc. But the seeds which we furnish are from prize-winning strains, guaranteed to produce specimens fit to enter in competition anywhere.

"No. 3792. B. TUBERCULOSIS (Koch). This half-hardy perennial is an old favorite, few family gardens being complete without it, but we don't highly recommend it.

" It is delicate, easily sun-blistered, and will not grow

in strong, rich soils. Besides, it is an exceedingly slow bloomer, often taking two or three years to produce any striking display. Pink-and-white blooms, however, very delicate and vivid when secured.

"We are obliged to quote a high price upon this line, for, while seeds are common, their collection is both difficult and dangerous, our agents being frequently overwhelmed in the sticky sputum bogs, or overcome by the noxious vapors rising from the cuspidor swamps where they are found. Only when spread around freely upon floors and walls, and allowed to dry, can the seeds be collected with any safety to our representatives. Though difficult to start and slow in blossoming, when once securely rooted, their growth is exceedingly sure and can be confidently guaranteed to produce a spectacle which will delight the heart of any connoisseur in the flowers of decay."

This is the sort of thing that the fly carries on some one of his six legs and in his well-packed trunk whenever he buzzes gently in at your window. If he is out of one, he is sure to be well stocked with another, to say nothing of a miscellaneous variety of staphylococci and streptococci from boils, erysipelas, and poisoned wounds; of diphtheria bacilli and scarlet fever scales and the germs of infantile paralysis whenever these diseases happen to be in the neighborhood; of the germs that putrefy meat and set up poisonous changes in milk and cause apples to decay and vegetables to spoil and bread and cakes to mould.

Two thirds of what, in the days of unenlightenment and lack of culture, we used to vulgarly term "bellyaches" and "colics" were due, not to the food itself, but to the nasty germs and bugs with which flies and other agencies had contaminated it, and which found our stomach and intestines nice, warm, moist, comfortable places to breed and riot in.

A fly in a house is as dangerous as a rattlesnake, as filthy as a louse, and as disgraceful as a bedbug. The time will come and now is when any modern, cleanly home will feel itself shamed and disgraced by the presence of a fly, and when every householder upon whose premises a brood of flies is detected will be heavily fined or sent to jail.

CHAPTER XIII

CRIMES AGAINST THE COW

WE have long known that cows were dangerous — that is, the better and instinct-guided half of us have. They do not trust themselves in the same field with one if they can help it, and, like Falstaff, are cowards upon instinct, so far as poor Bossy is concerned.

Now comes Science to explain the rational basis of that instinct. Their instinctive dread was just. Its only error was the direction which it took. They were afraid of the wrong part of the animal. It isn't the cow's horns that are dangerous, however crumpled they may be, but her milk — how dangerous we hardly as yet adequately realize.

Milk, as sold in many of our small city stores, contains more bacteria per ounce than sewage. One teaspoonful of it may contain more millions of inhabitants than there are in the whole of Greater New York. No wonder that we are waking up on the subject of dirty milk.

Every particle of this filthiness and deadliness is *of our own making*, the well-earned and richly deserved wages of our own greediness, carelessness, and filthiness. The cow and her milk are both as innocent — as they look. Appearances here, as elsewhere, are not deceitful, except where man has had a finger in the pie. Milk, plain milk, as the cow yields it, without any "improvements" in the way of dust, dirt and "bugs" is one of the purest and wholesomest foods of the race, and the only one on which we can live and thrive in the earlier and most critical stages of our career. Practically everything that is in it that shouldn't be there is what we have put there ourselves.

In fact, its "face" is our misfortune. It *looks* so pure and innocent and harmless. Its fragrance and its taste are inseparably connected with all the magic memories of our childhood; its aroma suggests daisies, buttercups and new-mown hay; it is almost impossible to believe evil of it. "Harmless as milk" has passed into a proverb, and its snowy fragrance has become the Teutonic equivalent of Matthew Arnold's Attic " sweetness and light." The sweet breath of the kine, the golden gleam of the straw, the tinkle of the brook through the meadow, the waving of the lush grasses in the summer wind: these are the associations which it conjures up.

Can this nectar of the Golden Age of Childhood be mentioned in the same breath with *sewage?* Sad to say, its very whiteness may become little better than whitewash, in the modern sense of the term, and its creamy opaqueness a screen for concealing all sorts of horrors. Clear water is dangerous enough, Heaven knows. But when you render it opaque and call it milk, there is practically nothing which it may not conceal.

Its very virtues are its own undoing. Man, alas! is not the only living creature that appreciates its high value as a food. There are others — millions of them — somewhat smaller, it is true, but even quicker to recognize a good thing when they see it, and take possession of it. And when they have bred in it for a few score generations it is literally alive with them. This is where it gets ahead of sewage, both in popularity and populousness. A quart of water could be left exposed to the air and sun for months without developing such a population of germs as a quart of milk will breed in as many hours. It is one of the most superb culture media for germs known, and a few score of them that are blown or dropped into it will in six or eight hours develop their hundreds of thousands.

The moral is: Keep out the first few *seed* germs. Figures are not fascinating, but they are sometimes illuminating. A teaspoonful of milk, if absolutely germ free when drawn, will, if handled in the ordinary barn or cowshed, then carried to the ordinary dairy, milk-room or cellar, show at the end of the first hour three thousand germs; of the third, fifteen thousand; the sixth, forty-five thousand; the ninth, one hundred thousand, and the twelfth, two hundred and fifty thousand. It makes little difference how thoroughly and hermetically it may be sealed up *after* the first contamination or "seeding" has taken place. The growth of its germ population goes on unchecked. The only way to check it is to boil it, pasteurize it, or expose it to a low temperature. This is why it is always a point of advantage to keep milk cool. An open jar or pan of milk, in any ordinary room or cellar in which it is kept, is a standing invitation to germs to alight and help themselves; and when once they have, at any stage of the exposure, they will go right on and multiply until they have reached the stage which all theatrical managers so long for, "Standing Room Only." The outlook for keeping milk clean would appear to be, in the language of the day, distinctly bilious. And so it was until a comparatively few years ago, but now, fortunately, we are prepared to meet the situation.

The first thing to be settled to clear the ground for our attack is, What are these germs? And where did they come from? The first gleam of consolation comes from the fact that only a very small percentage of them are disease germs; and of this small percentage a very small moiety comes from the cow. So that in ninety cases out of a hundred we do not have to sterilize the cow, but only the milk. It was at one time thought, and is still popularly believed, that the principal danger in milk consists in the infectious diseases conveyed by, or carried in it. But these are now known to form less than ten per cent of its dangers. *Ninety per cent of the injurious effects of milk are due to the germs contained in plain, common dirt*, barnyard manure, from the sides of the cow, the hands of the milker, the dust of the stable and the barnyard. These germs, setting up putrefactive changes in the milk, continue these changes in the food canal of the child. This turns digestion and nutrition into a process of self-poisoning, the child dwindles and droops, and the first mild infection that happens to attack it carries it off. The danger of conveyance of tuberculosis and typhoid through milk, though very real, is small compared with the results of these filth contaminations.

The danger from tuberculosis is serious, though much less so than usually believed, and every precaution which has been suggested in the way of thorough inspection of cattle, and the test by tuberculin of all that show any suspicious sign of the disease to the eye of the skilled veterinarian, should be absolutely and inexorably insisted upon. Even were there no danger of the direct transmission of this deadly disease from cows to children through milk, the use for human food, and particularly as the sole diet of babies, of the milk of any animal suffering from a wasting and loathsome disease, attended by the formation of abscesses in various parts of the body, accompanied by high fever, and running two thirds of its course toward death before it checks, dries up, or even seriously interferes with the flow of milk, should not be tolerated for a moment. Even though it be true that the milk of the tuberculous cow does not contain tubercle bacilli unless the disease has involved the udder, such milk cannot possibly be regarded as in a normal or a healthy condition, and its use for food is as objectionable upon sanitary grounds as the idea of it is repulsive.

All that is required is thorough and intelligent enforcement of systematic tuberculin tests, the destruction of infected animals, and the protection of healthy animals from infection, completely to stamp out this pest among cattle, a consummation which, from the monetary point of view alone, would be worth millions of dollars to the farmers and dairymen of this country, more than its carrying out could possibly cost. Tuberculosis in cattle must be exterminated, whether the bovine bacillus is ever transmitted to human beings or not. But there is little gained by overstating a case in order to carry conviction. Nor, is it either good policy or good morals to refuse to tell the whole truth to the public for fear they may misunderstand it or slacken their zeal. As nearly as may be summed up in a few words, the situation is this: —

First that experts — both human and veterinary — are frankly disagreed as to whether bovine (cattle) tuberculosis is at all readily transmissible to human beings. Most experts who have carefully and impartially studied the question, with the exception of a few enthusiasts and special pleaders, are practically agreed that the number of cases in which it is *known* to have been transmitted is exceedingly small, so that it is doubtful whether it causes more than from one to two per cent of all cases of human tuberculosis. That, as a source of danger in milk, it is small contrasted with the risks from filth-bacteria and other germs introduced into milk by human agencies. Fully half of the tubercle bacilli found in milk, butter, and cream are now recognized as of human origin, from dust containing dried sputum, from flies, handling by infected individuals, or from infected rooms. There is, however, no disagreement between even those holding the most extreme views as to the non-infectiousness of cattle tuberculosis to human beings, and those who believe it freely communicable, as to the campaign against tuberculosis in cattle. No milk coming from an animal suffering from disease should be for a moment tolerated as human food, whether directly infectious or not. The consoling feature of the situation, on account of which I have here alluded to it, is that ninety per cent of all the danger in milk comes from dirty and careless handling, and not from its source, the cow.

The transmission of typhoid through milk is purely and solely of human origin. Not only does the cow never suffer from typhoid fever, so that it is impossible that germs should be present in either her blood or her milk, but, even if she should drink infected water or sewage, it is quite impossible for the germs to pass through her body and appear in the milk. This has been put to the most rigid experimental tests a score of times, not only with typhoid bacilli, but with a number of other infectious germs, which might by various possibilities get into the drink or food of the cow, and invariably with negative results. The milk always remained absolutely germ-free.

But even if this point were in doubt, we have the further conclusive fact that every known instance of the transmission of typhoid through milk has been directly traced to its handling by a dairyman, or employee, who was suffering from the disease, or who had cases in his family which he was nursing, or from exposure to flies which had access to typhoid germs in the near neighborhood; or even from such infinitesimal pollution as the washing of the cans and milk utensils in water taken from an infected well or stream. The method now agreed upon, of keeping every possible contamination from human sources out of the milk, would absolutely prevent the transmission of typhoid, as well as all other diseases, except a small percentage of possible bovine tuberculosis.

The situation as to scarlet fever is practically identical. It was at one time regarded as possible that cattle suffered from a disease resembling scarlet fever, and germs resembling the group to which the organism of scarlet fever (which has not yet been positively identified) was believed to belong were isolated from the milk. But these findings were discovered to rest on errors and accidental contaminations, and it is now admitted that epidemics of scarlet fever traceable to milk are invariably due to infection of the milk from a case in the family of some one who has handled it. Boards of health nowadays keep a most watchful eye for the occurrence of cases of typhoid, scarlet fever, or diphtheria in the families of dairymen; and many of them require, as a condition of their permit to sell milk in the city or area controlled, that they shall file a certificate once a month from their family physician stating that he has examined the family and there is no contagious disease among them.

The danger, then, of the direct communication of infectious diseases is one that we are rapidly getting under control, and which, though real, is comparatively small, both as contrasted with the dangers from ordinary filth contamination, and with the total number of cases of the different diseases which actually occur.

This, then, leaves us free to concentrate our attention upon the single problem which will solve ninety per cent of all our milk difficulties and abolish ninety per cent of its dangers, and that is, simply *keeping dirt of every sort out of the milk from cow to consumer*. At first blush, when we consider the hundreds of different sources from which contamination can occur, and the millions upon millions of germs which lie in wait everywhere eager to plunge in and luxuriate in its fragrant coolness, this may seem like a utopian dream, a mere counsel of perfection. On the contrary, it is perfectly feasible, has a broad and substantial basis in results already accomplished, and is not merely desirable from a hygienic point of view, but practical and remunerative from a financial one as well. Dirt will soon come to be as unfashionable and as infrequent in the cowshed and in the dairy as it now is upon our faces and our table linen. When we recall that the earlier bacteriologic examinations of ordinary commercial milk taken from cans in the delivery wagon of the milkman or in stores showed from half a million to a million and a half of bacteria to the cubic centimetre — that is, from two million to six million to the teaspoonful — it can hardly be wondered that even sanitary enthusiasts were disposed to throw up hands of horror and dismay at the thought of even reducing their numbers to any appreciable degree, let alone preventing their occurrence. The caution with which they went at it in the first place strikes us now as positively amusing. It is a little on the order of the first temperance societies formed in New England. The members of these signed a pledge and registered a solemn oath to the effect that they would *not get drunk more than four times a year*, namely, Christmas Day, Sheep-shearing, Fourth of July, and Thanksgiving.

Similarly, our earliest milk reformers declared that all milk which showed more than half a million bacteria to the cubic centimetre should be regarded as dirty and unfit for human food. A few years later there arose a health officer of greater hardihood than usual, in Rochester, New York, who took a further step in advance, by declaring that within his jurisdiction no milk that contained more than one hundred thousand bacteria to the cubic centimetre should be regarded as "germ-free" and fit for human consumption. This has been known since as the "Rochester standard," and is the one which is now usually applied in our large cities.

But, of course, we could not long be content here; and realizing that the greatest danger and menace of milk was to young children, organizations of physicians and sanitarians formed themselves in different parts of the country for the purpose of inducing some dairyman to conduct his dairy in such a model manner as to produce a milk of unusual purity, for the use of nursing children, which they then agreed to use in their families and to recommend and prescribe for their patients. The cattle of the dairymen were to be inspected by competent veterinarians and tested with tuberculin; buildings were to be constructed in a special manner and kept in a given state of cleanliness, the dairies to be inspected at least once a month, and as often as the inspector or inspecting committee felt disposed to do so, without previous warning. In return for this, a certificate was issued to him, a copy of which could be pasted on each bottle of milk, stating that this milk had been produced under conditions favorable for purity, and was of a certain standard of wholesomeness. This came to be known as the "certified milk" plan, and is in extensive operation in all parts of the United States and of England. It works admirably, but, of course, in the nature of it, has never yet been applied to more than a comparatively small percentage of the total amount of milk produced. In order to check up the results of this cleanliness, regular bacteriological examinations of milk were made, and it was very soon found that the Rochester Standard, of a hundred thousand bacteria to the cubic centimetre, was far too low. This was rapidly raised, until ten thousand is now the maximum number of bacteria whose presence can be tolerated in milk for infants; and this will probably be reduced (and in some cases has already been reduced) to five thousand or even to one thousand.

In short, these methods, which are nothing more than simply strict, scrupulous cleanliness in the handling of the cows and of the milk, have reduced a population of over a *million* bacteria to the cubic centimetre to a *thousand!* And indeed, in many instances (as was the case in a certified dairy of this sort in the establishment of which I had the honor of assisting) counts would show as low as *two hundred and fifty* and *three hundred and fifty* bacteria instead of a million. Really dirty milk, by the way, will contain as high as four or even five million per cubic centimetre, while strictly clean milk will have as low as one hundred, or even fifty. It is therefore idle to say that milk cannot be delivered practically absolutely clean. It not only can be, but is, being so delivered in hundreds of dairies all over the country.

What is the method which has produced these magic results? Nothing miraculous, nothing wonderful or unusual in any way. Simply, Buffon's definition of genius, "An infinite capacity for taking pains." The cattle are first inspected by a veterinarian, and generally tested with tuberculin as a matter of routine, although in some cases this is applied only to animals whose condition may appear to his eye suspicious. Then the sheds in which they are to be milked are made with tight walls, with a good washable floor, usually either tarred or cemented and open to the roof, or with a tight floor overhead, so as to prevent the accumulation of dust in the loft and its sifting down into the milk or upon the coats of the cows.

Walls and ceiling are usually whitewashed, or else oiled and varnished and washed down with a hose twice daily after each milking time, as the floor always is. About half an hour before milking, the cattle are gone over with a currycomb and brush, and if there be any wet manure upon their legs or flanks this is washed off with a hose. This is to prevent dust, dirt, or bacteria falling from the coat and skin of the animal into the milk. Then, a few minutes before the milking begins, a man goes down the line with a pail of water and a damp cloth, wipes the udders and quickly moistens the hair of the flank on the side on which the milker sits. It is, of course, a necessity that all manure should be removed from the neighborhood of the barn at least once a week, and preferably daily, and that the cattle should not be allowed to stand or run in any yard in which there is mud or bogs of liquid manure, or filth of any description, which they can get upon their legs or sides. The milkers then wash their hands thoroughly in a small room provided for the purpose, don clean white duck or cotton suits and a cap to match (which are kept in a dust-tight closet), and proceed to milk. As soon as the pail is filled it is promptly carried into a milk-room which is kept scrupulously clean and free from dust, and poured through a cooler, which lowers its temperature to about fifty-five degrees, to check the development of stray germs. From this it is run into larger cans, which have been thoroughly cleaned and sterilized, and is tightly closed in and stored away in a cool place until it can be shipped to market or drawn directly into bottles, which are then hermetically sealed and placed in a cool place.

And what is the result? Milk handled like this will keep sweet at a reasonable temperature (below fifty-five degrees), not for days, but for weeks. Exhibition bottles of it have actually been shipped across the Atlantic and back again, and have been perfectly sweet at the end of the trip. Milk, like any other food, has no inherent tendency to sour, decay, or spoil. Such changes are all caused by the "bugs" that get into it. The old problem of spontaneous generation has again been tested and decided in the negative. Up to some two or three hundred years ago the basis for the classic belief that worms bred of themselves naturally in slime, was the fact that maggots would appear in meat when exposed to the air.

One day, about three hundred years ago, it occurred to a hard-headed embryo scientist to try the effect of covering the meat with close-woven wire netting. Result, no maggots. And this experiment, infantile in its simplicity as it appears to us, was the death-knell of the famous error of spontaneous generation. Pasteur's superb work on this problem was the basis of our whole magnificent system of antisepsis and asepsis, upon which modern surgery absolutely rests, and this is now being applied to the prevention of disease-producing changes in our foods. We are coming more and more to believe that, when a food has disagreed with us, the cause was not in the amount of that food taken, or in its over or under-ripeness, but from its having been contaminated by some definite germ, through careless exposure or filthy handling. Perfectly pure and germ-free food very seldom "disagrees."

Here, then, is our ideal, our flag which we have nailed to the mast: a clean milk, a pure milk, a germ-free milk, wholesome, nutritious, life-giving, one of the best and safest of all possible foods for infancy and childhood. What is the obstacle which now stands in the way of its realization? Chiefly a commercial one, the question of expense. As has been seen, there is no mystery or trick about its production. Merely strict "New England" or, better, "surgical" cleanliness and spotlessness, such as we insist upon on our tables, in our living-rooms and in our kitchens (more or less), and this appeals to us as both reasonable and sensible, as well as sanitary.

But it costs a little more in time and labor. And until the American public is willing to pay this additional two to four cents per quart it will continue to get cheap and dirty milk. A cynical colleague of mine once remarked that the public gets just as good milk as it deserves, in the sense of being willing to pay for it. While these model certified dairies are now in existence all over the land, and their value as an object-lesson is exceedingly great, and even those who do not patronize them are insisting upon their dairyman making at least a pretense of following their methods, they do not yet furnish more than five per cent and certainly not more than ten per cent of the total amount of milk now produced.

What is the reason? Chiefly and obviously, false notions of economy. Until any one has had practical experience as a milk enthusiast or sanitary officer, it is almost incredible the fuss which the average householder — even in perfectly comfortable circumstances — will make over an additional cent or two cents in the price of milk. I have known families in good, yes, wealthy, circumstances, who would purchase the munificent amount of two pints of certified milk per day at ten cents a quart for the baby of the family; while for the remainder of the children and the household these economists would buy a gallon of lactated sewage at six cents a quart.

Economy here as elsewhere, in the price of food, is one of the most dangerous of the petty vices. You can

generally depend upon it, when you are paying an unusually low price for a given article of diet outside of
certain seasonal variations, that you are getting a
dirty or inferior quality.

There is little need to point out how far ordinary
dairy, and even private, methods of handling milk fall
short of these standards. Much of it is due to sheer
ignorance and carelessness on the part of the dairymen and indifference on the part of the public. A cow
stable is expected to be a dirty, ramshackle, strong-
smelling sort of place. The yard surrounding it is
often innocent of drainage, and used as a place for the
accumulation of manure all winter long, until it is convenient to haul it out upon the land in the spring.

The trampling of the cows churns it into a bog of
mud and excrement, while from their breeding-place
in the piles of horse manure and other filth behind the
barn and pig-pen the flies swarm forth in their thousands in the spring and summer, to serve as myriad
conveyers of all kinds of filth to the milk.

The only reason why these conditions have not produced far more serious harm in the past is that the development of germs in milk, like other putrefactive
changes, takes time, and that where, as is usual on
farms and in country districts, the milk is drunk or
otherwise consumed within twelve or fourteen hours,
and often within five or six, of its production, there
has not been sufficient time for germs to render the
milk seriously unfit for food. But when, as is now the
case under modern conditions, the milk is shipped by
rail considerable distances, so that in our large cities

very little of it is less than twenty-four hours old before reaching the consumer, and a great deal of it thirty-six or even forty-eight hours old, then the situation becomes serious. This is the problem with which our boards of health are now struggling. Fortunately a majority of sanitary officers and of the medical profession are now thoroughly aroused to these dangers and eager for their removal. The chief problem is to educate the community up to the point of demanding clean milk and to being willing to pay the small additional charge.

Of course, the idea of economy is a totally false one, not merely from a sanitary point of view but from that of value received. The additional expense is not large, amounting, as most experts estimate it, to about the wages of one additional man to each thirty-five to fifty head of cows kept. Two to four cents a quart, according to the standards observed and the cost of feed in the locality, will amply cover it; and the consumer gets not merely protection from disease and death, which would be worth ten times this sum, but actually more than double this amount of additional nutritive value. In the first place, where cattle are submitted to this rigid inspection and given this excellent care, it does n't pay to milk and handle "scrubs."

Only cattle with good milking blood in them and giving a large amount and a high quality of milk can be profitably kept. In all certified dairies of my acquaintance, the additional per cent of butter-fat contained in the milk is alone worth the additional cost.

More important and vital yet, these myriads of swarming germs have not been idle, nor sitting about with
their mouths shut, while they have been multiplying
in that milk. They have been living on it meanwhile,
and while the milk to the naked eye and to the crude
chemical tests is still a mixture of water, casein, albumen, fat, and sugar, as a matter of fact a considerable percentage of the casein and other nutritive elements have been attacked and broken down by the
activity of these germs into substances which are not
only not nutritious, but actually poisonous to the organism. So that, just from the point of view of food-value,
milk which is swarming with bacteria is from ten per
cent to thirty per cent less valuable than it was in its
original condition.

If each consumer will first question his dairyman
about the methods used, or, better yet, go without previous warning and inspect the barns where his milk is
produced, and then and there offer him an additional
two cents a quart for really clean milk, or patronize
the dealer in his neighborhood whom he finds to be
producing the cleanest milk, the problem will soon be
solved.

"But," says some one who can no longer contain
himself, "what about pasteurization and sterilization?
If the trouble is due to germs, why not simply kill them
at once by boiling, and thus get rid at one stroke of all
the injurious consequences and dangers of dirty handling?" The answer to this is that pasteurization is at
best a choice between evils, a broken reed, which is
certain sooner or later to pierce the hand that leans

upon it. In the first place, it *will not clean dirty milk,* any more than running it through a straining cloth or combing it with a microscopic fine-tooth comb would. All it does is to kill the germs, leaving their already poisonous products practically unaltered. In the second place, its universal application would be a cloak for all kinds of careless, filthy, and unsanitary methods of production and handling of milk. Every careless farmhand, every greedy farmer, every unscrupulous dairyman would feel that he had been given a free hand to neglect any precaution which was irksome to him, because the milk was going to be pasteurized or sterilized anyhow, which would serve as a writ of indulgence and pardon for all crimes committed against it. Health experts look askance at pasteurization, except in large cities whose supply from four or five different states cannot be properly inspected on the farms and as a last resort for certain classes of milk for which consumers will only pay a low price, and which it is impossible to render sanitary in any other way.

Third, and most important, unless very skillfully used and carefully applied, it spoils the taste of milk so that children are unwilling to drink it. And the little rascals know what they are about. To their unspoiled palates, "Tastes good" means digestible and wholesome, "Doesn't taste good" means indigestible and dangerous. Sterilizing milk by raising it to the boiling temperature gives it a flat, disagreeable flavor, and often impairs the appetite of children who have to live upon it. Pasteurization, which is simply raising it to a temperature below boiling, but high enough to kill most microörganisms, was invented to remedy this defect. And this it does to a considerable extent. But it was found, not simply in private families, but also in homes and children's hospitals, that, while the babies fed on pasteurized milk no longer developed the acute intestinal diseases which were so fatal before, they often did not thrive and grow on it as they should, and many developed rickets or scurvy. So that no up-to-date children's hospital or home will to-day content itself with pasteurized milk, if it can possibly arrange to secure or stand the expense of a neatly clean supply of fresh, raw milk.

A little further investigation showed us that other changes, besides simply killing the germs, were produced in milk by exposing it to these high temperatures, which rendered it distinctly less digestible by children. Just what the nature of these changes is in detail is still under discussion. But one is that milk contains, in addition to its fat, proteid and sugar, a number of so-called *enzymes*, or ferments, which very markedly assist in its digestion in the human stomach and which play an important part in the changes which go on in the making and ripening of cheese. These *enzymes*, being living products, are destroyed or impaired by heating, as well as several of the proteids being coagulated and rendered less digestible.

In other words, milk to be perfectly wholesome and nutritious to a young child should be *eaten alive!* If you kill it, you have destroyed a considerable share of its value. This explains why milk which has been kept for a considerable period before being used, even though perfectly sweet, is less and less apt to agree with children for every six hours after the first ten, and after thirty-six hours is really unfit for use by infants.

The two great problems of our milk supply are: to keep it perfectly clean, and to get it to the consumer as quickly as possible after its production.

There appears to be little ground for the belief, occasionally mooted, that our modern milk supply is in any way inferior to that of fifty years ago, on account of the extraordinary specialization of our dairy cattle and the possible loss of constitutional vigor and stamina accompanying this.

It does make one gasp at first to realize that the modern Jersey or Holstein has been turned into a butter-making machine, a churn on legs, capable of turning out more than its own weight of butter per annum, or its own weight of milk every month! It does n't seem as if such a creature could have any room left for a heart or stomach, or any energy for such a thing as a constitution; though, as a matter of fact, these pure-bred cream producers, while unsuitable for beef purposes, are both healthy and long-lived. Nor is there any higher percentage of tuberculosis among them than among "scrub" cattle, which are stabled as large a proportion of the time.

It is believed that the better-balanced milks of less specialized breeds, like the Durham, Ayrshire, and Hereford, are more healthful, all-around foods for young children than the milk of the pure-bred Jersey, with its enormous percentage of fat and its exceedingly blue skim-milk.

But, apart from this, modern milk is far richer and fully as wholesome in every way as that of any age which has preceded it. An avalanche of public opinion in favor of pure, clean milk has started to move already, and woe betide those who from greed, filth or carelessness get in its track!

CHAPTER XIV

THE VACATION HABIT

THE best way to get a thing done well is often to do something else. It is easy to miss the mark by dwelling too long on your aim, or to drive the axe into your foot instead of the log by putting too much power into the stroke.

One of the secrets of success is to know when to stop and what to side-step. That is the chief advantage of a man over a machine. Whenever a man gets to working like a machine, meekly and mechanically grinding out the work that is fed to him by his boss, or his business, without taking a day or a week off occasionally to think it over and look at it from the outside and decide what's worth while and what is n't, then it is only a question of time when a machine will be invented to take his job. When it comes to patient, unremitting industriousness, a machine has a man beaten to a meringue. It is n't hours, it's ideas that count, in success in business as well as everywhere else.

Besides, it must be remembered that steady work is one of man's most recent accomplishments, biologically considered, and is proportionately dangerous. There is a world of painful historic truth in the indignant outburst of the old Oregon pioneer: "Durn you Easterners! We never hed to work fer a livin' till you come out here!" He lived in one of those golden valleys of the Pacific Slope where the woods were full of deer and the streams of fish and the glades crimson and purple with berries two thirds of the year round, and an acre of garden patch filled every gap in the dietary.

The two latest acquisitions of civilization have been habits of industry and the infectious diseases. And one is tempted sometimes to wonder which is the more deadly.

So there is no lack of convincing answers to the question — "Why is a vacation?" We might as well ask, "Why is sleep?" The steady and extraordinary growth of the vacation habit in American life rests on the soundest possible basis and is one of the most wholesome and encouraging signs of the times. Such junketings would have utterly puzzled if not horrified our Puritan ancestors and our agricultural forebears, as it does their survivors in the twentieth century. But it is a sign not of frivolity and idleness, but of harder and more efficient work than ever in the world before. We play more regularly and frequently than we ever did before because we are working harder and more enthusiastically in the intervals between. A vacation is not a vacuum nor a sign of mental vacancy.

The country vacation habit has come to stay for at least three good and sufficient reasons, any one of which would be enough to justify it permanently. First, because it is an excellent thing for a man to get clear outside of his business or profession for at least a month every year, and a day and a half every week, so as to get a good view of it from the outside and see it as it really is. Let him take time enough off out under the sky, among the woods and the meadows, the silver rivers and the singing brooks, to become a man again instead of a mere money-coining machine, and he will come back to his desk with a fresh taste in his mouth, an eye keen and clear to divide the important from the trivial, and a positive greed for attacking difficulties and solving problems.

The second reason for the vacation habit is that it restores to modern life that natural rhythm of work and rest, of busy season and slack season, that dependence upon season and weather and soil which was broken when we moved permanently indoors. It is almost impossible to run any business, which has to be carried on outdoors, six days out of the week and twelve months out of the year. The farmer, hard and monotonously constant the year round as his work is, has a period of months of enforced low pressure during the winter season every year, and days of enforced idleness every month on account of rain and storm and mud. Even the ditch-digger has his frost vacations and his rain holidays, besides those listed in the calendar.

Every activity of living stuff swings in rhythms. A period of rest and accumulation of energy, followed by a period of discharge in the form of work. No time for accumulation, no new discharge, save at the risk of overdraft and bankruptcy. Even the heart, that paragon of tireless persistency, that never skips nor stops until we stop, spends nearly half its time relaxing and resting. It is, literally, often the time which we waste that we gain. One of the most important practical questions to settle is what proportion of idleness will prove most profitable to us. How much time shall be spent in sagacious loafing instead of foolish busyness?

The third great reason for the vacation habit is that we work not in fractions, but as wholes. A man must not only put his brain but his heart and his body into and behind his work. The higher the pinnacle of efficiency to which we may raise one single faculty or power, the broader the basis of vigor and wide interests and enjoyment of life in all its phases we must put under it as a foundation, to keep it from tottering and becoming top-heavy. Shrewd and successful trainers have found that when an athlete is raising himself to the highest possible pitch in one particular feat, such as the high jump, for instance, there will come a period when he will reach a standstill and make no further progress. He must drop his jumping and run across country, or take an oar on the river, or box, or swim, give himself all-round athletic training for a couple of weeks. Then he can come back and within a day or two add an inch to his previous record.

The vacation habit brings the city dweller back to nature, back to that contact with the soil without which is no permanent health. Everything, from kings to cabbages, needs a root in the soil somewhere. It puts him in tune again with the wind on the heath, with the birds in the orchard, and the rivers in their rush. It shows him that the reallest joys of life are the simplest, the most natural, the cheapest — for they may be had for the asking, for the walking outdoors into — and the only ones that never grow stale and never bore us. It brings the city to the country and the country to the city, to the mutual advantage of both. It does almost as much, incidentally, for the farmer as it does for the city man and his family, giving him a new interest in life, new points of view, new markets for his produce right at his door, and putting a premium upon pure water supply and commodious and well-ventilated houses, running water in the house, and bathrooms, sewage and drainage, and the life-saving improvements of modern sanitation generally. It is hard to say whether the city man is coming to live more like a farmer, or the farmer more like the city man, or which has derived most benefit from the change. We may work in the cities, but we live in the country, as no nation ever did before.

Above all, never let school interfere with vacations. The holidays of a child are sacred. When the chestnut burrs are in session and the shagbark hickories drumming down upon their golden carpets, the wild grapes purpling in their clusters and the maples opening the leaves of their picture books of crimson and gold, it is no time for a growing child to be skewered to a blackboard or glued to a bench.

It was one of the sagest of the old Greek philosophers who sent a note to the schoolmaster asking that the boys be given a holiday, in order that they might learn something.

The groves were not merely man's first temples but his best schoolhouses, and are yet. Two thirds of all real education should be got out of doors. If a child is not making proper progress in school, take him out.

CHAPTER XV

THE instincts and the prejudices of the Cave Man die hard. For such countless generations has shelter been one of our chiefest needs, meaning as it did protection from the cold blast, the driving rain, the attack of enemies, that it has become one of our deepest and most ingrained instincts in any sudden danger to run to cover, as the fox hunts his earth.

It is little to be wondered at that upon such a basis civilized man should still make his "house his castle," the refuge to which he instinctively turns in any emergency. It is doubly natural that he should turn his eyes in this direction when the enemy that approaches is illness. A quarter of a million of years ago, the cruel Law of the Jungle taught him that to be sick meant to be eaten, — not merely by his natural enemies, but often by his own comrades. Hence the wounded animal crawls into the densest thicket that it can find, or into the farthest recess of its burrow, and the savage crawls into the darkest corner of his hut, to die.

Shelter, warmth, and concealment are the three things which even semicivilized man most instinctively craves, when mortally ill. What wonder, then, that the dawn of the Victorian Era, scarce seventy years ago, saw sick-rooms hermetically closed, darkened, overheated, the patient, if he had fever, piled with blankets, denied even the coolness of sheets, forbidden cold water, and permitted to drink only warm and nauseous decoctions of herbs and bitters?

Nature was cruel, Nature was not to be trusted, everything that the patient instinctively wanted was sure to be bad for him. In comes that glorified, systematized common sense which we call Modern Science, throws open doors and windows, lets in the sunlight, urges the patient to drink cool water by the gallon, covers him with the lightest of sheets, puts him to soak in cool water whenever his temperature rises above a certain pitch. Behold, the death-rate is promptly cut in two, and is now rapidly sinking toward one fourth of its former level in most diseases!

One of our first practical hints of the value of fresh air in the sick-room came during our Civil War, when it was noted that cases of both typhoid and pneumonia, which for want of proper hospital accommodation were cared for in tents, showed a distinctly lower death-rate than those in the hospital wards.

Naturally, the disease to which the method, not merely of letting air into the sick-room, but of taking the sick-room into the open air, was first applied, and has won its most magnificent victories in, was pulmonary tuberculosis, or consumption. This was due chiefly to two facts. First, that the patient was suffering from a disease of the lungs, which obviously impaired his breathing powers, and naturally it was advisable that whatever air he could get into his lungs should be of the purest and best possible. Secondly, that the disease lasted for months and even years, before it actually confined the patient to his bed, so that it was easy to arrange for his sitting out of doors, at least in the daytime.

It is difficult to realize, or even imagine, what an extraordinary revolution this new idea has wrought in the treatment of consumption, unless we either talk with some gray-headed physician or with one of our grandparents. However, it is not necessary to go so far back as this for typical instances. I can personally recall a case of consumption in a well-to-do and intelligent family in England, in which not merely every door and window was kept scrupulously closed and a roaring fire kept going on the hearth even in the early summer, but the room selected was the second of a suite, and the anteroom was also kept tightly closed, and every one coming in to see the patient, including his physician, was required to remain at least ten to fifteen minutes in its heated atmosphere until his clothing was sufficiently warm to remove all possible danger of "bringing a chill" into the inner room. Needless to say the patient died.

The change came gradually. Windows were opened, a grudging inch at the top during the daytime, in fear and trembling. Then the patient was carried on to the porch when the sun shone, and finally, completely out into the open. But it was long before we could rise superior to that awful bogey of the deadliness of "night air." As early as the days of the Crimea, Florence Nightingale had sharply challenged this superstition, with the short and pithy statement that

"Night air is all the air there is to breathe at night." The prejudice against it is a superstition, pure and simple, an inheritance of the days when the midnight mirk was peopled with ghosts and goblins and demons, ready to swoop in from the blackness and carry off the soul of the luckless sleeper, a feeling well illustrated in the title of our only surviving demon, the "Prince of Darkness." But it dies awfully hard. And it is difficult to make many of our patients even to-day believe that the coldest and dampest and "rawest" of night air is better for respiratory purposes than the best that can be had in a tightly closed, self-heated, and self-poisoned bedroom.

The next dragon of superstition which lay coiled across our path was the dreaded *Draft*. Fresh, even cold, air was an excellent thing, but it must be still, and with no perceptible motion. If it moved so that you could feel it blow upon you, then "Angels and ministers of grace defend us!" you were sitting in that deadliest of dangers, a *Draft*, and heaven only knows what terrible thing might happen to you! According to popular belief, drafts are capable of causing consumption, pneumonia, rheumatism, lumbago, neuralgia, and last but not least, that whole Pandora's box of evils, common colds and their consequences.

But this bogey has melted into thin air almost as completely as the night-air terror. As regards consumption, we now know that it is not caused by pure, fresh, outside air, however damp, raw, or cold, but by a definite bacillus, which can only breed and spread in close, airless, and sunless rooms. Let in drafts and sunshine, and you have made a room uninhabitable for the tubercle bacillus.

The other evils attributed to drafts are rapidly falling into the same category. Pneumonia is due to an equally definite germ, which can only attack a human body whose vital resistance is depressed by foul air, overwork, underfeeding, or bad habits, and our best results in the cure of it are obtained by putting our patients right out into the open air in winter time.

Rheumatism occurs in just as violent form in hot climates as in cold, and nearly as frequently, while as for the "Common Cold," at least three fourths of all cases are pure infections caught from a previous case, and their prevalence in winter is due not to the cold weather, but to the overcrowding and the overheating of houses, schoolrooms, theaters, etc., at this time of year, while at the same time our vital resistance is lowered by cutting down upon our summer life in the open air.

Even the sensation of chill which we experience when we are "catching cold," and which we believe to be due to some imagined lowering of the temperature, or hitherto unperceived draft, has in most cases nothing to do with cold air, but is merely the initial chill or rigor with which a feverish attack often begins. If you were to slip a thermometer under your tongue when the chills are running up and down your backbone and you are beginning to sneeze, you would find that it registered generally anywhere from 100° to 104°! The quaint old ethnic custom, found in every quarter of the globe, of saying whenever you hear any one

sneeze, "God bless you!" "The Saints protect you!"
"*Gesundheit!*" etc., — based as it was upon the naïve
belief that the soul left the body when you sneezed,
and that its place would instantly be taken by some
evil spirit unless the good spirits were appealed to for
protection, — had a real basis in fact. It was in error
only in supposing that an evil spirit was about to take
possession. As a matter of fact, it had already entered
the body in the form of a bacillus. In fact, the draft'
dread is, as Dr. Norman Bridge has aptly termed it,
the Draft Fetish of modern times, well-nigh as irrational and unfounded as the superstition of the Evil
Eye and the unluckiness of the number 13.

Outdoors is self-ventilating. It is only when we begin to cut chunks out of it with boards and bricks,
and inclose them box fashion between four walls, establishing a monopoly on a cubic section of the Universe, that we begin to get into trouble.

Outdoors, Nature will do our ventilating for us.
Indoors, we have to do it for ourselves. And with all
our "gude conceit o' oorsel's," we must admit that we
have n't made much of a success of it so far, either
practically or theoretically. With all our ingenuity
the best that we have been able to accomplish in the
line of ventilating is by abandoning our monopoly
upon our room space and calling in Nature to do the
job. In other words, by making our rooms indoors, as
nearly as possible, parts of all outdoors, by throwing
doors and windows wide, either constantly, or at frequent intervals, according to the temperature.

All attempts at or methods of ventilating a room at

second hand have so far proved unsatisfactory. In the majority of cases, the more elaborate and complicated and ingenious they are, the greater the dissatisfaction experienced with them by those who have to breathe the air. They work beautifully and ventilate to perfection, to the delight and satisfaction of their inventors and the engineers who operate them. But the children and the teachers in schoolrooms supplied by them tell a different story. They will deliver systematically, so many cubic feet per hour, per child, of a chemically pure mixture of oxygen and nitrogen, free from carbon dioxide, with all dust and impurities filtered out, sterilized by heat, cooled to the precise temperature at which it is to be inhaled into the lungs. —

But it is n't fresh air.

It is cooked air, killed air, with all the life and freshness taken out of it. What *Mr. Mantalini* would have called "a demnition product." It seems to be like sterilized milk or distilled water, — germ-free, — theoretically perfect, — but you can't live and thrive on it.

Practically, we must judge fresh air like the classic "handsomeness," not so much by what it *is*, but by what it *does*. If it makes those who breathe it under normal conditions *feel* fresh, it *is* fresh. If it does n't, it is n't. We must always remember that we are not ventilating rooms, but their occupants.

This is no reflection or criticism upon the inventors of systems of ventilation. On the contrary, it is a frank confession of our ignorance as hygienists, so far, as to exactly what constitutes "pure air," or, to put it more precisely, what the elements are which render air impure or unfit for breathing. The better class of inventors and engineers have, in the language of the day, "delivered the goods" according to our specifications. We were even more disappointed than they, to find that they did not fill the bill. But an honest confession is exceedingly good for the soul. And our comparative failure in our more ambitious efforts has led us to reëxamine more carefully and radically what are the qualities which we wish to secure, and what are those which we wish to avoid, in good air for breathing purposes. In other words, what is really fresh air.

Strange as it may seem, this comparative failure of our most elaborate and theoretical attempts at ventilation, while theoretically discouraging, is really just the contrary from a practical point of view. In short, it has led us to define fresh air as a working concept, as air which is simply what its name implies, *fresh* from outdoors. Wherever you get this into a room, you get good "lung food." Wherever you don't, poor lung food. In other words, the simple, everyday method of ventilating, which is within reach of ninety per cent of us, day and night, through open windows and doors, is the one that gives not only the best results, but the only satisfactory results. It requires constant and intelligent attention. It must be, as the artist Turner said of his colors, "mixed with brains." But that is one of its advantages. One of the things which we had forgotten, but which our failure to secure automatic and perfect ventilation without thought or effort, has brought us back to with emphasis, is that it is not only impossible, but against good hygienic policy to attempt to ventilate any room in such a way that healthy individuals will want to remain there more than three or four hours at a stretch, except when asleep.

Practically one of the best ways to ventilate a room is to turn its occupants out of doors at regular and frequent intervals. This is particularly true of school children, indoor workers, and busy housewives. Man is not able to live indoors. While his body engine is run chiefly by the bottled-up sunshine contained in his food, and its furnace draft is supplied by the oxygen of the atmosphere wherever found, he still must take a considerable proportion of both these sources of energy and purification at first hand in the open air.

Perhaps a very brief statement of the things that we have unlearned — the things that we know we *don't* know about fresh air and foul air — would be profitable here, for the purpose of emphasizing the value of a direct appeal to Nature and her methods.

It must be premised that this subject of ventilation is one of the most complicated and difficult which confronts the sanitarian, and that only the crudest and roughest outline of it can be presented here, and that it involves many necessarily dogmatic statements. In the first place, inasmuch as the burnings or combustions in the body, which constitute so large a part of life and its processes, are carried out by oxygen, which forms about one fourth of the bulk and of the active part of atmospheric air, it was naturally supposed that foulness of air was due to a diminution in the amount of oxygen.

Much to our surprise, the earliest of our systematic studies completely exploded this impression, since air was found to become impossible of respiration long before the percentage of oxygen had been exhausted below that which was necessary to sustain life. The foulest of indoor air in the worst tenement rooms still contains from twenty to fifty per cent more oxygen than is needed to support life. More than this, it was quickly discovered that our converse impression, that oxygen was literally the "breath of life," and increase of the oxygen in the air would increase the vigor and rapidity of life processes, was equally unfounded. While inanimate materials will burn in an atmosphere of pure oxygen with much greater vigor, and substances like a watch spring, for instance, which would not burn at all in common air, will blaze and consume with great rapidity in pure oxygen, life processes are not similarly affected. The mouse or bird, for instance, which is put under a bell filled with pure oxygen, while it will run around with great vigor for a few minutes, dies almost as rapidly and quite as certainly as if plunged into pure nitrogen, the other constituent of the air, or into water. In fact, its apparent signs of increased life and animation are merely the first symptoms of irritant poisoning.

So that the scores of well-meant efforts to supply an increased amount of oxygen in the air of schoolrooms and theaters have completely gone by the board, as they utterly failed to relieve the sensations of closeness, headache, and discomfort, even before they were found to be based upon a mistaken theory. Even the much-vaunted apparatuses for liberating ozone in buildings, advertised under the alluring caption of "Mountain Air in Your Bed-room," are on no better basis. For physiologists have now shown that the blood in the lungs will absorb oxygen at a comparatively fixed rate, determined by the demands of the body, and that this rate cannot be increased by increasing the amount of oxygen present in the air. So that, for instance, even the inhalation of pure oxygen in diseases of the lungs has yielded disappointing results, and is gravely questioned as to its theoretical basis.

Next after the oxygen-hunger theory came naturally that of the excess of waste products in the air, as constituting foulness. And as far the largest and most important waste gas thrown off from the lungs is carbon dioxid, or as it is often inaccurately termed, *carbonic acid*, it was natural to clutch at this as the cause of the injurious symptoms. A careful study of the percentage composition of expired and foul air, however, soon led us to a similarly surprising conclusion in regard to this gas. What made us the more ready to blame it was that it was known to be both poisonous and incapable of respiration, as is abundantly illustrated by its accumulation at the bottom of wells and in badly ventilated shafts and workings, where, under the expressive name of "choke damp," it has caused the loss of hundreds of lives of miners and well-diggers. Careful experimentation, however, both by the experimenters upon themselves and upon animals,

showed that long before the proportion of carbon dioxid in second hand air had reached an even mildly
poisonous level, the air had become utterly unfit for
respiration, and would cause headache, dizziness, and
sense of suffocation, and even fainting and collapse.
So striking was the disproportion that only about one
tenth of the amount of carbon dioxid necessary to
produce poisonous symptoms when mixed with pure
air is found to be present in the air of the foulest room
or experimental chamber.

As the well-known effects of breathing foul air were
so obviously similar to those of a depressant or narcotic
poison, it was next supposed that certain other excre-
tory substances in gaseous form which were thrown
off from the lungs or skin, much smaller in amount
than the carbon dioxid, but more intensely poisonous,
were the cause of the disturbances. But the most careful search for and study of these products has proved
so far almost equally disappointing. They are, it is
true, present, both in the air breathed out from the
lungs and in the air of foul or stuffy rooms where considerable numbers of individuals are present, as any
one with a normal sense of smell can very readily discover for himself. But they are only discoverable, in
any form as yet identified, in exceedingly small quantities, mere traces, in fact. And further, such of them
as have been definitely isolated are found to be but
weakly poisonous, even in considerable amounts. So
that in the amounts in which they are actually present, they can hardly be regarded as in any way injurious. Moreover, it is found that by the use of

vapors or sprays which precipitate or neutralize these poisonous products, the sense of oppression and suffocation was not in the least relieved nor the air made more breatheable.

One curious positive fact was, however, elicited, and that was that a very considerable element in the sense of oppression and suffocation was increased temperature, or heat. And that when this was reduced by the circulation of ice water or cold vapors through pipes surrounding the experimental chamber, the sense of oppression was strikingly relieved. Even such an apparently lifting-one's-self-by-one's-own-boot-straps sort of a procedure, as setting the foul air in rapid motion by means of an electric fan would also relieve the sense of suffocation. This was due to the cooling of the surface of the body by these currents which explains why the use of the electric fan, even in a comparatively tightly closed room, or the waving of an Indian *punkah* which simply swashes the air backward and forward, without causing any continuous current in one direction, gives such a relief from the sense of suffocation in hot weather.

In short, all chemical, scientific, or patent mechanical methods of treating the air, whether by the generation of oxygen or ozone, the precipitation or washing out of the carbonic acid, or nitrogenous excreta, have failed utterly to relieve the oppression and distress due to breathing foul air. And even the supply of a given number of cubic feet of washed and sterilized and warmed air will only in part relieve them, leaving us face to face with the present and long tested method of letting in an abundant rush of fresh air from the exterior as the only effective cure.

Of course, the objection will at once be raised that this method, simple as it sounds and effective as it unquestionably is, though all very well in summer time, is difficult of operation in cold weather. In a climate where "'t is always May," we may sit and work and sleep in rooms with the window or windows and even the door wide open, but hardly in our Northern December. This is unquestionably the most serious practical crux of the whole problem. One of the chief reasons why the death-rate — not merely from diseases of the lungs, but from all causes, is invariably in the North Temperate Zone anywhere from ten to forty per cent higher in winter than in summer — is this difficulty in combining a proper supply of fresh air with the modicum of heat necessary to life. The problem, however, is far from a hopeless one. In fact, the solution is already in plain sight: with a fair amount of intelligence, and not too much economy in the matter of fuel.

In the first place, like every other situation in nature, it has its compensations. We have already on our side in the winter time a natural force tending to promote ventilation, which is absent in summer, in the shape of the higher temperature of the indoor air. Every one, of course, knows that air, like most substances, expands as it becomes warmer. When it expands, it naturally becomes lighter and tends to rise above the colder air. This law is at the bottom of the well-known roaring draft, which can be not merely felt, but heard, and even seen, in an open fireplace with a brisk blaze going. Now, our houses and rooms are supposed to be water-tight and as nearly airtight as possible. At least it is the aim of the builder to make them so. But, practically, they fall very far short of this, not only on account of the innumerable possibilities for leaks and cracks around door and window openings, under the eaves of roofs, at the inlet or escape of ventilating pipes and the wide open chimneys, but also for the reason that most of our building materials are more or less porous or permeable to air. Wood, unless very heavily and frequently painted, is distinctly so; while a brick, as is well known, can be readily used for filtration purposes, and any form of pressure apparatus capable of raising the pressure of air can drive an appreciable current through a brick wall.

Consequently, our entire houses in winter time being warmed both by our heating and cooking fires, and by heat given off from the bodies of inmates, act as a sort of big slow-draft base-burner stove, sending up a current of warm air, from doors, windows, roof, chimney, etc., and sucking in through walls, windows, and other apertures a continuous current of cold air, to take its place.

So that we really secure in winter, with anything like an adequate amount of windows and doors, and a not too abominably tight and perfect house construction, a considerable amount of involuntary, or what might be termed natural, ventilation. This, however, is far from being adequate for our demands. And while we deeply regret to have to disturb such a hoary and venerable belief, with so many delightful and comforting assurances connected with it, as that perfect ventilation is obtained by an open fireplace, necessity compels us to state that the natural method of ventilation, either by an open fireplace or an ordinary stove, is neither adequate nor satisfactory. It is not adequate, because except in the leakiest of rooms, the amount of change made in the air is insufficient. And, second, and most vital, because the cold air that enters for the most part comes in at a level where it is of the least value for respiration, namely, from one to three feet above the floor, and is sucked directly into the fire and shot up the chimney; thus producing an unpleasant draft upon the feet and lower limbs while doing very little to purify the air at or above the level of the mouth, which is the only air in the room that we can breathe. In other words, the fire gets the bulk of the fresh air, and leaves the occupants of the room the foul air, which, being warm, tends to rise toward the ceiling. The fire gets plenty of fresh air free; but it does n't give any of it back for the use of the human occupants of the room. All the benefit they get is from such of the cold air as they may be able to catch during its rush toward the fireplace. Hence, while an open fire provides a much larger involuntary change of air than a closed stove, its mere presence in a room by no means solves the problem of ventilation for that room, as is often fondly supposed. It is a very pretty thing to look at, and an excellent means of providing healthful exercise, by causing the occupants of the room to take their turn in standing or sitting directly in front of it, turning themselves round and round, like meat on a spit, while so doing, to keep from being chilled on one side, and roasted on the other. But it is almost as much of a broken reed for ventilation as for warming in really severe weather. As an ornamental addition to a room already really warmed by furnace or steam heat, and as a temporary resource and addition to comfort during the inclement weather of spring and fall, when the entire heating system is not in operation, it is most excellent. But it can only be regarded as an more or less ornamental embellishment to methods of real ventilation and real heating.

That pitiable modern parody upon the open fire — the gas-log — is even less useful as a means of ventilation and may easily become an enemy in disguise. The combustion is so rapid, in proportion to the heat generated, and such large amounts of carbon dioxide are formed, that it does n't draw as well as the open wood or coal fire, with its slower and noiser and brighter combustion. So that while part of the poisonous gases of combustion pass up the chimney and draw a certain amount of air through the room in the process, another part are exceedingly likely, except in very well-built gas-grates, to pass out into the room. The strong tendency of modern builders is to economize on material, and turn the roomy, old-fashioned chimney into a mere eight-inch or even six-inch pipe. Further than this, in the large volume of gas poured out and the often inadequate expanse of surface over which it is burned, some part of the gas is almost certain to escape full combustion and to be given off, not as the comparatively harmless carbon dioxid, but as the deadly carbon monoxid, the gas which has such a deadly record in the many distressing fatalities from badly arranged gas-heaters in bathrooms and elsewhere. In a very considerable percentage of cases, a gas-log produces a sense of discomfort and odors which are distinctly disagreeable and oppressive, especially to one coming fresh from the open air. In fact, to be perfectly safe it is advisable to count the average gas-grate as adding to the pollution of the air, instead of diminishing it, and ventilate accordingly. Gas-stoves and heaters that have no flue should, of course, always be so counted and allowed for, if used at all. And even the ordinary gas-jet is a greedy competitor of the human occupants of a room, for whatever fresh air may be present.

In ventilating a room, the gas-jet can be roughly counted as an extra person, and the gas-stove or gas-log as from two to five such, though all of these produce from three to five times this amount of carbon dioxid.

Modern progress in civilization has in this respect been in the direction of improvement, for the electric incandescent light is far the most wholesome method of illumination which has yet been devised, adding no injurious element to the air, except possible very minute traces of nitric acid from the arc light. Nor is this advantage merely imaginary, as one of the London banks reported some years ago that among its several hundred employees, the absences on account of illness had been distinctly reduced since the substitution of electric light for gas. So that the extra labor gained had more than compensated for the increased cost.

The inevitable tendency of hot air to rise presents us with our most troublesome problems in indoor ventilation. It illustrates one of the penalties and responsibilities of monopoly. Out of doors it is the mainspring of Nature's great system of world ventilation. Without it, our climate would consist of a belt of scorching tropics and a zone of frozen North, with little temperate zone between. The air at the equator and in the tropics, heated by the vertical rays of the sun, rises rapidly from the earth's surface to the higher levels of the atmosphere. As it rises, it creates a partial vacuum, into which the cool air from the zones above and below rushes, to become heated and rise in its turn.

The risen hot air flows toward the Poles, becomes cold and falls to earth to be again sucked toward the equator keeping a perpetual aerial Gulf Stream flowing round and round both North or South of the equator and equalizing the temperature all over the globe. Local "chimneys" and "whirlpools" due to heating and cooling, known as the "lows" and "highs" of our weather charts, cause the winds and keep the air outdoors thoroughly sucked and perpetually in motion.

The same balancing process attempts to carry itself out indoors — with but poor success.

The heated foul air from our lungs or from our

stoves rises and attempts to escape, but is blocked by the ceiling. Most of the cool fresh air that flows into a room naturally, by doors, open fire-places, or windows open at the bottom comes in near the floor and stays there because it is heavier than the hot foul air above. If we keep the windows shut at the top and thus prevent the rising hot air from escaping, it will bank or dam up in the upper half of the room, so that it is unfortunately quite possible for us to be sitting with our heads, which do practically all the breathing for our bodies, in a stratum or upside-down "lake" of hot foul air, and our legs and feet in a pool of cold fresh air, which is of little more use to us for breathing purposes than if it were outdoors. Whichever way you turn, whatever device you resort to, you find yourself faced with this *impasse* — that you cannot keep the warm air down, any more than the good man of proverbial literature. It would take volumes even to describe the devices and systems which have been invented for the purpose of getting rid of this difficulty — the hot, hot ceiling, and the cold, cold floor. The more vigorously and effectively you heat your home, — and it must be remembered in all problems of heating and ventilation that it is not heat in the abstract we are dealing with, but heated or warmed air, — the more promptly it will rise to the ceiling and leave the floor cold.

One day, however, a great truth dawned upon the mind of a distracted householder, and that was, that the floor of one room is practically the ceiling of the room below. Follow this principle down through the house and into the cellar, apply it there, and the problem of floor heating, while still a perplexing one, is more nearly solved than it ever has been before. A cellar should not simply be a place high enough to hold a furnace and big enough to store coal and ashes, but a place for drying, warming, and ventilating the floors of the living-rooms above. A warm, dry cellar is literally and actually the foundation of a warm, dry, well-ventilated house. The evolution of the cellar is an interesting study of the slow development of human intelligence, devised originally simply as a subterranean frost-proof pit or cave under the house, in which could be stored, first, wines, and later, apples, potatoes, cabbages, and perishable fruits, together with milk, butter, and cheese. It was next utilized, when the absurd insufficiency of stoves and fire-places for heating purposes was recognized, as a convenient place to put the furnace, down out of the way. Then it was raised aboveground to make the furnace draw better, lighted and ventilated, until now it has become one of the most important sections of the house for sanitary purposes.

It should be lighted, heated, and ventilated, winter and summer, as carefully and scrupulously as any other part of the house. When this is done, we are rid at one stroke of dampness, with all its well-known rheumatic and other disease-breeding tendencies, of bad smells from decaying vegetables, accumulations of dirt in dark corners, leakage of sewage and other pipes, which are now in plain sight instead of buried in the earth; cold floors and all the injurious effects which come from dampness and moist decay all through the house.

The complaint that heating the cellar has spoiled its use for storage purposes is simply a proof of its advantages. For nothing could be more unsanitary, in this twentieth century, than to pile vegetables, cheese, and fruits together in dark bins and adjoining compartments, nibbled at and raced over by mice, rats, and cockroaches, imparting the odors of decay from cabbages and rotting apples to milk, cream, and cheese, and sending their combined aroma streaming constantly upward through the house on the natural upward automatic ventilation current of which we have spoken.

From a hygienic point of view, it is a matter of comparative indifference what is the source or character of the heat supplied to a room, providing it be abundant enough to permit of the free admission of cool, fresh air through open windows. The advantages of the different forms of heating — hot-air furnaces, steam, hot water — may be decided entirely upon the grounds of their efficiency, expense, and ease or difficulty of operation. Here again, modern improvements are not merely not unhealthful, but distinctly superior from a sanitary point of view, for reasons which have already been explained.

A stove as a means of heating must really be considered out of date; for every house should be provided with a cellar, both as a means of dryness and ventilation, and for warming the floors of the main living-rooms. With the improvements and simplifications that have been made in construction, any house of more than four rooms can be equipped with a furnace and heated by it at a comparatively trifling initial expense, and with actual saving of labor and fuel, to say nothing of coal dirt and ashes all through the living-rooms. Once get a proper amount of heat distributed about the different rooms, then, if your window space is properly arranged for purposes of lighting and ventilation the problem of fresh air is in your own hands.

Incidentally, it may be remarked that another of the advantages of furnace heat is that it warms the hallways and passages of a house, so that there is no longer that dread and acute discomfort from leaving a door partially open, which is a great practical advantage in winter ventilation.

The remaining difficulties which are to be faced, given these conditions, are the dread of a draft and the impression that changes in temperature are to be avoided, that equable temperature is ideal. Both of these rest largely on misconceptions, the first of which we have already discussed at some length. A current of cool, fresh air, in a well-lighted, well-ventilated room, even if it blows in moderate degree on the face or body, seldom does harm, and almost always does good. As to equable temperature and constant heat, this, instead of being beneficial, is unnecessary if not actually injurious. In studies of climate, from the point of view of health, the conclusion was reached some years ago, and is being strengthened every day, that while a mild and equable climate is of distinct advantage to invalids who are unable to endure shocks and changes, for individuals in average health, plenty of change, both between day and night, and between different seasons, is not only not injurious, but stimulating and helpful. Even in hospitals, where patients are compelled to remain in one room and one atmosphere day and night, it has been found beneficial to deliberately arrange for one or more variations of temperature in the course of the twenty-four hours. The night temperature is required to be at least ten degrees lower than day temperature. More than this, experiments in the extension of the open-air treatment for tuberculosis, typhoid, pneumonia, diptheria, and other diseases has led physicians to favor the frequent throwing open of both doors and windows in hospital wards during the day, with, of course, marked lowering of the temperature, and providing all wards with balconies and porches on to which the beds of the patients can be pushed out during suitable weather. So that even if your open window causes a draft, and you have to get up from your work or your sewing every half-hour or so to open or close it on account of the heating-up or chilling of the room, do not imagine that these alternations are risking your health or liable to do you any serious harm. It is n't healthy to sit perfectly still in any room, no matter how ventilated, for more than an hour at a stretch. And it is of great practical importance for as many of our living-rooms as possible and all our bedrooms in summer to be provided with doors or French windows opening directly on a porch, through which their occupants may step quickly into the open air at all hours. Any room which is lived in or worked in, no matter how elaborate and effective a system of artificial ventilation it may possess, should have doors and windows thrown wide open and the winds of heaven allowed to blow through it at least every two hours. Bed rooms should be kept in this condition all night long, through open windows, except in the stormiest and most inclement weather.

We have frankly confessed that we do not as yet know exactly what constitutes or causes air to be foul. Fortunately our difficulty is only a theoretic, not a practical, one. Though the element of foulness in air escapes in large measure our laboratory tests, we have one practical test at the disposal — I might have said in the hands — of every one of us, which is thoroughly efficient, and that is our sense of smell. If, on going into a room from the open air, we find that it smells "mousey," or stuffy, or close, then we may be sure that that room is not properly ventilated. We can, of course, unfortunately educate ourselves to stand anything, and the sense of smell is no exception. So that we must be prepared for the rejoinder, from those that have been occupying that room when we enter, that they "do not notice anything out of the way." The offensive odors have accumulated so gradually that their olfactory nerves have become deadened, so that they no longer affect them unpleasantly. If we would unhesitatingly and vigorously "follow our noses" in the matter of the air we breathe as well as of the food we eat, we should escape many a danger to health.

CHAPTER XVI

SPRING FEVER AND SPRING CLEANING

THE best cure for spring fever is to loaf in the sun or go fishing. It is Nature's divine intimation to halt for a few moments and watch how she Does Things. In one sense, spring fever is a penalty of civilization. To our savage as well as our animal ancestors, spring was a time of awakening from the winter's torpor, a time of throbbing pulse, of eager running hither and thither, of combat and mating and rioting. It was the real New Year, and should be ours instead of that pale, frost-bitten shadow of a shade which the almanacs have deluded us into anæmically celebrating in midwinter.

But now, with Puritan perversity, civilized man celebrates the real glad birth of the New Year in April with spring medicines and spring cleanings and the bankruptcies and heartburnings of Easter bonnets. And when, instead of caroling with the birds and gamboling with the young lambs and reveling in the young green of the grass and the scent of the woodland flowers, we feel depressed and headachy and fur-lined and bilious, we say we have spring fever, and proceed to dose ourselves with a "yarb" tea or a blood medicine. It is a slander upon Nature.

We have nobody but ourselves to blame for spring fever in any disagreeable sense of the term. The impulse to sit in the sun or roam the fields and woods and hills and watch Nature work her yearly miracle is wholesome and sound. Even if we are farmers, if we have done our winter work properly, we have the right to indulge it, and will be the better for so doing the rest of the summer. For the hard-worked business man, a week or even three days or a week-end vacation in the open air at this time of year will prevent a score of breakdowns and be worth a month in August.

Spring is not a time for work, but for rest and meditation and wondering enjoyment.

That curse of the walled house, that Bacchanalian orgy of the model housekeeper, spring cleaning, with its scrappy stand-up meals and its taste of soap in every dish, is the penalty paid for a whole winter's dirtiness, of windows never open, and often actually battened down and stripped. A properly kept house ought not to be any dirtier in spring than at any other time of the year, and never should be allowed to grow so filthy as to call for such a volcanic eruption of cleansing. It should be literally turned out of doors every day all the year round. Take up your dirt-and germ-catching and disease-breeding carpets, hotbeds for hatching stuffy smells and disease bugs, oil or paint your floors so that they can be wiped, not swept, really clean every day and washed down once or twice a week. Use rugs small enough to be readily taken out of doors and shaken and beaten, and your house will no more need a spring cleaning than you need a spring bath.

There is a classical story of a young lady who, hunting up the bathroom in a rural hotel, found a dust-lined tub and no hot water. Her indignant complaint was met by the landlord with the crushing reply that there "war n't no way of heating enough hot water, — an', besides, this hain't the right time of year to take a bath."

The right time of year for giving a house a bath is every week. Spring house-cleaning is a sign of dirty instead of spotless housekeeping, probably necessary when man was a cave dweller, but out of date now.

Let the real Gold Dust Twins, sunlight and fresh air, come into every room in your house the year round, and they will do your cleaning for you without any necessity for the fevered debauch of scrubbing-buckets and soap and snuffles in the first glad days of spring. The model housewife, in her frenzy of purification, with blood in her eye and cobwebs on her brow and whitewash on her tucked-up skirt, looks more like an avenging fury than the gentle and benignant goddess of the hearth. Small wonder that her husband flees to his club, her children to the neighbors until, her fury spent, she is ready to go comfortably to bed or to the hospital and leave the house in peace.

Tennyson assures us that: —

"In the spring a ruddier crimson glows upon the robin's breast;
In the spring the wanton lapwing gets himself another crest;
In the spring a livelier iris shines upon the burnished dove;
In the spring the young man's fancy lightly turns to thoughts of love."

But the fancy of the busy house-mother and the harassed head of the family turn to thoughts of spring medicines and blood purifiers. And sad and sufficient reason have they to do so, for this joyous season of swelling buds and of odors of paradise is the precise time of the year when the family doctor expects to be most nearly worked to death; when the death-rates of several of our great diseases, pneumonia, bronchitis, tuberculosis, meningitis, reach their highest pitch. This is the season at which we are most urgently warned against leaving off our winter flannels too soon, or sitting out on the porch in the evenings, for fear we will catch cold. All of which is due to the "explosion" of a series of poisons which we have allowed to go on piling up in our bodies all winter long, just like the dirt in our house up to spring cleaning. It is n't the fresh air and the mild weather or the drafts we sit in, or even the wet feet that we get in flower-gathering or fishing or duck-hunting, that give us these colds and other calamities; it is simply the "bugs" that we have been harboring in our own interiors through long winter months in stuffy bedrooms and dusty offices and workshops.

This can be positively prevented in the case of pneumonia, for instance, whose highest death-rate sadly, and paradoxically, is in late March, April, and early May. Its germ or "bug" has the peculiar power of living for weeks and even months in the mouths of healthy human beings without causing any trouble, until, from some cause or other, the vital resistance is lowered and it breaks through the breastworks and attacks the body. The mouths of large numbers of city dwellers have now been examined by city boards of health every month throughout the winter, especially in the crowded slums, and it has invariably been found that, whereas at the beginning of the winter not more than from two to five per cent of all mouths would contain the pneumococcus, this percentage went steadily up month after month, until, by March and April, fifteen, twenty, and even thirty-five per cent were found to be infected.

But there is another reason for this "explosion" which has given spring such a bad name as an unhealthy season of the year. Not only have the "bugs" been breeding and multiplying in our close-shut, under-lighted, non-ventilated, overheated homes and offices, but through the winter we ourselves have been living under these same suffocating conditions, and along toward spring the steady strain begins to tell upon us. In short, we have been encouraging the "bugs" and discouraging our own body cells all winter long.

In addition to this, in the poorer districts of the cities and in many of our comparatively comfortable country districts, our food supply, even when abundant, has been becoming more and more restricted and monotonous.

So that, along toward spring, the deadly monotony of bread and potatoes and salt meat and cabbage and dried apples and sweet pickles begins to pall upon us. We lose our appetites, begin to curse the cook and the grub, and then blame the spring weather. Hence, our craving for spring greens, for buds and shoots and roots, dandelion, hop-buds, pokeweed, anything that will taste fresh and crunch between our teeth. This

contributing cause of spring fever is no longer unavoidable with the superb advances in transportation
which lays the fruits of the tropics and the vegetables
of the South at our doors every month in the year.

But the best thing that the worried housekeeper can
do, where those resources are not yet available, is to
turn her grumbling brood out of doors for two or three
days on a camping, fishing, shooting, botanizing, or
tramping trip, to get an appetite, and see how the
complaints will subside when they come back to home-
cooking once more. The best cure for spring fever is a
spring vacation, and the next best to set your teeth
into every wholesome green thing that you can get
hold of.

CHAPTER XVII

VIVISECTION

EVERY living thing depends for its existence upon some other form of life — or death. Were it not for the pale, underground flowers of the soil, the bacteria, the grass could not live. If it were not for the grass, the browsing beasts of the field could not live. If it were not for the beasts of the field and the ripened seeds or roots of the grass, man could not live. On the other hand, there is the return circuit. The pale flowers of the soil feed upon the withering stems and leaves of the very grass that they nourish, as well as upon the flesh of the beasts of the field and on that higher flesh which, the Psalmist tells us, is as grass. To the table of these pale flowers we must all come, to pay the debt of our birth and to be born again into higher and more beautiful forms of life. The lap of Mother Earth is the great crucible of Nature into which sink our tired bodies, the ashes of all life's fitful fever, to be fused into new forms of life and beauty. The resurrection of the body is a fact of science. Omar was almost as true a scientist as poet when he sang: —

> I sometimes think that never blows so red
> The Rose as where some buried Cæsar bled.

The higher life feeds the lower and is fed by it. The browsing flocks and herds fatten the pasturage that they feed upon. As the old Spanish proverb has it

"The foot of the sheep is golden." Even man, the waster and the slaughterer, has preserved and brought into existence at least ten times as many lives as he has destroyed. Two thirds of the bird population of any given region will be found in the garden, the orchard, the meadow, and the cornlands, within half a mile of the homes of men. The prairie, the deep forest, the swamp, and the savanna are places of silence and solitude compared with the orchard and the garden. They are as thinly populated with bird life as they are with human. Moreover, though man has swept whole regions clear of deer, antelope, and bison, these creatures were but few to the square mile. On the other hand, he has repopulated each mile with hundreds of living creatures in pasture, in byre and fold, in cote and in hutch, for his own use and service. Many of them must die to serve him, as did the handful of wild things they replaced; but while they live their lives are free from the pinch of hunger and famine, the bitter bite of the frost, the lash of the sleet, and the dusty torture of drought. Their days are peaceful and happy, and their end, when it comes, is sudden and comparatively painless. Broadly considered, man has added at least ten times as much to the sum of animal life and happiness as he has taken from it.

Though man has exterminated several noble species of animals and birds and brought perilously near to the vanishing point a score of others, he is far from being only a destroyer. This is strikingly illustrated by the fact that, with the exception of his latest conquests, fowls and pigeons, the wild ancestors of his domesticated animals have practically ceased to exist in a state of nature. They, too, would be unknown and extinct, were it not for his preservation of them by domestication. Strange as it may seem, naturalists to-day are unable positively to put their finger upon the wild ancestor of the horse, of our cattle, of the dog, of the sheep, or even of the goat and the cat.

Man has on the credit side of his account in the great book of life not only countless millions of living things which he has protected and propagated with deliberate intent, but also a large involuntary credit of a slightly different sort. This is for the swarm of welcome and unwelcome pensioners upon his bounty — not only the feathered friends whose music and color are the choicest charms of garden and croft, and whose soft beaks could hardly earn them a living without the aid of his plough, but also the innumerable horde of rats and mice which can live only in his barnyards and granaries, and the swarms of rabbits and ground-squirrels and game birds which share his crops. Considering that in the United States alone man contributes — most unwillingly — in the neighborhood of twenty million dollars a year to the support of rats alone, he certainly has some standing as a preserver of animal life. Twenty million dollars donated to rats each year would have considerable weight as an offset, even before an animal court, to a few thousand guinea-pigs bred for and utilized in the laboratory.

Our debt to the animals is enormous, and one we are glad, yes, eager to acknowledge, but there need be no sense of humiliation, for we have conferred benefits as well as received them. The immensity of our debt to our kinsfolk in fur and feathers is a household word. Not even the dullest of us needs to be reminded of our priceless debt to the strength and swiftness of the horse, to the courage and fidelity of the dog. Our very lives depend upon the meat and milk and skins of cattle, upon the wool and the flesh of sheep, upon the products of the poultry yard, of the rabbit-hutch and pigeon-cote. Half our clothing is inherited from some other form of life, including that "excrement of worms," the shiny, shimmering silk.

But there is another portion of our debt to animals which is not so widely recognized and fully known — and that is our debt to them for our knowledge of our own body and its diseases. The poets assured us long ago that the proper study of mankind is man; but such is the confusing effect of what astronomers call the "personal equation" that, by a curious paradox, much of our "proper study" when conducted directly upon its subject went round and round in a circle. It was only when we began to study man through the animals that we made solid and substantial progress. Owing to the bitter prejudice against dissecting the dead human body, two thirds of our earliest real knowledge of anatomy was founded upon the dissection of animals. So true is this that, incredible as it may seem, certain of our bodily organs were named and originally described from their shape, coloring, and conditions as they appeared in animals. It was only in the fourteenth century that anatomy began to be placed upon a purely human basis by the dissection and study of the dead bodies of men. Though knowledge of the mere structure of the human body was thus put into fairly definite and reliable form, the wildest of confusion and conjecture prevailed as to its behavior during life, its physiology. The arteries were supposed to carry air to the different parts of the body, as their name to this day, Greek for "air-holders" literally "airteries" shows. The heart was the seat of the emotions, as every Valentine's Day still bears witness. The spleen was the abode of the angry passions. The nerves were supposed to be tubes carrying the vital fluid from the brain all over the body. There were four different kinds of fluid in the body — the red blood, the black bile, the "nervous fluid," and the lymph, which gave rise to the still surviving belief of the four temperaments — the Sanguine, Nervous, Bilious, and Lymphatic. Physiology, in fact, was a mass of fairy tales, of conjectures and legends. The first white light which entered this misty shrine of absurdities came early in the seventeenth century, when Harvey opened the chest of a deer and that of a frog and watched their hearts beat until he had succeeded in discovering that those organs were actually pumping blood, instead of throbbing with emotion.

Then, from observations upon the translucent membrane supporting the intestines in the frog, came the discovery of the passage of the blood through its tiniest channels, the capillaries. A little later, from the tiny milk-white streaks seen in the same transparent sheets in warm-blooded animals after a meal of milk or fat, the *lacteals* were discovered, and the method of the absorption of the fat of our food was explained. Finally, by further experimentation and observation during life or immediately after death in animals killed for the purpose, the whole system of the lymphatics — the closed sewerage system of our body cells — was discovered.

Similarly, as late as the middle of the eighteenth century, in such a highly important process as the digestion, the vaguest of ideas and most whimsical of conceptions prevailed until the experimental method was applied directly to the process. For sixteen centuries after Hippocrates, digestion was vaguely regarded as a fermentation, with so little definite idea of its character that, as late as Van Helmont, the theory was gravely advanced that it was like the raising of bread; that the intestinal canal never completely emptied itself, but always contained a small residuum which, like the baker's leaven, started the process in each new batch of food. This was of a piece with that infantile belief in many rural districts that a cow may "lose her cud," so breaking the invisible chain which keeps the food circulating through her stomachs, and paralyzing the processes of digestion. This idea was dissipated by causing birds and animals to swallow a piece of sponge with a silk cord attached, by which, after the sponge was saturated with the gastric juice in the stomach, it could be pulled up for examination and analysis. In later experiments a permanent opening was made directly into the stomach, thus providing a "peep-hole" through which the process of digestion could be watched.

A century and a half later two fortunate accidents occurred in human beings — one a gunshot and the other a stab-wound in the side which penetrated the stomach, leaving a permanent fistula through which the processes of human digestion could be directly observed. The results obtained were absolutely identical with those observed a hundred years before in animals. Incidentally it may be remarked that both of these men lived for years in vigor and comfort, with permanent openings into their stomachs, and they declared emphatically that, after the original wound had healed, they suffered no pain from their condition, and only slight inconvenience and discomfort from the numerous experiments and observations made upon them.

Since the discovery of antisepsis, this form of direct observation of the processes of animal digestion has been carried to a high degree of perfection. The animals are cared for with every precaution and care that would be given to patients in a private hospital; the rooms in which they are kept are sterilized and spotlessly clean; the operations are done like high-class hospital operations, under ether and with the strictest antiseptic precautions. The little pouch or pocket of the stomach or intestine to be observed is drawn completely out of the main course of the food canal, and the gap is stitched up. So all the processes of digestion and assimilation go on perfectly and normally in the animal, and a little supernumerary stomach or loop of intestine, which is attached to an opening in the skin, serves as a sort of pyrometer, or indicator, of the changes taking place in the main food canal. Animals under these conditions grow fat and frolicsome and live for years while furnishing daily information of the greatest practical value. Not infrequently they either die of some accidental disease, or, when the experiments are ended, have their fistulas closed by another surgical operation, and spend the remainder of their lives as pets in the homes of the investigators, or as pensioners of the laboratory.

Thus, one after another, the mysteries of our bodily functions have been opened up by the golden key of experimentation, the Baconian method — the lever of modern science with which the world is literally being moved. It is almost incredible how recent is most of our accurate knowledge of our own bodies. The bulk of it is not more than a century and a half old; much of it is not more than a quarter of a century, and all because this method was not applied before. The liver, the pancreas, the thyroid and other ductless glands, the brain, and the nervous system, all have yielded up their secrets.

This wonderful increase of accurate knowledge of our body and of its behavior in health was the broad and necessary foundation for our superb advances in control of its activities in disease, without which half our knowledge of bacteriology and pathology would have been useless or wasted. To take two instances at random, we can now pick out a certain type of congenital idiot, the cretin, who at twenty years of age has about the intelligence and development of a healthy child of two. Feed him with the dried thyroid gland of the sheep, and you change him into a sturdy, self-supporting, rational human being in a few short months.

From experiments made upon dogs and rabbits under chloroform, stimulating the surface of the brain, to see what portions of it control the different muscles, areas, and activities of the body, we can now locate the position of a brain tumor, a hemorrhage, or a depressed fracture of the skull, to a fraction of an inch, merely from the spasms, paralyses, or pain which it produces in certain regions of the body. Trephine the skull in that precise area and we can cut down upon and remove, in four cases out of five, the cause of an otherwise almost certainly fatal trouble. The difference between the new experiment-based physiology and the old deductive variety is like that between a knowledge of watch repairing, gained from opening the case and watching the wheels go round, and one based upon ingenious deductions from the movements of the hands and the color of the dial.

Our next great flood of light into the mysteries of our body temples came, not from the study of human beings, nor even of animals, but from that of plants, from the realm of botany. The great world-genius, Pasteur, who has only left us within a decade or so, in his masterly series of investigations which finally laid the ghost of the great problem of scientific thought, spontaneous generation, showed that every possible form of living activity, including fermentation and putrefaction, was due to the presence of previously introduced living organisms known as bacteria. A step further and it was shown that certain of the diseases of plants — notably the *phylloxera* of the grapevine, and a little later a disease of animals, the *pebrine* of silkworms — were due to the same kind of living germs. Instantly the genius of Lister leaped the gap and conceived the inspiration that wound infections, the suppurations and blood poisoning of surgical patients were due to the same sort of cause. Lister filled the air of the operating-room with carbolic spray, cleansed his hands, his instruments and the patient's body with powerful antiseptics, and his wounds healed without a drop of pus. The science of modern surgery was born and surgical fever became a thing of the past!

A link in the chain of absolute demonstration was still lacking. The mass of the surgical profession were "Missourians," or worse! Twenty years before, Semmelweiss in Vienna, and our own Oliver Wendell Holmes in Boston, had demonstrated practically the same necessity for cleanliness and antisepsis in another infectious disease, childbed fever. But they were unable absolutely to demontrate the cause of the inflammation and death, and their pleadings fell upon deaf ears. Now, however, the scene had changed, and the demonstration was readily afforded. Pasteur promptly took the discharges from suppurating wounds, spread them upon proper cultures, incubated them, and demonstrated the presence of a tiny organism which he termed the *streptococcus*. When he had isolated these organisms in pure culture he rubbed them into the wounds of animals and promptly produced suppuration and erysipelas. The most hardened mind could not resist such demonstration as this, and antisepsis in surgery was placed upon as solid ground as the law of gravitation.

Backed by such mathematical experimental demonstration, antiseptic surgery swept over the civilized world with the swiftness and irresistible force of an epidemic, including in its sweep the lying-in hospitals, which thirty years before had turned a deaf ear to the pleadings of Semmelweiss and Holmes, who lacked this support.

For a time it looked as if surgery were to have a monopoly of the benefits of the new-found science of bacteriology, but not for long. Less than ten years after the joint triumph of Lister and Pasteur, a young German bacteriologist, Robert Koch, announced the discovery, in 1881, of the tubercle bacillus. More than twenty years before Villemin had proved that consumption was contagious, by inoculating rabbits with tuberculous matter, but the discovery of Koch turned a hopeless struggle against a vague, incurable, terrible scheme of decay and decline of unknown causation into a fight against a definite, curable, preventable disease. Almost more important than the actual discovery of the bacillus itself were the broad, fundamental principles of bacteriologic research which his magnificent grasp and insight enabled him to lay down with such clearness and judgment that they remain to this day the canons of procedure in the search for the causes of disease. These canons were that any germ which was to be regarded as the cause of a disease must fulfill certain definite and indispensable requirements. First, the germ must be invariably present in the tissues and fluids of the body of those suffering from this disease; second, it must be present in no other disease conditions. Third, it must be capable of reproducing the disease when, after being isolated in pure culture, it is injected into the bodies of animals; and it must be again recoverable in recognizable form from the lesions and inflammations produced by it in the bodies of such animals. Upon this basis, and following these methods, there were discovered, within little more than a decade, the germs causing diphtheria, typhoid, anthrax, lockjaw, cholera, plague, malaria, pneumonia, influenza, and, a little later, sleeping sickness, meningitis, and hookworm disease. It is not too much to say that the results of these fifteen years have given man more control over his destiny, his health, his power of colonization, his happiness and his morals than those of any thousand years of his previous history on this planet. The greatest barrier to the colonization of the tropics by white races and the most potent cause of their degeneration in sub-tropical regions is malaria. One of the most weighty factors in poverty and dependency — yes, and in pauperism and crime — is tuberculosis. From one third to one half of our criminals are born of diseased or defective parents, stunted and warped by infections, reared upon poisoned water and decaying food, in sunless, airless hovels and slums.

For a time there was an echo of disappointment about these discoveries; they appeared to be of much greater scientific interest than of practical value. "What's the use?" asked practical men both in and

out of the medical profession — men who prided themselves on their hardheadedness and the fact that they
demanded results, not theories. "What's the use of all
this knowledge about the causes of disease if it gives
you no new remedies to cure them?" For a time there
was no answer, and, to make matters worse, the first
product of the newly discovered disease germs, which
was put forward as a possible cure for disease, the now
famous tuberculin of Koch, proved, temporarily, at
least, a distressing and disastrous failure. Bacteriology
and all its works were hotly denounced, not merely
in the lay press, but even in some medical editorial
columns, a little better than delusions, raising high
hopes only bitterly to disappoint them. But the bac-
teriologists, though disappointed, were not disheart-
ened; they improved their methods and returned to
the attack, with the cheering results that nine years
later, in 1890, Behring and Kitasato announced the
discovery of the diphtheria antitoxin.

The triumphs of this life-saving discovery are
already a household word. Within five years of its
general introduction it had reduced the death-rate
from diphtheria fifty per cent; within ten years, seventy-five per cent, while to-day the mortality of
diptheria cases given antitoxin within three days of
the beginning of the disease is barely five per cent,
as contrasted with an average mortality before the
antitoxin of over forty per cent. Antitoxin has now
been used for some twenty years all over the civilized
world with absolutely uniform results. In France
alone some three hundred thousand children are at-

tacked by diphtheria each year, and a nearly equal number in Russia, in England, and in Germany, and the death-rate has been reduced from forty per cent to a little over ten per cent — making a saving of nearly one hundred thousand children's lives in France alone each year — it can be seen what an enormous boon this discovery of the laboratory and of the experimental method has already been to humanity!

An item of somewhat earlier date on the debit side of our account with the animals, which must not be omitted from the ledger, is vaccination, though time and familiarity, those great levelers and buriers, have somewhat dulled our vision to its vast importance. Here was an antidote against a deadly infection, discovered a century before the science of bacteriology was born and more than a century before its germ was discovered — a prophecy of future triumphs. By a fortunate combination of lucky chance, observation, and that wonderful insight which we term genius, a thoughtful country doctor, Edward Jenner, noted that the dairymaids in his county who had caught from the cows they milked a mild pustular skin disease called cow-pox, upon their hands and wrists, did not develop smallpox, when exposed to it. After repeating his observations until he felt absolutely sure of the fact he inoculated the child of one of his more intelligent farmer patients, first with the pus of cowpox, and later with that of virulent smallpox. The experiment was a brilliant success, and within fifty years of its general adoption the method had reduced the death-rate from smallpox in Europe from hundreds of thousands annually to a few hundreds. Inside of a hundred years it had practically exterminated the disease which had a heavier mortality than any infectious disease except tuberculosis. No civilized country now has a death-rate from smallpox of more than a few score to a few hundred yearly, and three fourths of these are in individuals who have been unfortunate enough to escape vaccination. In 1907, for instance, smallpox caused fifty-nine deaths in the United States, while tuberculosis slew one hundred and fifty thousand. What experimental science has done to one disease within a century, it will do to the other in half that time! A century ago from twenty to fifty per cent of the population were pockmarked and from fifty to sixty per cent of the blind in our blind asylums had had their sight destroyed by smallpox.

Other diseases have diminished in deadliness under civilization, but none of them at a rate to compare with smallpox, for we have had no animal-born antidote against them. Other diseases, like the diseases of infancy, have become milder with the progress of civilization. But the great trinity of deadliest scourges that ravage humanity — cholera, smallpox, and the Black Death — still kill as many of their victims as they did in the days of Genghis Khan, unless we have been protected against them by some form of inoculation. As any health officer can testify from bitter experience, virulent smallpox to-day falling upon vigorous men in the prime of life and health, in our most highly civilized and healthiest communities, with ideal water supply, drainage, and food, still exacts its old, historic death-toll of from twenty to forty per cent if its victims be unvaccinated. Its fatality among those who have ever been successfully vaccinated, is barely five per cent. A vaccination scar, no matter how faded or indistinct, is to the smallpox demon what the splash of the blood of the Pascal lamb over the doorway was to the angel of the Plague of the Firstborn in Egypt.

The diphtheria antitoxin was, and still is, the greatest single curative result of the new knowledge, but it is very far from being the only one, as we sometimes hear critics of bacteriology complain. The diphtheria bacillus produces larger amounts of its poison or toxin, and excretes them more freely outside of its own tiny body into its cultures, the tissues of its victims, than any other disease germ yet discovered. Thus it has been possible by injecting it into animals to produce a high potency of the antitoxin in their blood, and thus provide an antidote strong enough to arrest and cure even the most virulent and advanced cases of the disease.

A typical instance of the weaker antitoxins is that of tetanus, an antidote for the horrible and fatal disease lockjaw. We have now developed by the injection of the tetanus toxin into animals an antitoxin which, though not powerful enough to cure more than a moderate percentage of advanced cases of lockjaw, has already greatly reduced the mortality from the disease by its preventive use in infected wounds and in very early stages of the disease. Incidentally, the tetanus antitoxin furnishes an illustration of the benefits which have accrued to animals from this experimentation, for this antitoxin is now habitually used in veterinary practice for the purpose of immunizing horses which may have been exposed to the disease. Similar serums have been made in the laboratory by the same methods for protection against anthrax and rinderpest, against hog-cholera and against glanders in horses, with the resultant saving of thousands of animal lives every year at the expense of a few score sacrificed in the common interest.

It is not too much to say that for a considerable percentage of our more serious infectious diseases some form of antitoxin has already been produced which, though still ineffective in severe and advanced cases, is exceedingly helpful in the early stages and in milder cases. A score of laboratories all over the civilized world are hard at work perfecting, developing and improving every one of these antitoxins.

For instance, in cholera, Haffkine has developed an antiserum whose use in India reduces the percentage of cases developing in those inoculated with it to about one tenth of that occurring among the uninoculated in the same villages and districts. The protective effect of the inoculation lasts about fourteen months.

For dysentery, a serum has been produced which in several series of two hundred or more cases has reduced the death-rate from twenty-five per cent to less than ten per cent. For hay fever, a disease caused largely by the pollen-dust of certain grasses and flowers, an antitoxin called pollantin, has been produced from animals, the introduction of which into the eye or nose of the sufferer has produced marked improvement in over fifty per cent of some two thousand cases. For bubonic plague, or Black Death, we have now a serum which, though comparatively powerless to cure this deadliest known pestilence, has a very marked effect in protecting persons against its attack. Among seven hundred thousand uninoculated persons in certain districts in India, there occurred fifty thousand cases of the plague with thirty thousand deaths. Of one hundred and eighty-seven thousand in the same communities who had been inoculated, only thirty-four hundred took the disease, and of these only eight hundred and fourteen died — a mortality of four tenths of one per cent. In the case of typhoid fever we have another mild vaccine developed by Wright, of Netley, the chief pathologist of the British Army Medical Department. This was used as a preventive during the Boer War, among the troops sent out to South Africa, where typhoid was known to be rife. Out of some two thousand inoculated, one hundred and sixty-two, or eight per cent, died of the disease. Of eleven thousand other troops in the same divisions and camps who had not been inoculated, eighteen hundred, or sixteen per cent died. The percentage of those who contracted the disease was about ten times as great among the uninoculated soldiers as among the inoculated. Since then almost every army in the civilized world has tested the typhoid vaccine and it has been used in nearly half a million cases, with a reduction of typhoid to the vanishing point as in our own army. Chantemesse, in Paris, claims remarkable results with a serum which he has produced by the inoculation of horses, reducing the death-rate in a thousand cases to four and three tenths per cent; while five thousand cases in the same hospitals and districts which were not inoculated had a death-rate of seventeen per cent.

Another disease for which a valuable antitoxin has been developed by the experimental method is snake-bite. This antitoxin, though of little practical importance 'in the temperate zones, is highly useful in the tropics. British India alone has reported twenty thousand deaths a year as due to snake bite. The subject is of great interest from a scientific point of view, for the reason that it was probably in this field that some of the earliest, if not the very first, practical applications were made of the modern method of securing immunity against a poison by giving a series of increasing small doses of it. Centuries ago the snake charmers of India had succeeded in giving themselves some form of protection against the bite of venomous serpents which they handled. There was, of course, an immense amount of deception about the process, but certain it is that a number of snake charmers in modern times have been bitten without apparent ill effects, by snakes whose bite was promptly fatal to rabbits and chickens, and produced very serious results in rash skeptics who allowed themselves to be bitten.

Building in part upon this and in part upon the new knowledge of antitoxins, Calmette and other experimenters have succeeded in developing, from the blood of animals inoculated with increasing doses of snake venom, an antitoxin called antivenine. This has been found exceedingly helpful in hundreds of cases of snake bite, saving lives which, without it, would almost certainly have been sacrificed.

Even in tuberculosis, in spite of the distressing disappointment resulting from the first use of tuberculin, varying forms of the products of the tubercle bacillus are now used in suitably selected cases with decidedly helpful and beneficial results, although none of them can claim to possess specific value as yet. This, fortunately, is not so serious as might be supposed, in view of the fact that we already have a fairly reliable cure for the disease in the now well-known open-air treatment. But, limited as tuberculin may be in its curative use, it has been of simply inestimable value for diagnostic purposes, enabling us to recognize the disease in those early stages in which alone it is almost certainly curable. Especially is this the case since the discovery by Calmette and Von Pirquet that a few drops of a solution of tuberculin dropped into the eye or scratched into the skin will in perfectly healthy individuals produce no results whatever, but in those who are suffering from tuberculosis it will promptly set up a reddening and inflammatory reaction. These reactions to tuberculin are now relied upon as our most valuable means of recognizing the disease before marked changes have begun in the lungs. Tuberculin has already been of as much value to humanity as any curative drug or serum that could be mentioned — with the exception of quinine, mercury, and the diphtheria antitoxin.

Last, but not least, has been the production by Flexner at the Rockefeller Institute of a serum which

has already produced most striking improvement in
the recovery rate of cerebro-spinal meningitis, popularly known as spotted fever. The method of its production is an interesting illustration of a distinctly
unexpected fact which has been a most serious obstacle to us in the development of antitoxins and in the
discovery of the causes of disease — that is, that not
infrequently there is no animal known which is susceptible to the disease that is being studied, and consequently no animal which can be infected with it. Many
unsuccessful attempts had been made to produce cerebro-spinal meningitis in animals, when it occurred to
Flexner that possibly those animals which were near-
est allied in blood and zoölogical relationship to man
might prove to be the pathologic missing link. Cultures of the meningococcus were accordingly injected
into monkeys, with the result that they promptly developed the full symptoms of the disease. Thus was
supplied the missing link in the demonstration that
this was the causal germ. It was only a step then to
the production of an antitoxin by injecting it into our
ever-useful friend, the horse. The antitoxin thus produced was then administered to monkeys which had
been inoculated with the meningococcus, and instead
of dying with the disease they promptly recovered.
After this procedure had been repeated a sufficient
number of times to feel sure of the result and to be
confident that it was safe to administer the serum to
human beings, it was tried in the first cases that could
be secured. The disease is not a very common one, so
that progress was slow; but up to date the serum has

been used in over a thousand cases with the almost uniform result that instead of from seventy to eighty per cent of the cases dying, as they invariably did before, from seventy to eighty-five per cent of them recovered; thus almost exactly reversing the mortality and recovery rate of the disease.

The latest development is a vaccine which is most efficient in protecting against this deadly disease. Vaccines are also in use against whooping cough and scarlet fever, with fine results.

Gratifying as have been the curative results of the antitoxins, vaccines and serums already developed, it is, however, not too much to say that, had none of these been discovered, the enormously increased power over the course, the spread and the causation of infectious diseases given by our accurate knowledge of their causes, of their life habits, of the places in which disease breeds and the channels through which it is transmitted to fresh victims, would have been worth a thousand times what our knowledge of bacteriology has cost in labor, time, money, and the sacrifice of animal life.

Even diseases like typhoid, tuberculosis, cholera, and pneumonia, for which no specific antidote has yet been discovered, show already a reduction of from twenty-five to seventy-five per cent both in their occurrence and in their death-rate when they do occur. Even if we should never discover a specific serum for typhoid, for tuberculosis, for cholera and for yellow fever, it is practically as certain as the sun rises and sets that we are in process of exterminating them entirely, and that their disappearance from civilized society is only a question of time.

Two most signal victories of this class were won in the case of malaria and yellow fever. It is only possible barely to allude to them here — indeed, little more should be necessary, as the newspapers are full every few weeks of reports of conquests over the two diseases. In one of these diseases, indeed, we already had an antidote, quinine, and though our new knowledge has given us no further curative agent in either, it has provided us with an absolute protection against them both, and put both well in the way of extermination. To put it very briefly, both were found to be due to parasites carried and introduced into the human blood by the bite of mosquitoes. This was demonstrated upon both animals and birds. Then a test upon human beings was demanded, and a score of medical volunteers, soldiers of modern science, stepped forward at once. In all of them the disease developed after they were bitten by infected mosquitoes, and the demonstration was complete. Two there were of those who offered themselves as victims at this altar whom we should add to our list of American heroes — Carroll and Lazear — for they paid the penalty with their lives. We thrill with pride when we think of the pension of two hundred and fifty dollars a month paid to Mrs. Carroll, and the noble sum of one hundred and twenty-five dollars a month which goes to Mrs. Lazear and her seven children. It required some three years of coaxing and lobbying, not to mention special bills, to wring these magnificent sums from a grateful and intelligent

Congress. These men by dying saved thousands of human lives in our Southern States from the recurrent invasions of Yellow Jack. What may appeal to us more, they saved millions of dollars' worth of damage to commerce and trade caused by quarantines and fever panics. But their orphans could n't get one thousandth part of the amount of protection from our noble Government that the feeblest and ricketiest Infant Industry can, by simply crooking its little finger.

Within five years of the discovery of the mosquito's part in yellow fever the disease was practically exterminated in its old hotbed and source of infection for the United States, Havana, and the single epidemic that has reached our shores since was stamped out with about one fifth of the usual mortality and panic. Never again, while health officers are reasonably efficient and intelligent, will a serious epidemic of yellow fever get foothold in these United States!

Similarly in the case of malaria, by cleaning up the small pools and puddles, any given district can practically stamp out malaria within its borders in a few years. Scores, indeed, have already done so. Of course it is brutally cruel. It represents an appalling waste and destruction of happy, singing, dancing life, millions of poor defenseless little mosquitoes; but then, alas! the gods demand a price for every boon.

Of course, to make an omelet one must break a few eggs, and this immense saving of both human and animal life, our enormous increase in health and happiness and social comfort, has been purchased at a price, and that price has been paid largely by our animal kinsmen. But as Sainte-Beuve remarked: "It is not necessary to calumniate even the Inquisition"; and even such brief review as we have here been able to take of the nature of our debt to animals and its results show that their sacrifice and suffering, while unquestionable and regrettable have been neither excessive nor unreasonable.

The great bulk of animals used for scientific purposes are guinea-pigs and horses — the former being extensively bred for the purpose. The procedures to which they are submitted are inoculations or infections with the germs or toxins of the disease under investigation. These inoculations usually involve about the amount of pain which attends the vaccination of a human being, as most viruses are introduced either by scratches made on the skin, by being mixed with the food, dropped into the eye, or injected with a hypodermic needle. The amount of suffering that follows is simply that which attends the development of the disease, and in many cases this is not allowed to run its full course to death, as the animals are killed as soon as it is certain that they have fully developed the disease. In other words, they suffer just about as much as if left to themselves to die of natural causes, except that their deaths occur somewhat earlier.

For every guinea-pig that has died by inoculated disease in the laboratory, at least one child — perhaps your child — has already been saved from death by diptheria alone. For every animal sacrificed in the laboratory, at least ten animals have been protected against painful and loathsome disease. Without the use of animals there would ever have been, at every step in the process, a fatal missing link in the chain of our evidence, and the superb advance of medical science of the last quarter of a century would either have been utterly impossible, or else have been less than one fifth as great and as helpful as it has been.

All things that live must die, and the utmost that we ask for ourselves as men is that we shall not have died in vain. The guinea-pig already has as noble a temple to his memory as that of many a martyr and liberator!

CHAPTER XVIII

THE MODERN FATHER

"IT is a wise son that knows his own father" and a rare father that knows his own son. The failure of the two generations to "get together" has been one of the daily tragedies of history. There ought to be a Society for the Promotion of Sociability between fathers and children.

Too often the average father does not know his boy at all, in the sense that he knows the men in his shop or factory, or his rivals in business, or his fellow townsmen. He has never studied him and gauged him and estimated his powers and tendencies as he has theirs. He just takes him for granted, either as a chip of the old block, a little replica of himself, a "living spit and image" of his grandfather, or as a shapeless lump of protoplasmic putty, which he will make a man of in such form and calling as seems to him best.

To the boy, the father too often is merely the "Governor" or the "Old Man," an obstinate and domineering sort of person — well-meaning and not unkindly at heart, but forming a sort of perpetual constitutional opposition to every proposal that does not emanate from itself, and playing the automatic wet blanket to every darling scheme of youth.

The perpetual paternal pose, "I am older and therefore I must know better," would goad a rabbit to revolt, even if the boy admitted the logic of the syllogism, which he usually doesn't — and an unprejudiced observer would often be compelled to agree with him.

Nowhere does the luminousness of William Allen White's shrewd phrase, "That type of ponderous folly of the middle-aged which we term mature judgment," stand out more vividly than in some of the chronic and historic clashes between paternal and filial judgment. What is wisdom in the old would be folly in the young; but naturally the old can't see it. Why can't each generation let the next live its own life and solve its own problems, unaided and unhindered save by its counsel, which the younger generation will be eager to have and value most highly if it is only left to itself and allowed to discover its value by a little harmless experience, instead of having it thrust down its throat unasked in solid chunks? To administer food with a stomach pump four times a day is not the way to stimulate an appetite for it.

In the old, unhappy days of battle, murder, and sudden death, to which with truly inspired idiocy we usually refer as the "good old times," when each particular family group, small and large, must literally hang together if they would not hang separately, the power of the father to enforce conformity to his policy was absolutely unlimited; and the family discipline of those days had literally "no nonsense about it." "Fathers were fathers" in those times, as we sometimes hear regretfully remarked. A father then, to successfully rear his children and literally save their lives, had to be, in the quaint but expressive phrase of our English cousins, "a bit of a brute."

The tradition was a painfully long time in dying out, even after all necessity for it had absolutely disappeared for centuries. One of the highest duties of a father was to chasten his children; so much so that even Jehovah announced himself, through his prophets, as intending to follow the same policy.

Under such distinguished auspices, and with the encouragement of such humane and enlightened relics of the Stone Age as "Spare the rod and spoil the child," the belief that the chief duty of man was a stern and severe discipline toward his hapless offspring grew and flourished, and the beating and starving and locking in dark closets of innocent and bewildered children became one of the chief virtues and an article of faith and practice.

Possibly it did not do the children much grave, physical harm, for the young human animal is most providentially tough — and it was the greatest relief to the parents. Few things are so soothing as to be able to "take it out of" some one when your equals or superiors have exasperated you and you are afraid to retaliate openly, especially when you can ease your conscience afterward by such pious admonitions as "Chasten thy son in his youth; beat his sides while he is young; spare not for his crying." To be able to relieve your own feelings and at the same time fulfill Scripture, even though Apocryphal, is a rare luxury. This was known as "doing your duty by your children," and, like most other forms of doing one's duty by other people, was a particularly spiteful kind of self-indulgence. The pious gave way to temper in the family circle, just as the profane gave way to drink — and with about equally disastrous consequences.

This sort of thing fortunately belongs to history now in our favored land, save in a few remote and benighted regions, and would be little more than a memory to laugh over were it not that it has left a black shadow behind it in the tradition that a stern rule and rigid discipline is the ideal régime for children, and that any departure from this ancient and barbarous standard will be ruinous to their character and utterly undermine both their vigor and self-control.

The argument is an unanswerable one: "All children of respectable families have been submitted to strict correction and discipline since the world began, and most of them have turned out passably well; therefore, if we leave off the discipline our children will grow up sluggards and shirkers." It may be respectfully pointed out that there is a flaw in the logic, since practically no children have ever been allowed to grow up without any form of discipline save the society and example of their parents, so as to see what sort of little monsters they would turn out. Such approaches as have been made to this natural and unregulated method of nurture have turned out exceedingly well, but they have only been approaches, so heavy hangs the dread of authority over us all. Our brains know better, but we are morally certain in our livers that they would grow up forgers and highwaymen — if not actually crosseyed and humpbacked.

We have the same ludicrously implicit faith that it is only what we do for our children that makes them turn out as well as they do, as the small boy had in the functions of a cat's tail. He was given that interesting animal as the subject of one of those tortures of the infantile Inquisition known as "essays in composition," and, after several trite and commonplace preliminaries, he achieved this masterpiece of insight and observation — strictly original: "A cat has a long tale which it raps round its pause when it sits down. I no a cat that has no tale and it is afrade to sit down in public for fear that its feet would skatter." Just where the wits and faculties of our amorphous offspring would "skatter" if we did not wrap and surround them with our most efficient and restraining family discipline, we do not and probably never shall know. We can no more refrain from "butting in" at every provocation than we can keep our tongue out of the hole where a tooth has been extracted, even with the certainty that a silver one will come in its place.

Interference just oozes out of parents like sap out of a maple tree in spring, and it would require great powers of self-control to maintain a consistent policy of "hands off," save in real emergencies or serious issues. The indifferent and wishy-washy father of to-day, with his lack of discipline and his unwillingness to compel his children to appear to respect him, whether they do or not, is inferior to the fathers of heroic times and the good old days of a couple of generations ago only in savagery and selfishness. In all other respects he is superior.

The father of to-day has changed for the better in another important respect. Fathers, of course, have always — in the vast majority of instances — loved their children, since the world began, and always will; but some of them in the olden days had considerable difficulty in making the children believe it. When the "stern old Roman" type of father, with his power of life and death over his family, began to decline, the *potestas paterna* began to assume another undesirable and even more galling though less picturesque form — the form of a claim upon the child's earning power and wages.

Like the other form of paternal tyranny, it had a perfectly natural and even rational origin. As the power of compelling obedience in the family was, in unsettled times, a military necessity, so this right of controlling the labor and earnings was an economic necessity for the support of the family group in pastoral and early agricultural times. It rapidly grew past this, however, until it finally developed into a right — which, like that of life and death, was formally recognized in law — of absolute control over the time and earnings of all children up to a certain definite age. In good hands it was little more than a reasonable and bracing method of training for life, but in bad or callous hands it developed into a grasping and grinding tyranny which the children not infrequently ran away from home to escape; whereupon, if they could be caught, they would be arrested and brought back and flogged like any other criminals.

Our fathers' generation, and even some of the older

members of our own, can readily remember the time when to "give a boy his time" before he was twenty-one years of age — in other words, to allow him to go out and work for himself and keep his own wages — was regarded as an act of great generosity and liberality on the part of the father. This tradition and custom was one of the influences which both permitted and promoted those fine large families of an earlier time, whose disappearance or shrinkage is now so absurdly lamented. It is still to be seen in all its glory in some of our Southern cotton mills, which are a perfect haven of refuge for that small percentage of the "cracker" and "tar-heel" class whose only visible assets are a few bad debts, six or eight dogs, and ten or twelve children, on which latter they proceed to realize in cash. It is an admirable arrangement for the father and the manufacturer — but pity the poor children! Fortunately this tendency to regard children as a cash asset is rapidly dying out in America — indeed, has almost disappeared, with the exception of a few instances like the foregoing; but it is in full swing yet in the mass of the population over the greater part of Europe.

Only a few months ago, when calling upon some artist friends in Florence, they were in despair because one of those rare jewels, whose worth can hardly be estimated in gold, — yea, fine gold, — a first-class cook, was about to leave them. An inquiry into the cause of her departure uncovered a pathetic little domestic tragedy. The servant girl, who was twenty years of age, was, it appeared, engaged to be married;

but, according to the romantic custom and tradition of the country, her lover's family felt that he would be sacrificing his self-respect if he married her before she had at least two hundred dollars. This sum she was within fifty dollars of having accumulated out of her earnings, and the day was set for the wedding, when suddenly her stern father appeared upon the scene with the news that her mother had met with a severe accident and was likely to be in bed for several months, if not crippled for life, and that she must come and keep house for him and her grown-up brothers until her twenty-second birthday.

Father and brothers were all earning good wages and were abundantly able to pay for a servant — indeed, there was a younger sister who would have been competent to take the mother's place, but she also was at work earning money which she was paying into the family exchequer; and, as they would have no legal control over the elder girl's time after about a year and a half longer, they were going to make use of her while they had the power, regardless of its effect upon her happiness. The girl was perfectly willing to go and keep house for the family; in fact, had no intention of refusing, should her mother's disability prove as serious as feared; but she was heartbroken at the thought of the delay which her period of labor without remuneration would make in her cherished plans.

It is really most gratifying to see to what extent this idea of making profit out of the labor of one's minor children has died out in America. It scarcely exists except in poverty-stricken and isolated communities and among our immigrant population. Even these last outgrow it with surprising rapidity when once they have fairly filled their lungs with the atmosphere of American life — so much so that, in some of the investigations as to the cause of child labor made by our American Committee on Child Labor, it was found, in some five hundred successive cases investigated, parental demands were responsible for only about thirty per cent of the evil. In nearly sixty per cent the children left school and went to work of their own accord, largely on account of the unsatisfying and purely literary and clerical type of instruction which they were given at the school. As a small "doffer-boy" whom I inveigled into conversation on a train put it: "I'd ruther be in the mill than in school; the work ain't so hard and it's more interestin'!"

It is no longer necessary for the American boy to regard his father either as a local representative of the Almighty and the personified "Don't!" in his scheme of life, or as a stern and grasping taskmaster. The American father has come down from his absurd pedestal of perpetual superiority and always knowing better, and is willing to meet and talk with his boy as man to man, and to treat his girls as charming little women in miniature, whose opinions and preferences are entitled to respect and affectionate consideration.

Family life has become a happy and peaceful republic, or a mild and humane constitutional monarchy, with the father as king and the mother as the power behind the throne, content to rest their authority upon the happy consent of the governed, reserving only a casting vote in a deadlock, and in extreme instances a practical veto through the power of voting or with-holding supplies — whether of skates or of hair-ribbons. It is wonderful how the children respond to it — what perfect little codes of morals and manners they form for themselves — much better and more graceful than any that could be imposed upon them — to say nothing of their being genuine and "dyed in the wool." They get a polish which won't rub off, even in the rough jostling of the outer world, and a set of principles that won't break down in after life, because they are self-made and self-supporting.

"But what becomes of parental authority in such a scheme?" some one will exclaim. The only earthly use of parental authority was to produce efficient, self-respecting children, with high courage and good character; and these can be secured far better under a rule of law and of reason than under one of sheer authority by brute force — whether personal or financial. It was not reason which led to the assertion of a supreme authority which must be maintained and a respect which must be insisted upon at all hazards from children, but tradition and selfishness, backed up by a large measure of self-conceit. "I intend that my child shall be a credit to me" was the attitude, though the thing we should have been most concerned about was that he should be a credit to himself.

We are desperately afraid that our children will not be so good as we are unless we strain every nerve to make them so, when, as a matter of fact, they will be better if we only give them the chance. The "reason" which leads parents to argue that they must know better than their children because they are older more closely resembles the cynic's definition of instinct in the classic dialogue: —

"What is reason?" "That which tells a man whether he is right or not." "What is instinct?" "That which tells a woman that she is right, whether she is or not."

If we fathers will be perfectly frank with ourselves we shall, I fear, be compelled to confess, looking back over our most acute clashes of opinion with our offspring, that, though we firmly and sincerely believed ourselves to be right — and often were — we were inspired more by a determination to uphold our own authority and back up our own opinion — "to save our face," as the Chinese say — than by a disinterested and dispassionate desire for the best good of our children. The battle was far more one between old self-conceit and young self-assertion than between venerable wisdom and youthful folly.

If you are really wiser than your child there is seldom much difficulty in demonstrating it, even to his satisfaction; and one of the most effective methods is to permit him a little harmless experience of the unwisdom of his own view. We may claim that we have a right to insist upon respect from our own children. As we sometimes tragically put it: "If they do not treat us with respect, who will?" In fact, there is the nub of the whole trouble: so many people don't; but we can make our own youngsters go through the forms at least. The only sure way to insure respect from your children is to be respectable. If you really are that you need n't worry. They 'll find it out and act accordingly.

Nowhere else can be found such devoted worshipers of the God of Things as They Are as healthy-minded children. They survey and transvalue everything with what Robert Louis Stevenson aptly calls "the pitiless eye of youth."

One great advantage of this modern method of democratic family government is that the father has to put some brains into it. It is no longer sufficient to provide liberally for household necessaries and school-ing, then give your orders and expect the family ma-chine to run itself within those limits, with a fair amount of supplementary and impromptu nagging, scolding, and chastisements. It is necessary to study most carefully the idiosyncrasies and powers and ten-dencies of every member of your parliamentary body, to know how to steady here, to stimulate there, to conciliate yonder, in order to be reasonably sure of a working majority in a crisis and avoid resort to the veto power as much as possible. To do this it is nec-essary to get thoroughly and intimately acquainted with your own children. It takes time and trouble, but it is astonishing how your respect for and confi-dence in them will rise when you have done it — to say nothing of theirs in you.

What we are pleased to term morality is inherent — the result of the struggle for existence — a necessary adjustment of ourselves to our surroundings — both personal and elemental. Make the life within the family circle as free and as happy and within a few degrees of as bracing as that in the world outside, and our children will grow into morals and grow into manners, and even habits of industry, just as naturally and as inevitably as they will grow into trousers and long dresses. Far from forming no moral standards of their own, it will not be long before you will find them pronouncing solemn judgment upon certain details of your own conduct; and you may have a hard time to justify yourself to the ruthlessly logical and clear-seeing eye of childhood. This is sometimes embarrassing, but it is exceedingly good for you; and you need not imagine there is anything new about it or that it would not have happened under the old-fashioned system of training or discipline. The judgments were formed just the same — only the youngsters were too discreet to pronounce them in public.

For this intimate acquaintance with and loving study of his own children the American father has better opportunities than ever fathers had before. This may seem an extraordinary statement in view of the wail that is raised on all hands about the incessant rush and bustle of modern life and the absorbing demands of the American man's business upon his time and energy. As a matter of fact, never was a man less of a slave to his business or handicraft or profession than he is to-day. Never was it more difficult to determine a man's occupation simply by studying his appearance — never more impossible to pick out a man upon the street as a merchant, a doctor, a carpenter, a broker, a machinist. A man is bigger than his trade to a degree that he never was before; and he has more leisure to devote to the things that are really worth while, such as the society of his wife and children, than he ever had in any age before. The very vigor and intensity and high pitch of efficiency with which he works make it necessary for him to have longer periods of rest and that recreation which is change of occupation and interest; in fact, we are beginning to find that in proportion as a man becomes superior to his trade the better he is at that trade.

Our proudest boast, and rightly, is the huge sum of money we spend every year upon education. We should spend no less money; but what we most need is to spend more of our own time in the education of our children. We often lament, with but little reason in either fact or judgment, the huge preponderance of feminine influence in our systems of public education, but we need have no fear of this if it be only supplemented by an adequate amount of masculine influence in the family life itself. What our children need and have a right to demand from us as fathers is not our money but ourselves. If the sacred business suffers thereby, then it must suffer — though, as a matter of fact, it won't, except perhaps in certain of its more savage and unscrupulous aspects. The Master's Degree in the university of life can never be granted to the man who has not held a chair in some family college.

We have heard so much poetic outpouring and "fond recollection" rhapsody about the superiority of the home life of a generation or two ago over that

of to-day that we are apt to overlook entirely the immense improvement which has actually taken place
in the atmosphere of the modern home. To a cynical
eye the most interesting comment upon the well-nigh
celestial glories and unearthly bliss of the childhood
homes of our parents and grandparents was how glad
they were to get away from them and the exceedingly
early age at which they usually effected their escape!
The twentieth-century child thinks nothing of staying
at home until eighteen, nineteen, or twenty-two years
of age, and continuing to enjoy himself thoroughly;
while the child of the eighteenth century who had
not either escaped from or been pushed out of the
family nest before he was sixteen, and often before
fourteen, was a rare exception; and, in the language of
the advertisements, "There's a reason!"

Part of this early thrusting forth from the sacred
shelter of the home into the wide, wide world was due
to the bad manners of fathers; part of it to the stern
necessity of that darling discipline and means of grace
of the successful classes, who have never experienced
it themselves — poverty, which compelled these little
ones to take the burden of life upon their tender
shoulders at this pathetically immature age; but no
inconsiderable share of it was due to a singular tradition, which grew up from Heaven knows where, that
the worst place for a child after twelve years of age —
especially a boy — was his own home! This tradition
is still in full swing on the other side of the Atlantic
and has a curiously equalizing effect in shortening the
home life of both the wealthier and the poorer classes,

in that, while the laborer's son leaves home to take an apprenticeship or a job at twelve or fourteen years of age, the boy of the merchant and professional classes also leaves the shelter of the parental roof at from ten to twelve years of age to enter one of those survivals of mediævalism — European boarding-schools. As the vacations of these institutions of learning are, to our American eyes, exceedingly short, averaging about a month in the summer and two weeks each at Christmas and Easter, and as the boy usually goes straight out into business or professional life on leaving school, it will be seen to what a large extent the children of the better classes, as well as of the poorer, for all practical purposes leave home and its influence behind them at the tender age of from ten to twelve years.

Reason and common sense are beginning to assert themselves a little, and the vacations in the best European boarding-schools are now lengthening until, in some cases, they reach nearly three months out of the year; but when the present generation was at school the conditions were far worse — only one vacation a year being allowed and that being of a month or less — and in the generation before this was cut down to two weeks. And, owing to difficulties of travel and distances to which children had to be sent, it not infrequently happened that the unfortunate little wretches did not come home at all for years in succession, but were left shut up in their boarding-school prison during the whole of their boyhoods or girlhoods.

Of course there were many homes of the humbler classes from which the children were not obliged to go out and earn their living at so early an age, or, if they did, in which they still lived at home; and of the better classes, in which the children were able to go to good day schools, or have good governesses or tutors at home. The effect of both these influences, however, in breaking up and shortening home life, until within the last fifty or seventy-five years, was very marked; and the decay of both, for which we can never be sufficiently thankful, has really for the first time provided an opportunity for full, adequate, and happy home life, for the affectionate and enjoyable association of parents and children.

Much of our abject dependence upon formal or public education outside of the home was due to the narrowness and imperfection of home life in the past, and the coming movement of the twentieth century is unquestionably to rely less upon public education and more upon high-grade, intelligent, thoughtful home training for the best and happiest development of our children.

No small responsibility for the spread of the boarding-school delusion must be accepted by fathers. It was so much less trouble to pay down a lump sum and shift all responsibility for their boys' or girls' education and training on to the shoulders of some supposed expert — save the mark! — than it was to undertake their training and submit to the burden of their companionship themselves. They were also largely to blame in another way, and that was in the extent to which they shirked the responsibility for actual and consistent family government and management, and left it upon the shoulders of the mother, confining themselves to stern and even ferocious interpositions with the strap and the slipper whenever things went openly and unmistakably wrong.

Thus, too often they came to be looked upon by their children as a sort of professional inflicters of punishment and family magistrates, and the threat, "I'll tell your father on you!" was one the significance of which there was no mistaking in a family fifty or a hundred years ago. This drove the mother unconsciously into an attitude of pitying protection and perhaps undue indulgence, and thus grew up the extraordinary old tradition that mothers would do nothing but spoil their children if they were left unchecked, and that it was better to send them out to boarding-schools, where they would be under the charge of indifferent and supposedly impartial teachers. This tradition still survives and was publicly voiced in the astounding statement of the head master of one of England's greatest schools a few years ago: "A boy's mother is often his worst enemy."

English boarding-schools, in fact, are a survival of the time when women were expected to be fools.

Instead of the influence of the home and parents upon children being on the decline in the twentieth century, it is greater than ever it was before and is increasing every day; and never was home life happier and more influential and more helpful than it is to-day. Now is the opportunity for fathers to redeem their shortcomings in the past, and nobly are they rising to it.

Never was there a time when fathers were more kindly and affectionately alive to the best interests of their children than to-day — more ready to sacrifice themselves for them and to do everything in their power to make their lives successful and happy. It would not be any exaggeration to say that the average father of to-day knows at least fifty per cent more of what his boy or his girl is thinking and doing and hoping than did the father of a hundred years ago. And the effect of this changed attitude, this improved relation, upon the atmosphere of home life is something delightful to see. There is plenty of room for improvement yet, however.

One of the most remarkable and hopeful signs in the business world to-day is the steady and progressive shortening of the hours of work. The business man, instead of feeling it necessary to be in his shop or factory by seven-thirty or eight o'clock in the morning, comes down at nine or nine-thirty and goes home at four-thirty or five, instead of slaving away until the six-o'clock whistle blows. Besides this, he has pushed his day of rest twelve hours in advance and holds his Saturday afternoon as sacred as his Sabbath. The laboring man, by combining with his fellows and fighting for the right to live like a human being, has succeeded in cutting down his hours progressively from twelve to ten, nine and even eight a day. Thus men of all classes have a better opportunity to be men instead of mere machines than ever before.

Nor is this a decline of industry or a sign of increasing self-indulgence on the part of the modern man.

Though often initiated for totally different reasons, — such as, for instance, a desire to make work go farther, so to speak, and provide places for more men on the part of the employees, — it rests upon the unexpected discovery, which one of our greatest political economists has rightly described as one of the most hopeful and cheering for the future of humanity ever made, that the efficiency of the worker and the amount and quality of the work done actually increase in proportion to the time allowed for rest, nutrition, and recreation. Of course it must be within reasonable limits; but, so far as the experiment has been carried, those limits have not yet been reached. Personally, I am inclined to believe that the improvement will still be maintained until at least a six-hour day has been reached.

The vital question is: Where is this new-found leisure on the part of the men and fathers of the nation to be spent? Some moralists and economists have been assuring us, with the utmost fervor and conviction, that it will be spent in drinking and dissipation; but the facts, as usual, are delightfully against them. Every careful and first-hand observer of modern life will agree that drinking, gambling, and dissipation of all sorts are distinctly and encouragingly diminishing, and that the place where two thirds of their newly gained leisure is actually being spent by men of all classes is in their own homes and gardens, or in open-air concerts in public parks, in places of recreation by seashore and river, White Cities, Coney Islands, moving-picture shows, many of them childish and frivolous, if you like, but — and this is a significant point — in company with and sharing the enjoyment with their wives and children.

Certain reformers, with their customary purblindness, are denouncing moving-picture shows, for instance, as corrupters of morals and a menace to purity of youth; but the most significant thing that has ever been said about them is the complaint of the saloonkeepers in a number of our larger cities that they are the worst things for cutting into their profits that have ever happened within their recollection — that the workingman, who has fifty cents to spend of an evening, instead of laying it all out in beer for his own enjoyment, brings his family downtown and takes them all to the moving-picture show.

In the nerve-racking and lung-poisoning long hours of labor of an earlier day, the father — whether business man or artisan — too often came home to his family so utterly exhausted and self-poisoned that he was entirely incapable of enjoying the society of his children. Indeed, his nerves were often so set on edge and his fatigue so great that the very shrillness of his children's voices and the little exasperating mistakes and annoyances that would arise rasped him beyond endurance, and made him no fit or improving companion for anybody. The only thing, in fact, that would appeal to his jaded nerves was drinking or gambling, and the one thing that would make him fit company for anybody was a couple of glasses inside him.

Never was there a time when so many men of all

classes of society were building and owning their own homes, however small or "cardboardy" and distressingly inartistic in appearance.

We lament much because we have got away from the healthful and wholesome country and are becoming more and more every year a nation of city dwellers; but we also become more and more a nation of city workers who live practically in the country; and that, from a sanitary point of view, is quite equal if not superior to living exclusively in the country.

The country is all very well in poetry and romantic literature, but it is a raw and melancholy sort of place to have to earn your living in. The average death-rate and disease-rate, as well as height and weight of children at all ages, in comfortable and even good working-class suburbs already is as good as that of the open country and in some instances superior to it. The home does not really become all that a home can be until it ceases to be a place for making a living.

A pathetically convincing illustration of the importance of the presence and even simple company of the father is furnished by the reports of workers in reformatories and institutions for boys who have gone wrong. A majority, of course, for obvious reasons, are full orphans and have had no parental care and influence at all. The next largest number are half orphans, having lost either father or mother; and, strangely enough, much more directly disruptive upon the home as is the loss of the mother, the loss of the father appears to exert an even more injurious influence upon the moral development of the boys.

Still more curious, it has been found, among those who have both parents living and a home of their own, that the next most potent factor in determining the balance of a boy's life is the nature of the occupation of his father, in respect to the number of hours a day and week which that occupation necessarily keeps him away from his home and family.

Some of the most distressing cases of boys going to the bad occur in families in which the father is necessarily away from home for many days out of the week or months out of the year, — as, for instance, in the case of sailors, railroad engineers, and traveling workmen generally, — even though they may be earning excellent wages and supporting good homes with ideal surroundings in every other respect.

There are fathers in all walks of life who are so busy making money for the boy that they lose the boy himself in the process. What shall it profit a man if he gains a whole million but loses his own son?

When the modern father fully realizes and lives up to his advantages in the way of greater control of his time, higher and broader intelligence, the disappearance of the boarding-school obsession and the decline of the necessity for regarding the labor of his children as an asset, home life will become something which, with all deference to the glamor of the past, it has never been before.

THE END

INDEX

INDEX

The Riverside Press

CAMBRIDGE . MASSACHUSETTS

U . S . A